OF LAND, BONES, AND MONEY

Under the Sign of Nature: Explorations in Ecocriticism

Serenella Iovino, Kate Rigby, John Tallmadge, Editors

Michael P. Branch and SueEllen Campbell, Senior Advisory Editors

OF LAND, BONES, AND MONEY

Toward a South African Ecopoetics

EMILY MCGIFFIN

University of Virginia Press
CHARLOTTESVILLE AND LONDON

University of Virginia Press
© 2019 by the Rector and Visitors of the University of Virginia
All rights reserved
Printed in the United States of America on acid-free paper

First published 2019

9 8 7 6 5 4 3 2 1

LIBRARY OF CONGRESS CATALOGING-IN-PUBLICATION DATA

Names: McGiffin, Emily, author.
Title: Of land, bones, and money : toward a South African ecopoetics / Emily McGiffin.
Description: Charlottesville : University of Virginia Press, 2019. | Series: Under the sign of nature | Includes bibliographical references and index.
Identifiers: LCCN 2018057194 (print) | LCCN 2018058604 (ebook) | ISBN 9780813942773 (ebook) | ISBN 9780813942759 (cloth : alk. paper) | ISBN 9780813942766 (pbk. : alk. paper)
Subjects: LCSH: Laudatory poetry, Xhosa—South Africa—History and criticism. | Laudatory poetry, Xhosa—Political aspects—South Africa. | Environmentalism in literature. | Ecocriticism.
Classification: LCC PL8795.7 (ebook) | LCC PL8795.7 .M44 2019 (print) | DDC 896.39851009—dc23
LC record available at https://lccn.loc.gov/2018057194

Cover art: Near Willowvale. (Photo by the author)

For the amaXhosa, their lands, and their poets

CONTENTS

	Acknowledgments	ix
	Introduction	1
1	A Brief History of isiXhosa Literature	19
2	Verse, Violence, and the Migrant Labor System	35
3	*Black Mamba* and the Durban/Rural Nexus	60
4	Versions of Silence	86
5	Literature, Iimbongi, and Ideologies of Development	115
6	Land Expropriation without Compensation and the Vocal Dispossessed	143
	Conclusion	173
	Appendix A. FOSATU, by Alfred Themba Qabula	181
	Appendix B. Isibongo Performed at the State of the Nation Address, 2016	184
	Appendix C. Izibongo Performed by Thukela Poswayo	
	Address to King Zwelonke, 4 December 2015	187
	Address to King Zwelonke, 11 March 2016	191
	Address to Chief Mthetho, 11 March 2016	195

Glossary	199
Notes	203
Bibliography	223
Index	241

ACKNOWLEDGMENTS

While this book owes its existence to many conversations over many years and the support of friends and scholars too numerous to list, I would like to thank several colleagues in particular for making such generous and valuable contributions to my work. Foremost among these is Catriona Sandilands, whose wisdom and thoughtful comments have been invaluable in shaping my thinking and this work. The insights offered by Thembela Kepe, Ilan Kapoor, and Byron Caminero-Santangelo at critical junctures of the project are deeply appreciated, as are my conversations with Jeff Opland and Russell Kaschula, whose pioneering, extensive, and rigorous scholarship on iimbongi I relied on throughout my research. The earlier work of Ari Sitas, Ruth Finnegan, and many excellent South African historians likewise merits special mention for its contribution to the present work.

I would like to express my deep gratitude to friends and colleagues in South Africa who helped shape and support this project. I am indebted to colleagues and friends at Rhodes University—in particular Dan Wylie, Heike Gehring, Jaine Roberts, Pamela Maseko, and the entire crew at the geography department—and to Lynne Grant, Petro Nhlapo, and the rest of the team at the National English Literature Museum for their assistance, insights, and friendship during my time in South Africa. The warm welcome I received from the extended Kepe family on my arrival in Makhanda helped root my work and strongly influenced its direction. Monde Ntshudu of the Department of Environmental Studies at Rhodes University traveled with me to Willowvale and introduced me to the

Busakwe family, who welcomed me into their home and community and made possible the fieldwork component of the research. Particular thanks are due to Nontlantla Busakwe, who was not only an excellent field assistant but also a kind and generous friend, and to Dumisa Mpupha who is always ready to assist with language, translation, and cultural commentary at a moment's notice or from the other side of the world. The iimbongi I spoke with in Willowvale, Bholotywa, Mthatha, East London, King William's Town, Makhanda, and Durban were generous with both their time and their knowledge, as were the many research participants from Willowvale and Makhanda who offered their invaluable insights on the imbongi tradition. I am particularly grateful to Thukela Poswayo, who generously shared his knowledge and the poetry that appears in this book. Without the participation and support of these individuals this work would not have been possible, and I owe them my most humble thanks. I'd also like to acknowledge the seminars at UHURU, the Unit for Humanities at Rhodes University, and the Reddits poetry series—two forums of friendly cultural and intellectual exchange that I particularly valued. Finally, thank you to Pauline, Jono, Daniela, Karen, and all the other good friends at the Oldenburgia Hiking Club for introducing me to the many landscapes of the Eastern Cape and helping to make my time in Makhanda such a pleasure.

This book began as a doctoral project and received invaluable institutional and financial support from the Faculty of Environmental Studies at York University. In particular, thank you to colleagues Anna Zalik, Sonja Killoran-McKibbon, Julie Chamberlain, and Erica Gajewski for excellent conversations and companionship and to Sharrieffa Sattaur, Josephine C. Zeeman, Lisa Dennis, Joseph Cesario, and Rhoda Reyes for assistance with the many logistical aspects of the work. Financial support from York University included a postdoctoral fellowship and several scholarships funded by private donations. I would like to extend my sincere thanks to funders and administrators alike for their ongoing commitments to higher learning. I also received financial support in the form of a doctoral fellowship from the Social Sciences and Humanities Council of Canada and an Ontario Graduate Scholarship.

Special thanks are due to the editorial team at the University of Virginia Press, including Boyd Zenner, Ellen Satrom, and Leslie Tingle; series editors Michael Branch, SueEllen Campbell, and John Tallmadge; and the two anonymous reviewers whose attentive comments have greatly improved the final work. An earlier version of chapter 3 appeared in a special Ecology and Labour issue of *Green Letters;* thanks to the anonymous reviewers and to guest editors Kate Soper and Martin Ryle for their editorial comments and to Pippa Marland for the meticulous correspondence. Similarly, an earlier version of chapter 5 appeared in a special issue of *Third World Thematics*, for which I would like to thank guest editors Thomas Anuerin Smith, Amber Murray, and Hayley Leck and the anonymous reviewers for their careful attention to the manuscript. Finally, many thanks to the Institute for Advanced Studies in the Humanities at the University of Edinburgh, where final work on the manuscript took place.

My friends in northern British Columbia are an ongoing sustaining force who have helped the work along in more ways than they will know. Among them, I owe particular thanks to François Depey, who has been a champion of the work from start to finish. Finally, this book would not have come into being without the ongoing love and support of my parents, Jane and Tim McGiffin, whose quietly radical commitments to justice, innovation, independence, and community continue to inspire me.

OF LAND, BONES, AND MONEY

Introduction

On a midsummer's day in 1970, in a lonely mountain valley northeast of Queenstown in what is now South Africa's Eastern Cape province, a man climbed into his parked car and set his tape recorder in motion. In the seat behind him, a poet began to speak. He first gave a brief introduction, then launched into an improvised poem in praise of his chief, homeland, and ancestors. His roaring, guttural recitation rose and fell for some minutes, at last rolling to a rousing conclusion. He stopped, and silence fell over the vehicle. Outside the car, beneath the line of rocky cliffs that stood above the valley, a small band of children stood listening, waiting to see what would happen next.

The oral praise poet, or *imbongi*, was David Livingstone Phakamile Yali-Manisi, a practitioner of an ancient poetic tradition that extends into the deep past and the uncertain future. His poetry, an isiXhosa genre known as *izibongo*, is a literary form layered with names of ancestors, animals, and plants and rich with idiom and allusion. As such, it is intimately enmeshed with the Eastern Cape landscape and the lives and afterlives of the people and creatures who dwell there. Take the following lines of Yali-Manisi's poem recited that calm December afternoon:

"Yish" goes the caterpillar,
eating mimosa, eating cat-thorn;
let's eat mimosa and leave it at that,
for our chief is reviled;
let's eat mimosa and leave it at that,

for our chief is uneasy.
He's Action, sitting tense on his legs like a bird:
when it squats they say it sits,
when it lifts they say "It's off."[1]

The lines, which immediately follow an opening stanza of grandiloquent praise that invokes the celestial spheres to describe the power and might of the chief, bring the poem thudding back to earth with the caterpillar's sardonic "Yish." Shifting his gaze from moon and stars to the humble insect perched among the yellow blossoms of mimosa and cat-thorn, Yali-Manisi charts a world of fluid relationships between tiny and vast, where each has a bearing on the order of things, and where even insects hold opinions worth listening to.

The man recording Yali-Manisi's voice was Jeff Opland, a young South African literary scholar on his first field expedition in the region. The encounter marked the start of what would come to be a thirty-year relationship, and it inaugurated Opland's lifetime of work compiling transcriptions and early publications of isiXhosa poetry. A substantial portion of Opland's significant archive has now been published in English translation, definitively extending the South African literary canon to include historically neglected authors and literary forms. Yet these works—and the rich linguistic and literary traditions from which they arise—are almost entirely absent from ecocritical scholarship.[2] This oversight warrants attention not only because the literature is intimately tied to histories of dispossession and disrupted environmental relationships that result from the imposition of colonial cultures and economies. It also expresses what Cajetan Iheka has described as "the interconnection and 'proximity' of human and non-human beings" particular to African literatures, in which "non-human life forms—material and supernatural" are essential citizens in the continuum of human and natural systems.[3]

Iheka's landmark work on African ecocriticism is one of the latest in a series of recent works that are helping to expand ecocriticism into a diverse, international movement concerned with the cultural priorities and convictions that have led to the profound environmental degradation that endangers our planet and with the many rich imaginings of alternative futures.[4] In the decades since its inception, ecocriticism has increasingly questioned the assumptions of North American environmentalism— including the ideals of wilderness, health, and the balance and stability of nature—pointing to their troubling associations with imperialism, ableism, and private property ownership and its affirmation of white middle-class privilege and anxieties.⁵ In the same vein, ecocritics have called into question variations of environmental rhetoric that reinforce conservative ideologies that are broadly aligned with Western neoliberal paradigms, including patriarchy, heteronormativity, white supremacy, individualism, and materialist consumption.⁶ Such disciplinary critiques have helped to bring about Cheryll Glotfelty's forecast that the movement will become "ever more interdisciplinary, multicultural and international" as it grows increasingly committed to social and environmental justice.⁷ From early international works such as Catrin Gersdorf and Sylvia Mayer's co-edited collection *Nature in Literary and Cultural Studies: Transatlantic Conversations on Ecocriticism, Nature, Culture and Literature* (2006) and Serenella Iovino's *Ecologia letteraria: Una strategia di sopravvivenza* (2006), a raft of international collections released over the past decade have extended ecocritical work to all continents and a variety of linguistic and cultural perspectives.⁸

By the early years of the new millennium, ecocriticism's growing concern with justice had opened a space for new critical work drawing together ecocriticism and postcolonialism.⁹ Postcolonial ecocriticism emerged from the need to engage both postcolonial and ecological concerns in challenging ongoing imperialism and its social and environmental consequences.¹⁰ This field of literary study coalesces around the term "justice," drawing together the social justice questions of postcolonial studies (exploitation, displacement, dispossession, and inequality), the environmental justice concerns increasingly taken up by ecocriticism, and the intersections and tensions between the two fields.¹¹ Specifically, it addresses the global systems of colonial oppression that have affected people, animals, and ecosystems and underscores the role of economic imperialism in producing both situations of human injustice and environmental exploitation and damage.

Byron Caminero-Santangelo's work in this field focuses specifically on how environmental degradation on the African continent resulting from "imperial capital operating with impunity" has "mostly been rendered invisible to the world as a result of the continent's extreme marginality both in imperial representation and in the world economic system."¹² He discusses how injustices of colonialism and foreign imperialism in Africa are perpetuated by globalized conservation movements that construct an image of charismatic megafauna and pristine wilderness as the "real Africa" even as they neglect the cultures of ecological care that have emerged over millennia of human dwelling within these landscapes. The result is "an emphasis on conservation that is often socially damaging, while many of the more difficult causes of environmental damage (i.e., histories of colonialism and legacies of intentional uneven development) are systematically ignored."[13] Caminero-Santangelo's work aligns with Rob Nixon's *Slow Violence and the Environmentalism of the Poor*, which tackles the twin problematics of slow violence and structural violence. Nixon argues that in seizing representational power, writer-activists put a human face on "outsourced suffering" to "give life and dimension to the strategies—oppositional, affirmative, and yes, often desperate and fractured—that emerge from those who bear the brunt of the planet's ecological crisis." Both Nixon and Caminero-Santangelo inform Brooke Stanley's and Walter Dana Phillips's call to embrace "a more inclusive literary canon" that allows for "the renegotiation of environmental literature and theory from African and global South perspectives."[14]

The scholarly discipline of ecopoetics, loosely characterized as "the incorporation of an ecological or environmental perspective into the study of poetics," includes multiple orientations and valences.[15] From early works such as John Elder's *Imagining the Earth: Poetry and the Vision of Nature* (1985), D. M. R. Bentley's *The Gay]Grey Moose: Essays on the Ecologies and Mythologies of Canadian Poetry, 1690–1990* (1992), and Terry Gifford's *Green Voices: Understanding Contemporary Nature Poetry* (1995), the critical field took wing during the decade straddling the turn of the millennium with a flurry of new books by Leonard Scigaj (1999), Jonathan Bate (2000), Bernard Quetchenbach (2000), Don McKay (2001), David Gilcrest (2002), and J. Scott Bryson (2005).[16] In 2001 the launch of the online journal *ecopoetics* heralded a shift toward nonrepresentational writing and innovative forms, while the first edited collection on the subject, *Ecopoetry: A Critical Introduction* (2002), drew women ecocritics into the conversation and grafted new concerns related to queer, postcolonial, and identity politics onto longstanding preoccupations with landscape, extinction, and the pastoral.[17] While there are no doubt gaps in this cursory overview, it illustrates how parallel strands of critical thought emerged simultaneously in different locations and grew into a critical movement as concern for the environment entered the mainstream critical consciousness. In his introduction to the 2002 collection, Scott Bryson acknowledges that the definition of "ecopoetics" is fluid. In the years since, the term has only become more unstable as new critical volumes have interrogated the concept of "environment" and carried the field beyond lyrical invocations of nature and wilderness and into the realms of context, experience and language, urban environments, and digital media.[18] Ecopoetics increasingly engages with poetry that grapples with human impacts on the natural world, human-induced environmental change, the entwinement of nature and culture, and the need to dismantle the constructed binary that, since the enlightenment era, has separated the two.

While ecopoetics is an engaged if not activist scholarship, a postcolonial ecopoetics—that is, multicultural criticism focused on the environmental politics of poetry produced by peoples living in what Jahan Ramazani calls "the shadow of colonialism," particularly in the so-called global South—has been slower to emerge.[19] This trend is likely linked to the underemphasis on poetry within postcolonial studies more generally that Ramazani and other literary critics note.[20] Poetry, with its complex structures, figurative language, and often arcane histories of form and syntax, perhaps has been seen as "less amenable to the historical and political imperatives of postcolonial studies than more seemingly documentary or socially mimetic genres."[21] At the same time this absence in the ecocritical scholarship is surprising, given that poetic traditions globally offer a rich archive of differing literary aesthetics and cultural orientations and express forms and styles of human thought and feeling adapted to cultures knit into local ecologies.

Recent collections have begun to address this scholarly gap, further extending the political and cultural ambit of the field. *Ecopoetics: Essays in the Field*, a new collection edited by Angela Hume and Gillian Osborne, highlights the increasingly intersectional nature of ecopoetics and draws science, animal and plant studies, and queer, disability, and race studies into a richly multidisciplinary conversation.[22] While not strictly limited to poetry, Sonya Postmentier's *Cultivation and Catastrophe: The Lyric Ecology of Modern Black Literature*, examines how twentieth-century black writers in the United States, Canada, and the Caribbean "have responded to environmental alienation resulting from the vexed legacy of the plantation, urbanization, and various forced and free migrations."[23] Similarly Meliz Ergin's recent work of comparative ecocriticism places Turkish and American poets in conversation in examining the entanglement of the social and natural spheres.[24] Stuart Cooke undertakes a similar work of comparative ecopoetics with his "multi-site poetics," which draws together Australian and Chilean indigenous writers.[25]

While much ecopoetic criticism draws on postcolonial perspectives, recent works increasingly consider how people outside of straight, white, able-bodied, anglophone epistemologies experience the natural world and engage poetically with questions of environmental justice.[26] In doing so, these books join a growing critical conversation that looks to the "many versions of environmentalism" for guidance in solving the manifold environmental crises we face. At least since Ramachandra Guha's 1989 essay "Radical American Environmentalism and Wilderness Preservation: A Third-World Critique," concerns about "narrow and inequitable conservation practices" have become a central aspect of critical environmental practice.[27] As globalization continues on its unyielding path and remote indigenous communities increasingly find themselves on the front lines of environmental struggles, the environmentalism of the poor—which centers on issues of justice, recognition, and participation "in situations where the environment is a source of livelihood"—is becoming the prevalent version of environmental action. Joan Martinez-Alier reiterates that indigenous peoples, "in their struggle to preserve their own livelihoods against mining companies, hydroelectric dams, biomass extraction and land grabbing, and oil and gas exploitation . . . have been since the 1980s and 1990s the backbone of the global environmental justice movement."[28] Faced with questions of how to act in an engaged and ethical manner in the face of an unfettered globalization, we can begin by recognizing and upholding the voices of marginalized and disenfranchised groups and supporting their insistence on just relationships.

This book intervenes in these conversations and imperatives, finding its place within the evolving orientations and definitions of ecopoetry as it considers a South African version of environmentalism and the poetry associated with it. In particular the book examines isiXhosa-speaking poets and their engagement with severe, long-term, and pervasive racial oppression and the inextricable relationship between human injustice and environmental exploitation in South Africa. Speaking from a class that was systematically excluded from owning rural estates or from enjoying recreational pursuits in pristine natural areas and instead forced to live in situations of environmental risk, these poets nevertheless voiced experiences of environmental proximity and natural beauty. The landscapes of their poems are complex assemblages of humans, animals, plants, and spirits that illustrate particular understandings of the relationships between these entities and call for an ethics of responsibility and care. By exploring the cultural politics of written and oral literature in amaXhosa society, this book looks to isiXhosa (and, in specific cases, isiZulu) literature as a force that has helped reimagine and recast power relations within an oppressive and unjust political economy and that can similarly help inform evolving relationships with the natural world. In challenging the extractive theft inflicted on their communities and environments under colonialism, apartheid, and neoliberal capitalism, the poets examined here voice their opposition to systemic injustices of exploitation and extraction.

In the process they express an environmentalism that recognizes the constitutive ties between capital, labor, and landscape, resisting not only the exploitation of black South African labor under the apartheid regime but also the environmental injustice that this subjugation represented. Their work expresses an explicit concern with "lived environments, the social implications of environmental change, and the relationships between representations of nature and power."[29] In doing so, isiXhosa poets also express the struggles and triumphs of the laborer, the migrant, the dispossessed—the actual producers of wealth—who remain systematically excluded from cultural and environmental representation in South Africa and beyond.

In much the same way that isiXhosa literature confronts colonial, apartheid, and neocolonial thought with alternative imaginings, vernacular African literatures more broadly have the potential to disrupt and resist the ongoing hegemony of colonial languages and institutions. In demanding justice and articulating the need for decolonization, equality, and the democratic distribution of wealth, poets articulate possibilities for transformed relationships with one another and with the world around us. Through an investigation of oral and written isiXhosa literature in translation from the late nineteenth century to the present, this book argues that even authors whose work does not deal primarily with natural settings and landscapes in a way familiar to Western readers nevertheless possess a keen sense of environmental realities and a particularly cogent awareness of the political structures that have so degraded the environments of their homelands.

"*Imbongi*" (plural, *iimbongi*) is the term among isiXhosa-speaking peoples for the oral poet. Referred to in English as a "praise poet," the imbongi performs in an improvised eulogistic genre known as *izibongo;* the singular *isibongo* refers to a specific poem.[30] Izibongo, deeply evocative both of place and of the ancestral presences that continue to inhabit those places, ties people into a lineage and form of dwelling that extend into past and future. Through the poet's voice, language becomes a healing medium that strengthens connections to land and lineage, often producing or enabling a flow of emotions in listeners. The poetry is active; it performs both spiritual and material work as *umoya*, the spirit that inspires the poet to speech, moves from the landscape through the body of the poet and into the air, traveling in linguistic form to listening ears. There is an earthly physicality to the poetry—spoken most often in the open air at public gatherings, it is by nature an inclusive art form that welcomes its listeners into the communal experience of cultured and attentive dwelling.

Iimbongi are prophetic artists, visionaries in a spiritual as well as an intellectual or artistic sense. As performance artists, they are visible interlocutors with culture and power and are, at the same time, agents of sound, enacting words as events that revive the power of orality and restore the weight and magic that traditionally inhere in the spoken word.[31] In oral poetry, spoken words unfold aurally across time rather than visibly in space, as dynamic and ephemeral occurrences.[32] By delivering brief, living words and the imperative message they contain, iimbongi and their art disrupt notions of space and time, progress and development, possession and distribution that have advanced alongside the rise of the printed word and an increasingly global capitalism. In doing so, they make present and visible more ancient ways of relating to time, language, and landscape and draw listeners' focus to the implacable natural forces that ultimately organize human lives.

Yet even as their orality links them to nonliterate ontologies, iimbongi have a dynamic rapport with the printed word. The British missionaries who arrived in the Eastern Cape in the early nineteenth century soon developed an orthography for the isiXhosa language that enabled the printing and distribution of religious texts and the dissemination of Christian and European ideologies.[33] By the mid-nineteenth century several isiXhosa newspapers and publishing houses had been established, and although these remained largely mediated and censored by the colonizing class, they also enabled the circulation of particularly African interpretations and disputations of history, politics, and contemporary society.[34] In embracing print and, more recently, digital media to circulate their words, iimbongi sustain a dynamic relationship between written and oral, vision and sound, traditional and modern, rural and urban, and they blur these categories into a fluid and multifaceted continuum. By creating conceptual and material linkages, iimbongi extend the potentialities of individual life in postcolonial, late capitalist South African society beyond everyday concerns. As they call forth ancestral presences and evoke the responsibilities associated with homeland and lineage, they voice new possibilities for human identities, offer kinder ways of relating to land and environment, and suggest possible social and political futures.

Poetry in general is a linguistic and literary mode that enables a rich expression of humanity's imaginative and empathetic potential and that facilitates lyric perceptions of matter in ways beyond what our linguistic systems permit. Through the hinge of metaphor, poetic language articulates an ethics of inclusivity and ecological dwelling, preserving "difference in community" and "the particularities of things in their larger contextual relationships."[35] Working with the limited instrument of language, metaphor can produce a form of understanding in which we are able to perceive relationships between seemingly distinct subjects through their juxtaposition, a process in which we "see, simultaneously, similarities and dissimilarities: we experience things as both metaphysically distinct and ontologically connected."[36] In their representative and affective power, "poems are material events and fields of force" whose imaginative work involves "world-making" and "rearrang[ing] categories of thought" that can help reconceive and reconstruct "the human relationship to the more-than-human world."[37]

While literature in general and poetry in particular operate discursively, engaging with ideas and ideologies, the emotional effect of poetry, the work it does, is also tightly linked to its materiality. Textual elements—pattern, repetition, style, tone, alliteration, metaphor—are of fundamental importance because of what they contribute to the audience's emotional understanding of the words. The sounds, beats, and rhythms of spoken language, and especially poetic language, are not simply discursive: they are physical experiences with material effects. This is particularly true of izibongo, a performed, spontaneous form that is visual as well as aural, often voiced unexpectedly and often at high volume by a figure who may be dressed in skins, beads, porcupine quills, traditional garments, or other distinguishing attire. The isiXhosa language is poetically alliterative, richly textured with clicking and aspirated consonants, and abundantly endowed with evocative idioms and poetic terms that are experienced physically and conceptually by both audience and performer. Each performance is novel, and poems are tailored to the people and events at hand. The combined effect of sound, language, and visuals works on its audience on deep levels, and listeners are at liberty—they are, indeed, expected—to voice their enthusiasm for the performance with cheers and ululations that amplify the physical work of the poem. These material aspects affect the emotive, intellectual, and perceptual qualities of the work such that poetry exists as both a material and symbolic entity in which meaning is inseparable from form, sound, rhythm, and texture.

When it is transcribed, much of the physical effect of izibongo is lost, as is the active exchange between the participants and the performer. To some extent the rhythm and sounds of the oral poetry are captured in the text and can be reproduced by reading aloud. However, once the transcribed poem is translated, the text bears little resemblance to the original performance. The drastic change in the texture of sounds, sentence structure, and words fundamentally alters the meaning and effect of the poetry, since "a word is able to denote only through its complex interrelations with other words . . . because poems are peculiarly compressed structures of language which exploit to the full the crisscrossing affinities between their various elements."[38] It is difficult to translate form, content, and meaning simultaneously, particularly since figurative language and idiomatic expressions vary markedly from one cultural and linguistic context to another. Translators are generally forced to make compromises between language and meaning that may profoundly affect the readers' understanding of the text and their overall experience of the poem. Jeff Opland describes how, in translating isiXhosa texts into English, he often struggles with the best way of conveying figurative language that would be meaningless if translated literally.[39] Much is lost in translating a figure of speech that may involve creatures or objects specific to amaXhosa landscape and culture into a familiar English equivalent.

These many complications could be seen as good reasons for a literary critic to stick with written poetry in his or her own language. On the other hand, the omissions of oral and vernacular literatures in ecocritical scholarship merit close attention given the broader race-based exclusions and inequalities that are a central aspect of contemporary society. South Africa is a prominent example of racialized, uneven development that has produced vast disparities in material and social wellbeing between different social groups. At the same time, South Africa is also a vibrant example of a terrain of struggle in which an oppressed and exploited class has consistently used its resourcefulness, wit, imagination, and courage to advance its liberation agenda. As centuries of extractive capitalism have fundamentally reordered South African landscapes and human relationships with them, the same period has seen iimbongi voice alternate ways of thinking and seeing. The South African case, which provides a poignant example of the ongoing social and environmental costs of racial injustice and of the power of liberation movements to effect real ideological and political change, also illustrates the urgent need for research into the ways geographies of power and inequality are actively constructed, contested, and reshaped through discursive and creative means and how oral and vernacular language texts in particular offer insights into the priorities and worldviews of subaltern classes that often speak but are rarely heard.

In examining the ecopoetics of isiXhosa poetry, my intention is not to impose yet another Western literary theory onto an African literature. Rather, with environmental considerations in mind, I have aimed to listen to these poets, their poetry, and their communities, and I suggest that attention of this sort can contribute to an emerging postcolonial ecopoetics.

This work is grounded in a definition of literature as a vast realm of meaning and understanding that offers a vital connection between people and the environments they inhabit.[40] By seeking out and discussing both written and oral texts originally published or performed in a vernacular African language, I hope to expand the range of literary genres and languages considered by ecocriticism and ecopoetics. This project also widens the boundaries of South African postcolonial ecocriticism beyond poetry and fiction published in English, which has been the central focus of South African ecocriticism to date, by drawing on and extending the scholarship on the shifting social and literary role of the amaXhosa imbongi. Unlike the novel and other written forms that have been the focus of postcolonial studies, poetry is a global literary genre that predates colonialism. It is particularly well developed in oral cultures and is the literary genre that people in sub-Saharan Africa are most likely to encounter.[41]

At the same time, although this book brings together several years of reading, explorations of the South African landscape, and discussions and interviews in villages, townships, and cities, the work is constrained by important limitations. First, the need to impose some boundaries on my investigation of a large body of literature led me to focus on a limited range of poets working in a particular style. My interest in the imbongi *zomthonyama* tradition, particularly in rural areas, and the writings available on the topic carried the work in a particular direction. I leave it to future scholars to investigate the dynamic forms of isiXhosa oral poetry as it unfolds in townships, urban centers, universities, arts festivals, and slam poetry venues across the country, blending languages and forms in the process. Second, as a white, anglophone, Canadian, female scholar from a settler-colonial background conducting research on a culturally specific and traditionally male poetic form, my personal situation is clearly far removed from the topic at hand. South Africa has a very particular and complex history of which I have had no direct experience, and the oral nature of isiXhosa poetry is entirely different from the written forms I am trained in. These separations no doubt substantially affect my interpretation of this poetry and the life experiences it describes, particularly given my very rudimentary knowledge of the language.

To address this second set of shortcomings, I undertook an in-depth study of isiXhosa grammar and lived for several months in situations of linguistic and cultural immersion that helped me to better understand both the amaXhosa culture and the nature and restrictions of my own positionality. Although I am unable to understand and speak the language, I feel that my grasp of its aural rhythms and grammatical structures and my work on the translations included here have enabled me to provide a useful critical commentary. However, the linguistic and cultural barriers restrict my ability to discuss literary style and nuanced uses of the language. They have likewise prevented me from situating written or performed works within a broader literary context, since my experience of the poetry is confined to works available in translation and to the interviews and performances described in the chapters that follow. Finally, despite my efforts to learn about and experience firsthand the environments and cultures of these poets, my critique remains rooted in my own Anglo-Canadian epistemology.

In spite of these limitations, this book nevertheless offers an attentive consideration of the work of important South African artists who have not yet been considered by ecocritical scholars. As a multilingual poet accustomed to reading and speaking other languages, I approach the work first and foremost as a fellow artist with a keen interest in the sounds and structures of language and in language's capacity to liberate the human imagination, awaken our capacity to perceive and appreciate beauty, and cultivate our spirits for the courageous work of responding to damaging cultural and political forces. My life history has also given me an understanding of social structures that exclude particular groups from environmental and cultural narratives. I was raised and continue to live in small, resource-based communities in British Columbia among people who make their living as physical laborers in land-based extractive industries. Like South Africa, this Canadian province is divided and contested postcolonial terrain where historical violences continue to inflict themselves on present lives.

Despite my inability to part ways with the nominal categories that have shaped my own identity and positionality, these categories themselves are not static. In my own case, the research process has dramatically altered my knowledge and understanding of racial dynamics, histories, and contemporary experiences of oppression rooted in race and gender. This research has also had a significant impact on my understanding of my place within the complex, racialized matrix of my own decolonizing settler colonial nation, and indeed within a racialized world in which northern nations such as my own benefit from the ongoing exploitation of others. The research has deepened my understanding of my complicity with the privileges that racial disparity has afforded me and has informed the means by which I can actively resist structures of privilege and oppression. This deepened and sensitized awareness was one of my main interests in undertaking this project in the first place.

The work presented here draws on all of these perspectives, introducing interdisciplinary methodologies that incorporate the commentary of iimbongi and their audiences into the text.[42] In keeping with the themes of agency, language, and voice that form the core of this study, I have chosen not to edit these voices for grammar or clarity. There are many versions of spoken English, and while the structure and cadence of English spoken by the research participants may be unfamiliar to some readers, I feel that it would be inappropriate to alter their words simply to make the transcriptions conform to a particular version of grammatical accuracy.

As this book makes clear, I owe my understanding of the poetry not only to the work of previous scholars (and my own interpretations of it) but also to the poets themselves and to the many anonymous villagers and township residents with whom I spoke. In compiling their voices, I have sought to offer a multifaceted portrayal of the poetry as it is experienced by many different people at various locations throughout the Eastern Cape. When it comes to the thorny question of how white scholars from foreign contexts might speak about other cultural traditions with sensitivity, I hope the work presented here, despite its inevitable shortcomings, might begin to offer an answer.

Ecopoetics and the Imbongi

The Eastern Cape landscape and its people have experienced violent and overwhelming changes over the past two hundred years. During that time, as people and their cultures have adapted, so too has the izibongo genre. Past scholars have written on the shift of traditional poetry out of rural realms and into urban ones and have marked its movement from the courtly realm of chiefs and kings into the that of elected officials. It is blended with other genres—rap, hip-hop, slam poetry—to create lively and compelling hybrid performances that are often shared through digital media. The present work contributes to discussions of changes while at the same time noting that alongside them, certain trends abide. Izibongo remains rooted in expressions of praise for land and lineage and of reverent dwelling with both. Its "rhythmic, syntactic, and linguistic intensifications" are among "language's most direct path of return to the *oikos* . . . an answering to nature's own rhythms, an echoing of the song of the earth itself."[43]

Chapter 1, "A Brief History of isiXhosa Literature," introduces the historical and ecological contexts in which the work takes place. Beginning with a succinct history of the Eastern Cape province from before the arrival of Europeans to the end of the nineteenth century, a basic introduction to the isiXhosa language, and some notes on the biogeography of the Eastern Cape, the chapter moves into a more detailed discussion of iimbongi and the izibongo genre, discussing its political role and affective power. Drawing on the work of literary scholars and historians, the chapter describes the cultural origins of the imbongi and the izibongo genre and then presents the political context of the study with a sketch of the early British colonial period in what is now South Africa. It argues that over this period, extractive capitalism, segregation, and the migrant labor system have ordered South Africa's present geographies and social configurations.

Chapter 2, "Verse, Violence, and the Migrant Labor System," examines the imposition of extractive capitalism on the peoples and landscapes of South Africa from the discovery of gold in the Witwatersrand in 1886 through the first three decades of the twentieth century. Within this context, the chapter examines recent translations of poetry written by Nontsizi Mgqwetho, one of South Africa's most prolific and least-recognized female poets and the only woman to have produced a substantial body of poetic work in isiXhosa. The chapter discusses her collected poems and comments in detail on her direct literary engagement with political events in Johannesburg in the 1920s and her contribution to isiXhosa literary culture. It also looks at the ways in which the politics and concerns that Mgqwetho expresses in her poetry reflect how individual experiences of South Africa's social transformations were highly mediated by gender. Finally, it shows how her work directly contests the colonial and apartheid policies that enabled the exploitation of black South Africans and their environments and that actively produced situations of underdevelopment and environmental degradation throughout the country.

Chapter 3, "*Black Mamba* and the Durban/Rural Nexus," begins with a discussion of South African political history from 1948 through the 1980s, outlining the structural conditions prevalent in South Africa during the latter half of the twentieth century and the labor movement that arose in response to these. From here, it moves into a discussion of the work of Alfred Qabula and Nise Malange, poets who became prominent cultural and political figures within the South African labor movement through their writing, performances, and cultural activism. The chapter shows that the political texts produced by these poets and their colleagues in the workers' cultural movement were also deeply environmental in their evocation of both rural and urban environments and in their call to listeners to defend the beauty of their homelands. These texts speak directly to the cultural politics of the extraction, dispossession, and accumulation that underpinned South African industrialization. Through the skillful use of language and metaphor as well as the adaptation and deployment of traditional forms, the worker poets created oral texts with tremendous cultural and emotional resonance. The language of the poems brought the cultural imaginary of the rural realm into industrial Durban, depicting environments that were energizing and empowering not only in their natural imagery but also in their invocation of history, memories, and ancestral presence.

Chapters 4, 5, and 6 consider the changing role of iimbongi in the postapartheid context and explore ways in which the genre interacts with the politics of land and development. Chapter 4, "Versions of Silence," considers questions of censorship in South African poetry and politics, from apartheid to the present. Despite a well-documented tradition and contemporary practice in which iimbongi perform the role of political and social critics, many iimbongi feel limited in their current ability to speak truth to power. This chapter probes the silences surrounding the iimbongi's words, examines interstitial spaces within izibongo, and asks what is not said and why. Drawing on existing scholarship, conversations with practicing iimbongi, and textual analysis, the chapter considers the contemporary role of the amaXhosa imbongi within postcolonial, postapartheid structures and the vocal popular struggles that have shaped the social and political landscapes of contemporary South Africa. Looking at poems produced for the annual State of the Nation Address, it discusses how the poetry is limited by both censorship and commodification yet nevertheless works within these constraints to engage in a veiled yet potent political critique. Turning to the general absence of female iimbongi, the chapter concludes by linking this to social factors that, as in the past, continue to erase the presence of women and inhibit their voices at every level of society.

Chapter 5, "Literature, Iimbongi, and Ideologies of Development," looks closely at aspects of the imbongi tradition that have received little scholarly attention: namely the ritual or spiritual significance of these poets and the role of both iimbongi and their literature in development and decolonization in contemporary South Africa. In particular, the chapter takes up Graham Huggan and Helen Tiffin's assertion that "one of the central tasks of postcolonial ecocriticism as an emergent field has been to contest—also to provide alternatives to—Western ideologies of development."[44] Drawing on interviews with people living in and around the rural town of Willowvale in the former Transkei, with residents of

Joza township adjacent to Makhanda (formerly Grahamstown), and with fourteen iimbongi from various communities in the Eastern Cape, the chapter shows how the ongoing practice of spiritually rich literature has a profound effect on audiences, contributing directly to people's spiritual and emotional wellbeing and to the social development of communities. It argues that the iimbongi's spiritually significant literature affirms African agency, creativity, autonomy, and vision, helping effect a shift from a development paradigm based on economic growth to a holistic paradigm that considers a full spectrum of human and environmental wellbeing.

Finally, chapter 6, "Land Expropriation without Compensation and the Vocal Dispossessed," draws together political concerns related to politics of land in South Africa, placing particular emphasis on the complex and multilayered cultural politics surrounding dispossession as expressed through oral literature. Looking at the rise of neoliberal ideologies over the past two decades of democracy and their influence on South Africa's land reform program, the chapter joins scholars calling for redress of historical injustices that benefits disenfranchised groups. I also join those who call for a cultural response to neoliberal discourse more generally, emphasizing the role of artists and intellectuals in tackling the cultural and environmental vacuum in neoliberal politics. The chapter begins with a brief overview of factors involved in land politics in South Africa and then moves on to close readings of historical and contemporary isiXhosa poetic texts. It explores the potential of oral poetry to help articulate an alternative political economy of land that extends beyond narrowly defined market relations to acknowledge other values—symbolic and spiritual, for example—that land holds. Like the previous chapter, it argues that the affective power of izibongo derives from details of the craft: an imbongi's choice of words and metaphor, the rhythm of the language, the performance style. The chapter presents these details with an eye to the way that they combine to create a particular expression of land that is stronger and more powerful than the words alone would suggest. In this way, iimbongi help tighten connections to landscape, kin, and heritage not only by informing people about their history and ancestral responsibilities but also by involving them with the emotional valences of these concerns.

The concerns explored throughout these chapters take on an added significance when seen as part of larger-scale patterns of privilege and exclusion and their devastating consequences for environmental justice. South Africa's drastically skewed distribution of wealth and access—which, despite the rapid growth of a black middle class, remains defined by race—resembles a contemporary global order in which a collection of elite white nations have defined the institutions, histories, and mythologies underpinning international culture and politics. The history of South Africa, with its institutionalized racial segregation and apartheid that operated in the service of capitalist expansion, sheds light on the workings of a global system that, in confining racial others within disadvantaged peripheries, perpetuates a system of racial injustice that is in many ways reminiscent of apartheid. Given capitalism's long history of reconfiguring landscapes and human relationships with them—and Western concepts of "nature" that are entwined in these worldviews and have often been deployed in support of colonial and capitalist agendas—this book argues that the isiXhosa literatures explored within its pages, which assert non-Western perspectives and criticize colonialism and capitalism in all of their iterations, are key examples of African environmental literature that are of deep significance to ecocritical and ecopoetic thinking.

1 / A Brief History of isiXhosa Literature

Okukwazi onako nje
Sel' udume wacand' izwe,—
Lemihlaba, eliwonga
Uzizuze ngabani na?

With all your information
still famous across the nations—
who was it who gave you the means
to acquire these lands, this status?

—WILLIAM WELLINGTON GQOBA

Prior to European contact, the tip of the African continent that forms present-day South Africa was peopled by a variety of cultural and ethnic groups. The various San or "bushman" nations (e.g., !Kung, |Xam, ǂKhomani), are descendants of the earliest human inhabitants of the region who had lived in southern Africa for some two hundred thousand years.[1] These peoples lived for generations as hunter-gatherers who ranged across southern Africa before they began to be displaced by the pastoralist Khoi people. The origins of the Khoi are unknown, but they are thought to have migrated from present-day Namibia or Botswana with domesticated herds that they had acquired through contact with pastoralist peoples in these regions.[2] The Khoi settled throughout the area that is now the Western Cape and were the first South Africans to come into contact with Europeans—first the Portuguese, followed by the Dutch—as the latter arrived and settled in the area around Table Bay. Around CE 1500, Bantu-speaking peoples joined South Africa's ethnic blend as they moved south with their cattle from the Great Lakes region of East Africa. Their arrival was part of an enormous, incremental human migration that began around 3000 BCE in the borderlands of what is now Nigeria and Cameroon, eventually resulting in the settlement of most of the African subcontinent by agrarian peoples.[3]

This brief historical sketch hints at the relationships that humans have developed with South African landscapes over millennia, illustrating how human modes of living and interacting with the environment of the region changed continually as new migrants introduced different livelihoods, languages, cultures, and spiritual practices. Yet all of these peoples lived in close contact with the diverse biogeographies of the lands they inhabited. It was not until the arrival of Europeans from the late fifteenth century onward that changes to human ways of relating to each other and to the landscape around them became increasingly drastic.

In precolonial times South Africa was home to dense populations of large mammals—elephants, rhinos, giraffes, many species of antelopes, zebras, buffalos, and lions—enormous quantities of birds and fish, and some of the most complex and diverse plant communities found anywhere in the world. The arrival of Europeans, with their horses, firearms, and superior killing capacity, quickly saw the region's large, diverse populations of mammalian fauna diminish to a shadow of what they had been.[4] European settlers went on to transform the landscape itself, establishing towns, cities, and networks of roads and railways, converting complex ecosystems to simplified cropping systems and setting up extractive industries that altered not only the biota of the country but also vast expanses of its very bedrock. Grazing by the settlers' large herds of cattle and sheep intensified the environmental effects that had begun with the earlier arrival of African pastoralists. The speed of change increased drastically in the late eighteenth century as the British took control of the Cape colony and began a relentless annexation of land and resources. As colonial administrations parceled the rural landscape into private allotments, human settlement and transhumance patterns changed dramatically, reflecting concurrent processes of upheaval in Britain and Europe.[5] Newly introduced plant species proliferated, and the erection of tens of thousands of kilometers of fences changed the movements and presence of game and the seasonal movements of pastoralists, all transforming precolonial ecosystems.[6]

This chapter introduces the people at the center of the present study, namely the amaXhosa and their poets. Drawing on previous scholarship and my own fieldwork, I offer a sketch of the environment and language of the amaXhosa, reserving historical events following the arrival of Europeans for subsequent chapters. From these background considerations that are important to the study, I move into a general discussion of the tradition of the iimbongi and the izibongo genre based on past scholarship. The research I present in subsequent chapters complicates some of this previous work, placing renewed emphasis on the importance of the spiritual and healing roles of the iimbongi and their poetry and questioning the role of activist poets in a political climate that stifles dissent.

The amaXhosa and Their Poetry

The term amaXhosa designates a diverse group of isiXhosa-speaking kingdoms—including the amaGcaleka, amaRharhabe, amaMpondo, abaThembu, amaBomvana, amaXesibe, amaMpondomise, and amaMfengu—whose traditional lands cover much of South Africa's Eastern Cape province.[7] EmaXhoseni, the lands traditionally inhabited by the amaXhosa people, is a fertile and biodiverse region that consists largely of temperate grasslands on shallow clay soils that are better suited to livestock than intensive cropping.[8] Like their amaZulu neighbors to the northeast, the amaXhosa lived as settled agrarians who set cattle at the heart of their culture—a lifestyle for which their undulating landscape, with its varied blend of well-watered bushveld and pasturage, is ideal.[9] EmaXhoseni spans four climatic zones running parallel to one another between the Indian Ocean and the mountains that separate the coastal zone from the dry interior plateau. While many amaXhosa settled in the coastal area, the majority lived in the highlands beyond, settling amid smaller mountain ranges along river basins that boast rich soils, mixed pasturage, and abundant rainfall.[10]

Each of the amaXhosa kingdoms takes its name from an ancestor from which the lineage is descended, and each traditionally occupied a different area: the amaGcaleka and amaRharhabe resided in the south between the Sundays and Mbashe Rivers; the amaMpondo dwelt near the border of what is now KwaZulu-Natal; the abaThembu claimed the northern interior of the province, and so on.[11] Each kingdom has its own unique history, genealogy, dialect, and set of cultural and livelihood practices specifically adapted to its home place. While some scholars have highlighted these differences by limiting their definition of amaXhosa to those groups who trace their lineage to the ancestor uXhosa (i.e., the amaGcaleka and amaRharhabe kingdoms), in this study I use the term amaXhosa to refer to all groups that speak the isiXhosa language.[12]

The amaXhosa kingdoms are in turn made up of chiefdoms, villages, and clans. Chiefs, particularly the paramount chief (king), preside over their territories by sacral and hereditary rights.[13] Traditionally, and in many regions of the contemporary Eastern Cape, everyone lived in a chiefdom, and the relationship between chiefs and their people was, and remains, complex. As direct descendants of the ancient founders of the chiefdom, chiefs are endowed with profound obligations to oversee and provide for the solidarity of the community and the welfare of its members. In contemporary times, chiefs remain much more than symbolic figureheads; in rural areas in particular the chief continues to hold layered significance, in a sense embodying the spirits of landscape and community and helping to maintain harmonious relationships between these entities.[14] At the same time, they are problematic figures whose hold on undemocratic power has been harshly criticized by a variety of commentators.

Clans are a further grouping in amaXhosa society. The clan name, *iziduko,* is additional to a person's surname and reflects a further ancestral affiliation shared with a larger group than the immediate family, linking a person to the genealogy of the clan and to other clan members in their local community and beyond. (For example, Nelson Mandela is often referred to by his clan name, Madiba, as a gesture bestowing honor on both Mandela and the ancestor for whom his clan is named.)[15] Due to traditional exogamy rules that forbid intermarriages between members of the same clan, neighboring households in both rural and urban areas tend to have a variety of clan affiliations.

The second-most widely spoken language in South Africa after isiZulu, isiXhosa is one of four closely related Nguni languages in South Africa, including isiXhosa, isiZulu, isiSwati, and isiNdebele. The Nguni languages are in turn part of the Bantu language group spoken by peoples across sub-Saharan Africa, an area stretching from the Cameroon coast east across the continent to Kenya and south to the Cape, a distribution that reflects past human migrations.[16] The total number of languages in this group is unknown—largely because in many cases it is difficult to draw a clear line between languages and dialects as distinctions developed in other locales are often inappropriate for African contexts; however, linguists put the number of languages at about five hundred, which are spoken by some 240 million people in twenty-seven African countries.[17] When Bantu peoples reached the lands that currently comprise South Africa around the beginning of the sixteenth century, they encountered indigenous Khoi and San peoples, and the interaction between the groups resulted in the transmission of clicks into the Nguni languages. In many Khoisan languages the percentage of click words may be over 60 percent; in isiXhosa and isiZulu, clicks are present in about 15 to 17 percent of words.[18]

IsiXhosa is an agglutinative language in which various prefixes and suffixes are joined to root words to alter their meaning. For example, *ukufunda* is the infinitive form of the verb "to study" or "to read," *ndiyafunda* is the gerund "I am studying," while *andifundi* is the negative "I am not studying." *Umfundi* is a student, and *umfundisi* is a priest; *ukufundela* means "to study for," and *ukufundisa* "to teach," while *ukufundisana* means "to teach each other," and so on. Like other related languages, isiXhosa nouns fall into classes. Most Bantu languages have about fifteen or sixteen noun classes arranged in about ten singular/plural pairings.[19] IsiXhosa itself has six singular classes, six plural classes, and two abstracted classes that lack plural forms. In isiXhosa the noun is the dominant part of speech that determines the form of subject and object, possessive pronouns, adjectives, and verbs, which each must in turn adopt specific concords depending on the class of the noun. Concords are drawn from the noun prefix and contain similar combinations of sounds.[20] The examples below illustrate how prefixes are added to noun, verb, and adjectival stems to create concords within sentences:

Umntwana **w**am **om**hle **u**yadlala. (My beautiful child is playing.)

Abantwana **b**am **aba**hle **ba**yadlala. (My beautiful children are playing.)

In these sentences, the root word for child, –*ntwana,* changes class depending on whether it is singular or plural, while the prefixes of associated adjectives, possessives, and verbs are altered accordingly. Similarly,

Inja **y**am **e**ntle **i**yadlala. (My beautiful dog is playing.)

Izinja **z**am **ezi**ntle **zi**yadlala. (My beautiful dogs are playing.)

Clearly, the arrangement of concords makes the language highly alliterative. The agglutinative structure also enables any given word to express a single object or idea or to contain complex sets of relationships and ideas in a compound that may be the equivalent of multiple English words. The result is that in many cases complicated concepts or even simple actions can be expressed much more succinctly and eloquently than in English. For example, during an interview with King Zwelonke, I asked a question that he had answered previously, and Zwelonke's graceful reply was "*Besendibethile*" (We have already discussed that). This single word contains the verb, the past tense, the collective subject of the action, the direct object, and a sense of polite formality and eloquent dignity captured in the slightly archaic form. The isiXhosa language is thus well suited to poetic diction in its musicality, inherent alliteration, and subtle conveyance of conditional, subjunctive, past, and future tenses. Like any language, it is also rich in idiom and figurative constructions, many of which derive from the amaXhosa peoples' connections with their environments.[21]

The isiXhosa language includes fifteen click consonants that are often used alliteratively by iimbongi. In the written language, clicks are denoted through combinations of roman consonants. Principally, there are three clicks enunciated with varying degrees of nasality or aspiration. *C* alone or in combination with other consonants (*ch, nc, ngc,* etc.) denotes forms of the frontal click, in which the tongue is sucked against the back of the front teeth to make a "tsk" sound. *Q* (*qh, gq,* etc.) indicates a palatal click, in which the tongue is sucked against the roof of the mouth and then snapped away sharply to produce a loud pop or egg-cracking sound. *X* (*xh, nx,* etc.) indicates a side click, in which the side of the mouth is clicked against the molars. In the isiXhosa language *h* is always voiced and indicates aspiration: thus *ph* is an aspirated *p,* rather than an equivalent of *f,* while *th* is an aspirated *t,* not the English dental frictive of "this" or "thin." *R* or *rh* is a guttural sound produced in the back of the throat, similar to the Scottish *ch* in "loch." Other consonants unfamiliar to English readers are the combinations *dl, hl, tl,* and *ntl.* In these combinations, the consonants are voiced with the tongue pressed against the front teeth while air is blown out on either side.

Since the arrival of Europeans in South Africa, African languages have steadily absorbed words from their languages. This applies to objects and concepts that were unknown prior to colonization and thus required new words (e.g., *ikhaphetshu* from the English "cabbage") as well as preexisting terms for which a word with English or Afrikaans origins may be substituted (e.g., *ndirayiti,* "I'm all right," in lieu of the traditional *ndiphilile,* "I'm fine"). In other cases, new words have been created as required by changes in society and technology. *Isithuthuthu* (motorbike) is a well-known example, the alliteration reminiscent of the sound of the engine. Linguistic hybridity is particularly evident in urban and peri-urban areas, where the mingling of languages and cultures has resulted in lively slang terms. One example is *ublomer phi?,* a slang variant of the standard isiXhosa *uhlala phi?* (Where do you live/stay?) that derives from the Afrikaans *blom,* "to bloom." While iimbongi make use of these urban language forms, they are also celebrated for their use of "deep Xhosa," archaic forms of the language unalloyed by the colonial languages of English and Afrikaans. The use of deep Xhosa, with its words and phrases that are often uncommon in everyday speech, is an important aspect of the affective power of iimbongi and their work.

In amaXhosa society oral poetry and imbongi have a long association with leadership and play a respected role in social commentary and political critique.[22] Historically associated with chiefs and monarchs, iimbongi have traditionally acted as court poets who work in a panegyric poetic form known as "praise poetry" that is common to various cultures in southern Africa. Panegyric, a particularly sophisticated and well-developed poetic genre in sub-Saharan Africa, is a eulogistic form, an "intermediary between epic and ode, a combination of exclamatory narration and laudatory apostrophizing" that may also incorporate clever invective, either stated overtly or couched in metaphor.[23] Traditionally, the local imbongi was a political figurehead, unique in his license to publicly criticize leadership with impunity.[24] As mediators between public and political realms, iimbongi observe, interpret, and represent society in ways that help maintain social organization and balance. Their multiple roles include contributing to cultural cohesion, maintaining cultural tradition, holding leaders to account to the people they serve, and inspiring courage and unity among community members, particularly in times of strife.[25]

The standard translation of iimbongi as "praise poets" or "praise singers" and their poetic genre as "praise poetry" is misleading in the amaXhosa context; a nuanced and political artistic genre, izibongo is as likely to be laced with barbs as praise, and it deals "with praise and blame as twin aspects of truth-telling." The central aim of many izibongo is "to fearlessly evoke the subject's true character."[26] Nevertheless, the English terms capture the spirit of the poems, which are traditionally a blend of artful critique and laudatory apostrophe: they are lofty in diction, rich in figurative language, and replete with references to historical characters and events. While there are many contemporary exceptions, izibongo are traditionally eulogistic in nature rather than epic or narrative, as is more common to oral traditions of the West (for example, the *Odyssey* or *Beowulf*). Perhaps most importantly, they are spontaneously composed in direct response to the circumstances, events, or people at hand.[27] These events are becoming increasingly diverse, and iimbongi are invited to perform not only for traditional leaders and contemporary politicians but also at festivals, weddings, funerals, and other public events.

The allusive and sophisticated language that characterizes izibongo is vital to its most studied social role, in which the poetry serves as a means of communicating important social and political information. In cases where such information risks enflaming volatile situations, the imbongi's skillful use of idiom and figurative language is vital.[28] Rich in metaphor, allegory, imagery, proverbs, and allusion, the language of the imbongi enables political commentary that is often elliptical or implied rather than overt. Meanwhile, the unexpected juxtapositions and linkages invite a momentary departure from the everyday world, inspiring new insights and ideas by enabling the poet's audience to perceive reality in novel ways. While much of the commentary is clear and resonant to the imbongi's

Fig. 1. The imbongi Thukela Poswayo performing at a wedding near the town of Engcobo. (Photo by the author)

audience, the culturally specific nature of the poetic devices means that the full power of the words is muted or even inaccessible to outsiders. The recitation of names—surnames, clan names, ancestral names, praise names, names of prized oxen and cattle—forms the backbone of the izibongo genre, further complicating it for outsiders unfamiliar with specific lineages and histories. However, as Opland points out, praise names are often commemorative of a person's attributes or accomplishments and may refer to specific events.[29] The original reference may be lost over time, while the enigmatic praise name remains. This means that the names may be obscure even to amaXhosa audiences, though their literal meanings may inspire curiosity and speculation.

It is especially important to note that in amaXhosa society the imbongi fulfils a complex role that spans spiritual cosmologies and healing practices as well as the political and social roles that have been particularly emphasized by literary scholars.[30] Certain conventions surrounding iimbongi reflect these spiritual aspects. For example, iimbongi may carry assegais or knobkerries, and their distinctive attire—which may include, for example, skins or traditional fabrics, beads of particular colors, distinctive skin hats or beaded headdresses—can be reminiscent of that worn by *amagqirha* (traditional healers). Similarly, the roaring, guttural voice often used in performing izibongo is much like that of the amagqirha, who are moved by a similar spirit.[31] While female amagqirha and iimbongi are becoming more common, historically women have been unable to serve as iimbongi because of traditions that circumscribe their speech, forbidding them from uttering the names of living and ancestral chiefs.[32] While they are becoming less common in contemporary South Africa, traditional forms of respectful speech, known as *hlonipha,* involve complex vocabularies that prevent women not only from speaking the names of their husbands' ancestors (and by extension their own married surnames) but also words that are alliterative with these names, leading to intricate languages of substitution and allusion. As the izibongo genre is based on the incantation of genealogies, praise names, clan names—invoking beneficent ancestral spirits by pronouncing their names—there is clearly a conflict of traditions when it comes to women and poetry.

IsiXhosa shifted from being a purely oral language following the arrival of missionaries with the Church of Scotland in 1824. The missionaries established themselves in Gwali, later named Lovedale, where they set up a printing press and began the publication of scriptural materials. They settled on the lands of Chief Ngqika and his people as the chief was sympathic to their cause. The history that determined the location of Lovedale, the subsequent relationships that developed between the missionaries, the amaNgqika, and the people of surrounding chiefdoms, and the recurrent violence of the Frontier Wars during the time that Christianity was introduced on the Eastern Cape are subjects too complex to recount here, and several excellent accounts exist elsewhere.[33] Suffice it to say that as a result of Ngqika's hospitality toward the missionaries, the latter based an orthography for a written isiXhosa upon the dialect of the amaRharhabe. In 1850 Wesleyan missionaries founded a short-lived monthly magazine in King William's Town that was followed by several periodicals based in Lovedale.[34] While these publications provided a venue for intellectual exchange and literary development, missionary control of their content dramatically limited the scope of the materials printed and curtailed any printed critique of growing European power in the Cape.

The State of South Africa

From 1488 onwards, South African history is a story of immense social upheaval and cataclysmic change in the relationship between humans and the natural landscape. The arrival of the Portuguese—followed by the Dutch and the English—on South Africa's shores was part of a process of forceful capitalist expansion at a global scale that was driven by Europe's need to accumulate land, labor, and materials to fuel industrial growth. As in other colonial contexts around the world, these processes would profoundly transform the landscapes and societies of South Africa, and in many ways the South African experience is simply another variation of the continent's violent experience of divide and conquer, seize and remove.[35] Yet the permanent and substantial presence of white settlers in South Africa, the size and global importance of its extractive industries, and the emergence of the apartheid order set South Africa apart. In particular, the brand of capitalist despotism that took shape in South Africa was acutely marked by relentless accumulation and geographical reconfigurations that produced stark internal disparities to the advantage of those wielding economic power.

In 1795 the early colonialism of the Portuguese and Dutch gave way to intensifying imperialism following the seizure of the Dutch Cape colony by British forces. Over the next century the South African landscape increasingly became reordered in the service of extractive capitalism, first through the conversion of vast tracts of land to privately owned farms and then through the establishment and rapid expansion of the gold and diamond industries linked to the City of London.[36] As capitalism took root in South Africa and grew, its development followed a standard trajectory in which the leading economic sector gradually shifted from agriculture to minerals over the course of the 1800s and then to the secondary and tertiary industries of manufacturing and services over the course of the twentieth century.[37] The construction of race and the promotion of racism was far from incidental to this development but rather was a consubstantial component that concentrated wealth in a few hands and prevented racialized groups from sharing in the growing prosperity of the nation.[38]

Racial policies shaped South Africa's culture and defined the development of its physical and institutional landscapes, laying a foundation of systemic discrimination that culminated in the apartheid regime.

While the seeds of inequality were planted with the arrival of the first Europeans on the Cape, it was not until the discovery of diamonds in Kimberly in 1867 and gold in the Witwatersrand in 1886 that industrialization—and its uneven distribution of benefits—got underway in earnest. The mining magnate and politician Cecil John Rhodes—who founded the De Beers diamond company in 1888, became a parliamentarian in 1890, and served as prime minister of the Cape Colony from 1890 to 1896—exemplified the tight linkages between capital and the South African state that have existed since the early days of British colonialism. One of Rhodes's primary motivators in politics and business was his professed belief that Anglo-Europeans were destined to greatness as, to quote his last will and testament, "the first race in the world."[39] Reasoning that "the more of the world we inhabit the better it is for the human race," Rhodes advocated vigorous settler colonialism to ensure "the birth of more of the English race who otherwise would not be brought into existence."[40] Regarding Africans in the Cape Colony, he wrote, "We have got to treat natives, where they are in a state of barbarism, in a different way to ourselves. We are to be lords over them. These are my politics on native affairs, and these are the politics of South Africa. Treat the natives as a subject people as long as they continue in a state of barbarism and communal tenure; be the lords over them, and let them be a subject race and keep the liquor from them."[41] These writings reveal the degree of Rhodes's white supremacy that, combined with his influential position in South Africa and England, placed him squarely in the position of "architect of apartheid" who laid the foundation for a century of institutionalized racism.[42] Rhodes's writings also make it clear that although apartheid is often blamed on the rise of Afrikaner nationalism in the early twentieth century, segregationist thinking is much older than the National Party (NP), and Afrikaners were certainly not alone in viewing themselves as a superior race.

Throughout Rhodes's tenure and into the decades that followed, racial economic disparities were increasingly imposed through a series of policies, including restrictive land acts that reconfigured settlement patterns and people's relationships with landscapes and environments. This geographical reordering was accompanied by increasingly draconian pass laws (a kind of internal passport system) and influx controls that regulated the movements of black South Africans. The first pass laws, enacted in

1896, aimed to address the problem of workers abandoning the appalling conditions of the town and worksites that had sprung up around the mines. As industrialization progressed, pass laws began to serve the opposite purpose, preventing dispossessed and impoverished rural people from relocating to urban areas. The laws effectively segregated male laborers, who were granted access to the Witwatersrand and other urban worksites, from their wives, children, and elderly relatives, who were confined to rural reserves where they survived mainly through subsistence agriculture. While traditional lifeways in rural areas changed, they did not disappear, and their persistence enabled the expanding capitalist system to offload reproductive and environmental costs.[43] These dynamics produced a separation of—and in many cases an opposition of—urban and rural, in which the urban, industrialized realm was viewed as the site of progress while the rural remained an undeveloped backwater. Such thinking reflected a colonial teleology that assigned these realms and the people associated with them to differentiated slots on a constructed social hierarchy. Apartheid, which emerged from this racialized matrix, intensified the systemic racial segregation and associated violence of the preceding centuries and furthered a series of segregationist laws that ensured the economic success of the white ruling class and lifelong poverty for other racialized groups.

While systematic racial oppression is the most familiar characteristic of South African apartheid, a simplified racial construction conceals the dialectical interrelationships between labor and capital, society and environment that are apartheid's foundation. These relationships are the subject of ongoing debate that this presentation does not mean to simplify, but of particular interest to this discussion is the revisionist critique of earlier historical accounts that emerged in the 1970s.[44] As class consciousness emerged on shop floors around the country, Marxist scholars in South Africa began to articulate an understanding of apartheid as an integral component of South African capitalism. The emerging scholarship viewed apartheid not simply as racial segregation and domination but also as domination of capital over labor that directly benefitted capitalist growth.[45] Viewed through this lens, the regime therefore represents a structurally imposed system of legalized racial violence that enacts a prolonged onslaught against labor, society, and the environment by a particularly despotic brand of racist capitalism.[46] In seeking any means possible to sever intimate human relationships with the landscape, apartheid represents a system of profound environmental injustice that reconfigured geography in the service of capital accumulation, embedding unequal relationships in the very landscape.[47]

Literatures of emancipation and agency represent one of many responses to this brutally unjust regime and played an important role in the quest for independence. Throughout the African continent, traditional and contemporary arts have long been powerful expressions of cultural identity that constitute a collective challenge to cultural imperialism as they bolster popular resistance, strengthen independence movements, and call those in power to account.[48] In the climate of extreme censorship and police brutality that defined apartheid South Africa, poets faced banning orders, violence, detention, and the very real possibility of death—authoritarian reactions that attest to the political power of their art.[49] In embracing their vocation, poets responded with courage and humanity to the transformation of landscapes and societies to spaces of industrial capitalism, to the extraction and industrialization of human bodies that enabled this transformation, and to the resulting upheaval in relationships between humans and their environments that affected people not only at social and material levels but at the psychic, spiritual, and creative levels as well.[50]

Iimbongi are complex political and intellectual figures who, since colonial times, have articulated the fraught and at times ambiguous relationship between amaXhosa people and white society. Their public performances recount national histories and local genealogies while probing the nature of the human condition and the conundrums of contemporary politics and environmental change.[51] Their poetry takes an expansive view of humanity and the richness of its emotional, imaginative, and empathetic potential, offering a lyric ethics that enables the perception of matter in ways beyond what other, more linear literary forms permit. In a postapartheid landscape, iimbongi offer an alternative view of land and place, disrupting colonial versions of private property ownership and disordering languages of management that construct lands, waters, ecosystems, and even humans and their communities as "resources" and sources of "capital" to facilitate economic growth.

This ongoing cultural resistance is vital because, despite the hope of liberation movements and the promising early years of the new administration, the end of South African apartheid has not brought about a radical reorganization of wealth or the successful establishment of long-term, effective programs to address pressing social and economic needs.[52] Instead, the advent of South African democracy coincided with the emergence of a reconfigured capitalist society that produces "three times more dollar millionaires than the global average and the fourth most in the world."[53] The social and economic conditions of contemporary South Africa reflect the interruption of a radical liberation movement by capitalist interests that curtailed a more democratic distribution of South Africa's wealth and forestalled full decolonization of its institutions. As a result, recent years have seen the South African political landscape rocked with unrest over issues ranging from inadequate housing to university fees to language politics.

Such discontent is becoming increasingly symptomatic of the neoliberal capitalist order. This global trend began in earnest in the decade preceding South Africa's transition to democracy, and as a result the independence movement shifted to accommodate new economic and cultural demands. Neoliberalism is a "macroeconomic doctrine" and a "theory of political economic practices" that promotes the ideals of individual liberty, the creative power of entrepreneurship, and the invisible hand of the market as the best ways to advance human wellbeing.[54] Achille Mbembe notes that it involves "the production of indifference; the frenzied codification of social life according to norms, categories, and numbers." Neoliberal ideology holds that markets must be free of government interference to operate efficiently; the role of the state is primarily to create a hospitable institutional environment through the removal of trade barriers and financial regulations and the creation of markets in sectors where they do not yet exist.[55] Meanwhile, "public values and any consideration of the common good are erased from politics, while the social state and responsible modes of governing are replaced by a punishing state and a Darwinian notion of social relations."[56] In South Africa these ideologies produced "adherence to free market economic principles" rather than "the radical participatory project many ANC cadre had expected."[57] Now, in democratic South Africa as elsewhere, three decades of neoliberal policies have produced a situation in which upper and middle classes fare well at the expense of poorer ones and where a formerly radical independence movement has been transformed into a neocolonial state.[58] These trends have contributed to South Africa's emergence as one of the most economically polarized societies on the planet: according to World Bank data, the poorest 40 percent of the population earns less than 4 percent of the wealth in circulation in the country while the wealthiest 10 percent earns more than half.[59]

As South Africa and many other cases illustrate, despite the enthusiastic uptake of neoliberal policies by various nations around the world since the 1980s, neoliberalism has proven a lackluster economic strategy and contributes little to overall growth. Instead, its real power lies in its ability to funnel wealth away for poorer nations and classes toward richer ones. This process of redistribution has been enabled through what David Harvey terms "creative destruction," which involves "the dismantling of institutions and narratives that promoted more egalitarian distributive measures in the preceding era" and depends on the transformation of "social relations, welfare provisions, technological mixes, ways of life, attachments to the land, habits of the heart, ways of thought and the like."[60] As neoliberalism has become the dominant political and social reality for a large portion of the world's population, its values and discourse have overflowed from the economic realm, promoting the monetization of social life and the environment and engendering a preoccupation with the profitability of all aspects of productive and reproductive processes.[61] The result has been a fundamental shift in social narratives and cultural priorities and an overall reordering of our expectations, experiences, and interpretations of the world.[62] This shift has had profound environmental consequences, as "connections between neoliberalism, environmental change, and environmental politics are all deeply if not inextricably interwoven."[63] Neoliberalism has been particularly damaging to the African continent, where it represents the latest iteration of an ongoing social and environmental pillage by colonizing and neocolonizing nations.

The neoliberal discourse of the ruling and middle classes does not align with the sentiment of the majority of South Africans who fought and sacrificed for a socialist vision involving the democratic distribution of the nation's land and wealth. In the years following the 1994 elections, the euphoria of democracy soon gave way to a widespread sense of disillusionment over social and economic realities and the failure to realize progress toward a more equitable distribution of the country's considerable wealth. General disappointment at an unjust economic structure that has failed to change appreciably since the end of apartheid has found expression in rounds of often violent citizen protests.[64] Gillian Hart claims that these "escalating struggles over the material conditions of life and livelihood are simultaneously struggles over the meaning of the nation and liberation, as well as expressions of profound betrayal."[65] At the same time, the African National Congress (ANC) has won a strong majority in each of five democratic elections in which the majority of the adult population has voted, and the party has shown reasonable competence, leading other authors to argue that the narrative of a "betrayal" or "sell-out" is simplistic.[66] Rather, the full story is tangled and complex, and many combined factors have prevented socialist—or at least egalitarian—ambitions from being realized. In any case, the ruling party's shift from leftist to neoliberal values over the past two decades has been accompanied by soaring levels of corruption and crime in the country as the gulf yawns wide between a prosperous elite and an impoverished and excluded majority.

Although apartheid is a specifically South African phenomenon that exhibits cultural and historical particularities and formations that distinguish it from the institutional racism found in other locales, the case of South Africa provides a valuable lens from which to view broader patterns of racist capitalism. In the segregated, heavily policed, and profoundly polarized terrain of the contemporary world, an independent and liberated black African continent engages with the global economy on terms dictated by the white countries of Europe and North America and according to historically established disequilibria.[67] Within the global economy, Africans remain economically excluded and culturally maligned.[68] They are on the losing end of inequitable trade relations and have been the victims of illegitimate debt and poor policies imposed by the global North.[69] With notable exceptions, Western media persist in portraying Africans as dependent, impoverished, and culturally simplistic and the African continent as a dangerous site of constant violence and dysfunction—constructions that perpetuate paternalistic, if not outright racist, beliefs.[70] These portrayals and the beliefs they foster act insidiously on the minds of westerners and serve to justify neocolonial interventions in African nations by states and corporations of the global North.[71] A critique of the history of modern South Africa therefore has important elements in common with a broader critique of industrial society and the unjust relationships between Africa and the global North. Culture and discourse play an active role in maintaining and legitimizing configurations of the global political economy by obscuring the underlying historical and political causes of the African continent's ongoing struggles. Yet at the same time, a growing crowd of prominent creative voices from Africa and its diaspora are increasingly demanding that many other truths be told.

2 / Verse, Violence, and the Migrant Labor System

> *I look at an ant and see myself: a native South African, endowed with a strength much greater than my size, so I might cope with the weight of racism that crushes my spirit.*
>
> —MIRIAM MAKEBA

An early photograph taken on the Witwatersrand shows a row of round, thatched-roof houses on an open savannah, speckled with low trees, that rises smoothly to a rocky promontory.[1] In the foreground, in front of the tall reed fences surrounding the huts, a figure in traditional dress leans on his staff while a younger man in trousers and jacket sits on the ground looking up at him. In the quiet, pastoral beauty of the scene, the two figures hint at the profound changes taking place around them. The men rest on the cusp of a colossal transition from the lifeways that had existed on the South African landscape for generations to a new order defined by capital, racial privilege, and colonial law. In 1886, a year after the photograph was taken, the discovery of gold nearby would lead to the founding of Johannesburg. Ten years later, the total multiethnic population of Johannesburg would reach seventy thousand. In 1895 Lord Randolf S. Churchill wrote of the city, "Around, wherever the eye reposes, it is arrested by mining shafts, hauling gear, engine houses and tall chimneys. Johannesburg presents a very English appearance, that of an English manufacturing town minus its noise, smoke and dirt. The streets are crowded with a busy, bustling, active, keen, intelligent-looking throng. Here are gathered together human beings from every quarter of the globe."[2] The same year, William Basil Worsfold commented, "The sudden growth of Johannesburg is the more remarkable when we remember that at first every nail, every plank, every brick, every morsel of food and every drop of drink had to be carried up to the desert plateau, for a hundred miles or more, on ox-waggons. The average pace of the ox-waggon is a mile and a half an hour.

To-day, however, the railway has brought Johannesburg within forty-nine hours of Cape Town, and seventeen or eighteen days of London."[3]

In a span of slightly over twenty years, the landscape of Johannesburg and its surroundings changed profoundly as the city's growth drew increasing numbers of people from the surrounding region and from distant sites abroad. These transformations were wrapped up in new forms of mobility as ox-wagons gave way to railways that enabled the transport of large quantities of goods and as people became increasingly mobile on the landscape. By 1920 over two hundred thousand black mineworkers lived on the Witwatersrand, part of a vast migrant workforce that formed the backbone of South African industry.[4] As workforce dynamics shifted over the early decades of the century, rising tensions culminated in 1922 in the Rand Revolt, which marked a decisive shift in politics and race relations.

Alongside major social and political developments unfolding in the late nineteenth and early twentieth centuries, changes in the literary landscape altered the terms and methods of intellectual engagement and debate.[5] In particular, isiXhosa literature was increasingly appearing in print, most notably in newspapers and other serial publications that had become staples of the South African literary landscape since their first appearance in 1837. Over the second half of the nineteenth century, these publications grew into a major forum for intellectual and literary exchange that drew on oral modes of expression.[6] As well as expressing social and political concerns of the times, isiXhosa writings through this period reflect shifting ideas of gender, family, and community and of changing relationships with landscapes and natural environments even as connections to homeland and heritage stood firm.[7]

The works of Nontsizi Mgqwetho are prime examples of such writing. Mgqwetho, a poet from the rural Ciskei who made her home in Johannesburg during the decade in which she wrote and published her poems, is "the first and only female poet to produce a substantial body of work in Xhosa," yet very little is known about her life.[8] Published regularly in the Johannesburg newspaper *Umteteli waBantu* from 1920 to 1929, Mgqwetho's poems confront the pressing social issues—ranging from the oppression of women to cultural and territorial dispossession—of a period defined by the precipitous rise of extractive capitalism and urbanization.[9] Written for vernacular-language newspapers, Mgqwetho's poems are explicitly directed toward an isiXhosa readership familiar with oral izibongo.

Yet even as her poetry denounces the social ills wrought by the upheavals of her time, Mgqwetho acknowledges the complexity of the circumstances in which they were written. These very changes brought new freedoms and reordered social structures; opened new spaces and channels of communication, debate, and literary production; and enabled a freedom of speech and creativity that would not have been possible a generation earlier. Thus, her engagement with the tumultuous social and political changes of her times is astute and nuanced: she rails against injustices imposed by whites yet also points to the various failures of blacks, including complicit silence, rampant jealousy, and a lack of unity due to internecine strife and overbearing patriarchy.[10]

Like the laborers she joined on the rapidly urbanizing Witwatersrand, Mgqwetho was a rural transplant who found herself living in an unfamiliar industrial environment according to a new and unstable set of social and cultural norms. In his anthology of her poetry, Jeff Opland introduces her as a member of the Rharhabe kingdom and the Chizama clan. Evidence suggests that she hailed from the small town of Peddie or the neighboring village of Tamara in the Ciskeian region of the Eastern Cape; however, these and other details of her life are speculative.[11] Mgqwetho's poetry suggests close ties with a rural homeland despite her life as an urban woman on the Rand. As Opland writes: "Animals feature prominently, too, the sheltering wing of a mother hen, the spots on a leopard, the stalking lion, the cow yielding only dribbles of milk and the hyenas that Christians turn into at night. Although she writes removed from her home country, her imagery is that of the countryside, rural rather than urban."[12] With both rural and urban elements present, Mgqwetho's poetry draws together the landscapes and concerns of the two realms; rather than painting them as divided jurisdictions, the poems reveal a continuum in which urban nodes are linked to the rural by a fluid movement of people between rural homes and urban workplaces, knitting the cultures and psyches of the two realms.

As well as drawing on rural themes and lifeways, Mgqwetho's poetry encapsulates concerns about environmental justice and changing human relationships with the environment in a broad sense. In engaging with the politics and social upheaval of her time, Mgqwetho is fundamentally concerned with the structural conditions and relationships leading to the chronic degradation of people and their environments. Her poetry, rooted in her oral culture and its proximity to the many inhabitants of her rural homeland—whether human, animal, or supernatural—highlights the multimodal transformation of South African landscapes and peoples by an increasingly global capitalism.[13] Crucially, it responds to a fractured and racialized environment and the systematic violence imposed on racialized bodies.[14]

This chapter discusses the work of Nontsizi Mgqwetho within the context of the conditions and events of the historical period in which she lived, showing how the social upheaval and resistance of her times permitted her, as a rural woman from an oral culture, to voice her politics well beyond her community through print media. Beginning with the discovery of gold in the Witwatersrand in 1886, I present the colonial and capitalist policies that supported the development of extractive capitalism in South Africa and the deepening segregationist politics that culminated in the establishment of apartheid in 1948. In this historical discussion, I pay particular attention to the Witwatersrand gold industry, which became the world's largest by the early twentieth century and underpinned South Africa's expanding world trade.[15]

The environmental devastation wrought by the gold industry not only fundamentally changed the local environments of the Witwatersrand but also contributed to drastic changes to human communities throughout southern Africa and to their relationships to land and nonhuman nature, profoundly altering natural environments throughout the entire region.[16] Within this complex terrain, black resistance to the politics of segregation was a form of class struggle that also combatted racial, cultural, and environmental injustices.[17] Mgqwetho's poetry, intimately tied to the gold industry and to the political and economic factors that enabled its rise, offers a window into the emerging South African state and its creation of a proletariat through divisive and violent coercion that set the stage for the apartheid order that would follow. These processes mirrored larger global processes of racial exclusion and environmental oppression being established through imperial expansion and resource extraction to ensure the ongoing prosperity of the global North.[18]

The chapter also explores some of the formal shifts that isiXhosa poetry experienced as it left the traditional realm and increasingly became a form of expression and activism for a much broader public. Mgqwetho, like other poets of her time (and the half century leading up to it), adopted certain formal elements of Western poetry, such as regular stanzas and rhyme schemes, even as she maintained traditional imagery and metaphors. Through the nineteenth and twentieth centuries, as isiXhosa poetry shifted from being an exclusively oral art form to one that is also written and printed, published poets reached wider and more ethnically diverse audiences than oral poets, who remained largely tied to place-specific venues and customs. The rise of independent black newspapers and print media permitted new freedoms in terms of literary production and distribution, fostering critical thought and facilitating lively cultural and political debate. In particular, the newspaper medium opened new possibilities without which Nontsizi Mgqwetho, a rural woman, would have been much less able to pursue a poetic practice.[19] Individual experiences of South Africa's social transformations were highly mediated by gender, and the particular politics and concerns that Mgqwetho faced as a woman are prominent in her poetry. In examining Mgqwetho's work, I consider the intersectionality of race and gender, looking at the impacts on women of colonialism, the imposition of capitalism, and the resultant migrant labor system as expressed by one of the only black female writers of the time and place. Finally, I consider Mgqwetho's writing as environmental activism by examining its direct contestation of colonial and apartheid policies that enabled the exploitation of black South Africans and their environments.

Historical and Social Perspectives

The discovery of gold in the Witwatersrand in 1886 was a watershed moment in South Africa's history. Within ten years geological surveys had determined that the deposit was the world's largest, a vast reef of uniformly low-grade ore plunging forty miles underground.[20] The low concentration of gold, the depth and vast dispersion of the deposit, and its distance from transportation centers made extraction both expensive and labor intensive; since the end price of gold was tightly controlled, the industry's profitability relied on the availability of cheap labor.[21]

By 1889 South Africa's mining industry had organized a Chamber of Mines that upheld a labor procurement enterprise based on its belief that "an abundant supply of cheap labor drawn from the colored races is of supreme importance, and without this aid there do not appear to be any great potentialities for the shareholder, the white mine employé [sic], or the country at large." The chamber also remarked that "the native of South Africa is an excellent and powerful muscular machine, and if he can be obtained in sufficient numbers and induced to remain on the mines for extended periods we do not desire to look further afield." That is, thanks to the subcontinent's latent labor supply, indentured labor would not need to be imported from distant parts of the British Empire. The chamber went on to urge that "without delay everything that is possible shall be done by the Government in placing at their disposal all the 'muscular machines' procurable from the whole of British South Africa, and such more northern parts of the continent as are within reach."[22]

Despite its size, the latent labor pool in nineteenth-century South Africa appeared unlikely to be of help to the industrialists as it consisted of autonomous and self-sufficient agrarians and pastoralists with little interest in working in the new extractive industries. Early industrial expansion was a boon to black agrarians, who enjoyed brisk sales and high prices as the growth of mining towns increased the demand for their agricultural goods. Yet industrial growth and, by extension, the South African colonial government depended on cheap labor, and the need to remove labor from the landscape and send it underground became increasingly pressing. The Chamber of Mines duly urged that "legal and moral pressure" be enacted to compel people into wage labor in greater numbers and for longer periods.[23] Following the discovery of Kimberly diamonds in 1867, and particularly after the discovery of Witwatersrand gold in 1886, mine owners, white farmers, and the colonial government colluded to bar black producers from access to land and markets while increasing tax demands.[24] The colonial government imposed a stock sequence of colonial policies—taxes, dress codes, cultural prohibitions, religious exhortations, and confinement to land reserves—designed to erode self-sufficiency while manufacturing reliance on the cash economy.[25]

The process of crushing the independent peasantry was already well underway across much of the subcontinent by the time the Chamber of Mines issued its exhortations. In the Eastern Cape the traditional lifeways of the amaXhosa were violently disrupted by the arrival of European settlers from the late eighteenth century onward.[26] Between 1779 and 1879 Afrikaner and British colonialists waged nine frontier wars against the amaXhosa people, over the course of which the border between the settlers and the amaXhosa territories marched relentlessly eastward.[27] The Eighth Frontier War (also known as the War of Mlanjeni), waged from 1850 to 1853, would become "the longest, hardest and ugliest war ever fought over one hundred years of bloodshed on the Cape Colony's eastern frontier."[28] By the end of this long and grievous conflict, many decades of violence had sapped the strength and leadership of the amaXhosa nation, exposing it to potential disaster. The tragedy that struck arrived with the prophesies of the young Nongqawuse, a niece of Mhlakaza, a chief councilor of King Sarhili. Sarhili was in turn the son of the beloved King Hintsa, who had been killed and beheaded through the treachery of Sir Harry Smith in 1835 during the Sixth Frontier War. Importantly,

"This Mhlakaza was not just a councillor, he served his people as a diviner, living at Gxarha where the Kei enters the sea."[29] Following in this lineage of seers, Nongqawuse had a vision of two strange men who asked her to relay a message to her people that would restore the former strength and wellbeing of the amaXhosa and would help drive out the white settlers:

> Tell them that the whole community will rise from the dead; and that cattle now living must be slaughtered, for they have been reared by contaminated hands, since there are people about who deal in witchcraft.
> There should be no cultivation, but new grain pits must be dug, new houses must be built, and great strong cattle enclosures must be erected. Cut out new milksacks and weave many doors from buka roots. So says chief Napakade, the descendant of Sifuba-sibanzi. The people must leave their witchcraft, for soon they will be examined by diviners.[30]

Mhlakaza passed the message on to the amaXhosa, who felt that the lung sickness rapidly spreading among their cattle was proof that the beasts were indeed tainted. In response to Nongqawuse's prophecies and the growing desperation of the period, thousands of amaXhosa killed their cattle over the course of a mass slaughter that lasted thirteen months, from April 1856 to May 1857, and resulted in the death of some four hundred thousand cattle.[31] The famine that followed brought disease, starvation, and an exodus of amaXhosa from their lands: the government census taken at the end of 1857 reported a drop in the population of British Kaffraria from 104,721 to 37,697 over the space of twelve months.[32] The catastrophe marked the end of eighty years of amaXhosa resistance and destroyed the independence of the Xhosa nation; in the years that followed almost all of the remaining lands of emaXhoseni were lost to white settlers.[33]

Altogether, conflicts, disasters, and dispossession under the capitalist expansion of the nineteenth century resulted in the upheaval and restructuring of South African rural environments and compelled the emigration of landless peasants to industrial centers; by 1904 some 53 percent of whites and 10 percent of blacks lived in towns and urban areas.[34] These demographic shifts were further escalated when the infamous Natives Land Act of 1913 established racial segregation throughout the newly minted Union of South Africa. The reserve system created under the act set aside 7.3 percent of the land base as reserves for blacks and prohibited them from residing or owning land in nondesignated areas.[35] Despite the increase of this total area in 1936 to 13 percent under the Native Land and Trust Act, the act of 1913 remained the most effective measure to date in promptly forcing thousands of black South Africans off their traditional lands and into the labor market.[36]

By designating only 13 percent of the land base for the country's entire black population, the land acts prevented all but a handful of families from surviving as independent farmers, while the remainder were driven to seek wage labor.[37] At the same time, to prevent an influx into the cities of dispossessed and impoverished blacks, increasingly draconian pass laws prevented all but employed, pass-holding blacks from relocating—even on a temporary basis—out of the reserves and into urban areas. The resultant overcrowding in the reserves led to crises of poverty and malnutrition as the densely populated agricultural lands became increasingly eroded, overgrazed, and unproductive.[38] As mounting numbers of able-bodied men were drawn into mining labor, the reserves came to serve as zones for the reproduction of labor and as dumping grounds for bodies (women, children, the elderly, and differently abled people) unnecessary for industrial profit.[39] Together with the industrial limbo of urban worker compounds and hostels, reserves formed part of a network of spaces that isolated and controlled black labor.[40]

In a matter of decades reserves, relocations, and pass laws effectively converted a large segment of the black South African population to a migrant proletariat geographically separated through the use of violent force from the white owners of the means of production. At the same time, the era's increasingly pervasive rhetoric of "civilizing" black South Africans through this process of urbanization and segmentation masked an intensive assault on their economic autonomy. Systematic attacks on black cultural institutions that celebrated traditional livelihoods and environmental relationships were part of a larger process of weakening traditional economies, generating dependency, and coercing people into the labor market.[41]

As Mgqwetho's writings make clear, the social transformations that unfolded in southern Africa were not unequivocally negative nor universally condemned by blacks. Many people in rural and urban areas alike saw opportunities in the changing economy and embraced the Western education and cultural interaction that it offered. Women in particular had a complex relationship with the emerging capitalist order. Urban South African society was largely a space of exclusion that took shape in the absence of black women, who remained systematically barred from it. Largely confined to rural reserves that they could not legally leave without a pass, most women eked out a subsistence living punctuated by the often violent homecomings of their itinerant husbands.[42] Yet for women such as Mgqwetho, who found their way into urban spaces and turned the assets of urban society to their advantage, the changing social conditions offered an alternative to the very different pressures of traditional rural life.

Histories of colonial South Africa and the emergence of the migrant labor system have tended to overlook the women's involvement in events. As in other contexts, the emergence of capitalism in South Africa is generally framed as a process of vying masculinities in which male conquerors dispossessed other men of their lands and traditional livelihoods and coerced them into white industries. Such histories omit women's experience of capitalism's assault on landscape, bodies, and society. They also overlook the effects that women's experiences and resistance efforts exerted on social and environmental transformations and the popular resistance to them. As Jeremy Krikler makes clear, white women were very much a force in the Rand Revolt and the events surrounding it, although they are largely excluded from historical accounts. Using time-honored stereotypes and gender relationships to their advantage, women played an active and often violently aggressive role in the strike, fundamentally challenging gender norms in the process.[43] Meanwhile, black women in the urban realm were active in church groups and labor movements, finding their way into situations they had been excluded from in traditional society ruled by complex social codes and gender roles.[44] For example, adopting pseudonyms for some print publications, Mgqwetho found possibilities for vehement political engagement that would have been closed to her in the more traditional rural spaces that restricted certain forms of speech to men and where anonymity was impossible.

By the early decades of the twentieth century, South African society began to buckle under the strain of increasingly untenable social conditions. The First World War had brought an astronomical increase in living costs as prices rose by almost 50 percent between 1917 and 1920.[45] By the end of the war, nearly half of South Africa's gold mines had been rendered unprofitable by wartime inflation.[46] In many rural areas agricultural productivity had begun to decline as over-cropped soils became depleted, and in September 1918, South Africa was hit by the global influenza pandemic that sent a third of the mining labor force to hospitals and brought calamity to rural communities. The war also threw labor dynamics into turmoil. As white workers enlisted, exiting the labor pool, skilled labor became increasingly scarce and costly, yet the color bar, which placed specific restrictions on blacks, prevented white labor from being replaced with black.⁴⁷ Instead, the mining industry maintained two parallel working classes: a rigidly controlled class of unskilled migrant workers coerced off the landscapes of southern Africa, and skilled white workers enticed to the remote industrial outpost of Johannesburg from Europe and other parts of the British Empire by high salaries.⁴⁸ When fifteen thousand black mine workers walked off the job demanding higher wages in July 1918, violent police clashes followed and the Chamber of Mines reiterated its commitment to the color bar enshrined in the Mines and Works Act of 1911.⁴⁹

In an earlier attempt to counter the increasingly oppressive and segregationist white government, blacks had formed the South African Native National Congress in 1912, the party that in 1923 became the African National Congress, the familiar ANC. The party's roots were far from radical: its early leaders were Western-oriented, mission-educated Christians who aimed to join the middle class as equals then gradually extend these benefits to the rest of the black population.⁵⁰ Yet their efforts to advance equality and the economic wellbeing of black South Africans through rational argument and constitutional means met with little success. Not only did they fail to win any substantial ground from whites determined to maintain the status quo, but also, mired in organizational incapacities and financial constraints, they were unable to garner mass support from blacks.⁵¹

Instead, the situation for blacks steadily worsened. In September 1919 five London banks instated the gold standard, fixing the price of gold on the world market and making it impossible for South African companies to pass their high extraction costs on to consumers. Gold prices temporarily rose before dropping by nearly a third, which triggered an industry crisis. For mines to remain profitable, owners estimated that they would need to replace some ten thousand white mine workers with blacks, who were paid a tenth the wage on average. Such a move would equate to the collapse of the color bar and instigate the upheaval of a carefully maintained social and industrial order. Instead, the Chamber of Mines announced that it would replace only two thousand white workers with cheaper black workers. Yet even this smaller shift left thousands of white workers facing the threat of an imminent loss of livelihood in precarious economic times. Rising tensions between workers—both black and white—and mine owners culminated in the Rand Revolt of 1922. The movement began as a walkout in response to the chamber's announcement and quickly flared into a general strike and then an armed rebellion in which insurgents attempted to take control of Johannesburg. Prime Minister General Jan Smuts imposed martial law, and the ground and air troops of the Union

Defense Force quelled the violence within a week, forcing mine workers into unconditional acceptance of the owners' terms. Smuts drew intense criticism for his handling of the revolt, and in the 1924 election was defeated by the Nationalist and Labour Parties.[52]

New acts by the Pact government, a coalition led by J. B. M. Herzog, deepened segregation by protecting the jobs of white workers and voters while securing a continued supply of cheap labor from throughout the region. Hertzog's Industrial Conciliation Act, which commenced in April 1924, excluded blacks from membership in registered trade unions and prohibited registration of black trade unions. Over the next fifty years, upwards of two hundred thousand laborers annually would travel to the Rand from the northern colonies of Bechuanaland (now Botswana), Southern Rhodesia (Zimbabwe), and Mozambique and from as far away as Northern Rhodesia (Zambia) and Nyasaland (Malawi), where the tariffs on labor exports generated a welcome source of income for colonial governments.[53] As the demand for labor spread into these northern areas, the mining industry exploited conditions of poverty and desperation, coercing laborers from pastoral and agrarian lives destabilized by colonialism into an alien and dangerous industrial environment. Once on the Rand, these men became the chief source of profit for white shareholders and mine owners, largely in Britain, Europe, and North America.[54]

Clearly, although apartheid officially began with the election of D. F. Malan's Nationalist Party in 1948 by a slim majority, an array of contributing factors had been brewing for decades. Racism was part of the fabric of British colonial thought, and segregationist strategies were systematically established through the labor, settlement, and military policies of the political and economic establishment. As these policies were meted out, whites reiterated their power over blacks dispossessed through white imperial power and a variety of conspiring calamitous events, including the loss of both their lands and their independent livelihoods.

Mgqwetho's Ecopoetry

It was into this turbulent social context that Nontsizi Mgqwetho emerged, earning a reputation as Mbongikazi, the woman poet, through her oral performances before going on to publish her first poem in the isiXhosa newspaper *Umteteli waBantu* in 1920.[55] Over the decade that followed, she would go on to publish nearly one hundred poems that spoke directly to the issues of her time, calling for an end to white domination and for unity among her people in addressing the struggles and injustices they faced.

Her poetry laments the confusion and conflict that, by the 1920s, had come to define the amaXhosa experience: internecine strife and jealousies, spiritual and cultural upheaval, alcoholism, exploitation, and abuse at the hands of whites. In its attention to these and other concerns, her work is also intensely environmental. In Mgqwetho's poetry the entanglement of human, animal, and spiritual realms reveals the ecological orientation of rural amaXhosa society and its proximity to nonhuman entities. Meanwhile, her indictments of colonial society and its ecologically devastating industries and her calls for Africans to return to their rural homelands and cosmologies are in many ways consistent with Cajetan Iheka's observation, in the context of Amos Tutuola's *The Palmwine Drikard*, that "anticolonial resistance resides precisely in naturalizing Africa, by yoking together the human and nonhuman worlds threatened by a colonialist, rational ideology."[56]

For example, in "I Afrika ihleli Ayiyangandawo!!" ("Africa stayed! She's nowhere else!!") she writes,

I Afrika ihleli ayiyangandawo	Africa stayed! She's nowhere else!!
Kangela enceni wofik' isahluma	Look how the grass continues to sprout.
Kangela imitombo yamanz' isatsitsa	Look at the springs still bubbling with water.
Kangela yonkinto imi ngendlelayo	Look all around, it's all in its place!
Uti "Mayibuye?" makubuye wena	You say "Come back"? *You* must come back!!
Nezizwe zomhlaba zix'witana ngawe	You're profit to all the earth's nations:
Zipuma e Node zipuma e Sude	they come from the north, they come from the south,
Kwasempumalanga nase Ntshonalanga	out of the east and out of the west.
Zip' intombi zenu? Izwi liyintoni	Where are your daughters? What do you say?
Sigqibe lomhlaba sishweshwe zihange	"We roamed the countryside, shacked up with gangsters,
Site nzwi nendlebe butywala bomlungu	we're up to the ears in the white man's booze."
Kodwa yen' umlungu akabudl' obetu.	But the white doesn't drink a drop of yours.[57]

In these stanzas Mgqwetho evokes the pastoral imagery of rural Africa and then angrily derides not only the exploitation of black South Africans, whose lives and bodies are abused for foreign profit, but also the complicity of blacks themselves in this process and in upholding an unjust colonial culture with no interest in reciprocity or mutual learning. It is impossible for the land and nation of South Africa to enjoy the wealth and freedoms of its past without the commitment of blacks to a different future than that offered by whites. Here it is not South Africa that has changed but rather the minds and hearts of her compatriots. In this poem, as in others, Mgqwetho makes her political point through natural imagery juxtaposed with descriptions of urbanization and its social transformations, suggesting that "coming back" to Africa may mean a return to rural ancestral homelands from the cities that are manifestations of the false promises of whites.

At the same time, Mgqwetho makes it clear that, despite their complicity with the new white society and their exploited and downtrodden position within it, blacks have plenty of vigor with which to make real change if they desire it:

Ingonyama yobumnyama isagquma	The lion of blackness still roars
Napakati kwetu zizwe ezimnyama	from the midst of our black nations:
Masivumise ke nase zazulwini	let's seek the truth from those above,
Zabafa kudala nabafa kutsha.[58]	those long dead and the recent deceased.

In these lines, from the poem, "Ingonyama! Yobumnyama Isagquma!" ("The lion of blackness still roars"), Mgqwetho reminds readers of precolonial cosmologies in which people live closely with benevolent ancestral spirits who are ready to lend their assistance when called upon to do so.

Yet even as she calls for a return to traditional African values, Mgqwetho resists turning unequivocally to anticolonial pastoral tropes that might suggest an easy route to healing and redemption by reviving indigenous cultural values.[59] This overall sense of ambivalence is expressed both in her oeuvre as a whole and in individual poems or stanzas. For example, in "Ingxoxo yo Mginwa ku Magqoboka!" ("A Red debates with Christians"), Mgqwetho takes the position of a traditionalist berating Christians:

Aninalutando aninayo nani	You're bereft of love, bereft of all,
Kodwa nizibiza no Tixo wotando	yet you proclaim a God of love:

Lonkolwana yenu yokusikohlisa	that faith of yours stands just as tall
Mina ingangam ndiguqe ngedolo	as I do down on my knees.
Nakufika kuti tina bomaqaba	If you ever try to come near us again,
Tina sakunoja siti niyinyama.	we Reds will roast you like meat.
Anditsho ukuti Izwi lika Tixo	But I'm not saying the word of God
Ukuteta kwalo akunanyaniso.[60]	is entirely barren of truth.

While she avoids reinventing the precolonial past as a romanticized world of bucolic beauty and harmony, she nevertheless champions the traditions and beliefs of the Reds, those amaXhosa who have not converted to Christianity, and urges a widespread return to precolonial roots. In "Utywala Sisiqu Sempundulu!" ("Liquor's the lightening bird itself!"), Mgqwetho unfurls fiery denouncements only to throw them into ambiguity in her closing stanza.

Anditsho ke ukuti busisono	I don't insist that drinking's a sin,
Ndingatsho nokuti abusiso isono	then again, I'm not saying it's not;
Kodwa ke konke okudaliweyo	there's a lesson for us
Kuti—kunentshumayelo yako.	in all that occurs.[61]

In both poems Mgqwetho alternately praises and castigates Christianity and modern society, pointing out slippery ambiguities. Similarly, in "Umfula! Wosizi!!" ("The stream of despair"), she writes,

Izwi nabelungu kade lafikayo	Long ago the whites brought the word;
Sixakiwe lilo kuba linxa zonke	we're confused that it bends with the wind:
Liko ngaku Tixo kuti ligalele—[62]	over there it's with God, over here it flogs us.

Rather than endorsing a return to a non-European past, she embraces the Christianity that is the legacy of white conquest while problematizing interpretations of the scriptures and their malleability to suit particular agendas. She also denounces those who have embraced colonial ways for personal gain despite the social division that results.[63]

Yet even as the upheaval and urbanization of the nineteenth and early twentieth centuries wrought havoc on social life, they also opened possibilities for Mgqwetho that were unheard of for women of previous generations. Not only did she learn to read and write, but she applied these skills with verve, becoming one of the most accomplished poets of her time and place. Stepping into the opportunities that a changing South Africa afforded her required a large degree of fearlessness, which Mgqwetho clearly possessed in ample quantity. Her poetry suggests that she rode a wave of change, leaving her rural homeland and stepping into a new life on the Rand as a childless, unmarried woman. Given the traditional worldviews and spiritualities that would have tightly circumscribed women's lives during her time, her visionary dissension involved a degree of courage that contemporary commentators may overlook. From her debut poem in *Umteteli waBantu*, Mgqwetho acknowledges the gendered politics of this new territory and launches herself in regardless, from her first poems establishing herself as an imbongi with the right and indeed the duty to criticize openly. As she points out in "Imbongi u Chizama" ("Chizama the poet"), poets have always been male; only now, in "the land of thugs and booze," is it possible for her to respond to her calling and express herself freely.

Hamba Sokulandela,	Go and we'll follow you:
Kuba tina simadoda nje asizange	no female poet
Siyibone kowetu imbongikazi	came from our house:
Yenkazana kuba imbongi inyuka	the poet who rouses the court
Nenkundla ituke inkosi.	and censures the king's always male.
Hamba Sokulandela,	Go and we'll follow you!
Nezi mbongikazi Tina sizibona	We first encountered these female
Apa kweli lo laita ne bhekile.	poets
	here in this land of thugs and booze.[64]

The changing social landscape opened new possibilities for expression that were unavailable in the traditional realm, where defying the rules and cultural norms associated with speech brought harsh physical consequences. In "Pulapulani! Makowetu" ("Listen, compatriots!"), Mgqwetho tells us,

Taru! Nontsizi intombi ka Sandile	Mercy, Nontsizi, Sandile's daughter,
Mntana wenkosi kwinkosi zakwa Ngqika	child of the Ngqika paramount.
Kubonga amakosi not amabhungexe	You were thrashed by kieries on Ngqika plains
Watshiswa zinduku kumataf' akwa Ngqika.	for praising chiefs and *not* commoners.[65]

The lines illustrate the physical consequences women faced in daring to practice as iimbongi. As Thulani Nxasana explains, "Mgqwetho was censured and assaulted by kieries (which only men carried) for attempting to praise chiefs. This was taboo in Xhosa society and she was disciplined for doing that; women could bonga (praise) but only imbongi could praise chiefs or hold the status of imbongi."[66] Women were prevented from becoming iimbongi, a poetic tradition rooted in naming, because of the limitations on their ability to utter names. Traditionally, women were forbidden from uttering the names of the chiefs or their ancestors, while married women show respect for husband's ancestors through hlonipha (respectful) speech that involves avoiding particular words because of their association with the forefathers. In households that adhere to this tradition, avoided words are substituted with synonyms to form a richly allusive language that informs and extends isiXhosa poetry.

The arrival of Christianity and mission educations introduced new spiritual teachings that altered many people's relationships with both ancestral spirits and the spoken word as they challenged the power and primacy of both. It is surely no coincidence that not only did Christianity negate ancestor veneration, but the print media that missionaries introduced also brought about a shift in understandings of literature and in the power dynamics surrounding the possession, circulation, and transmission of words, names, and knowledge. Furthermore, Christianity loosened the traditional bonds within families and communities by providing an individualist alternative to communal modes of living.[67] On the whole, the religious beliefs and the print medium introduced by missionaries changed the dynamics of language, destabilizing and reconfiguring traditional relationships between men and women, youth and elders, living and dead, as they upended notions of culture, intellect, and eloquence. For Mgqwetho, the anonymity offered by urban society and the literary medium of newspapers made it possible for her to breach taboos. Nxasana points out that her liberated speech would not be tolerated in rural society, where "her father or husband, if she were married, would be addressed and instructed to keep her in line and discipline her." As a woman "she would be relegated to a passive and subservient position."[68]

With her defiant debut in *Umteteli waBantu,* Mgqwetho signaled her audacity with respect to amaXhosa tradition and its adherents and conveyed her willingness to speak out in her own terms—despite the potentially dire consequences that such "speech" might bring. In doing so, she straddled the complex transition from traditional to modern and from oral to written text, and she captured the changing meanings and spiritual understandings that such transitions entailed. Walter Ong notes that "deeply typographic folk tend to forget to think of words as primarily oral, as events, and hence as necessarily powered." Spoken language is inherently dynamic, "a mode of action and not simply a countersign of thought" that can convey power over things.[69] Seen in this light, taboos that restrict the utterance of names to specific people and occasions are relevant in maintaining a harmonious social order.

Considering the power and importance of names in amaXhosa society, Ashlee Neser's claim that "for Xhosa poets like Yali-Manisi, Mqhayi and Mgqwetho, there is no contradiction in using print to harness the rhythms, authorities and ways of speaking offered by oral genres" seems to overly simplify matters, particularly when considered alongside her competing claim that "written izibongo must, in Opland's sense, fail as sacred invocation because it solidifies its expression and publishes community in profane contexts of print circulation."[70] While there may not be a *contradiction* between written and oral, the two media clearly differ profoundly and serve different purposes, audiences, and resonances. Much more than simply harnessing the rhythms of speech or defying gender norms, Mgqwetho's poetry calls into question fundamental understandings about the nature of the spoken word and the power of names to call forth the ancestral shades, and it challenges accepted notions of who has the right to exercise such power and under what circumstances. For these reasons, Mgqwetho also has a complex relationship with both the oral and the written word: the former, with its tight linkages to traditional beliefs, limited possibilities for her as a woman; writing and print publications opened possibilities of expression that would not have been available in her rural home. Her work explores shifting equilibria of freedom and responsibility as literary media and traditional environments transformed.

Clearly, Mgqwetho's relationships with tradition and modernity are complicated; she is unpredictable in terms of both compliance and defiance, and these instabilities are reflected in her poems. In some poems, for example, Mgqwetho defers to tradition, writing, "Amagama enkosi ayandipazamisa" (the names of kings confuse me) or "Ndifungo k'ok'o nobawo ndizalayo" (I swear by my shades, and my father who sired me), thus avoiding the contentious act of naming.[71] Whether such avoidance was a bid to appease her audiences or the ancestors themselves is unclear, but it is certain that for a strong believer in both Christian and amaXhosa traditions, Mgqwetho's acts of defiance may have exposed her not only to physical harm from men with kieries but also to the potential malevolence of offended ancestral spirits.

In her poems Mgqwetho also makes it clear that her understanding of and relationship with tradition is much different from that of her male peers. When she calls for a return to traditional values, it is with full understanding of the complications associated with these values—the constraints and unfreedoms they impose that are felt unequally by different members of society. Mgqwetho is under no illusions about the restrictions and limitations of precolonial amaXhosa society; rather than romanticizing, she complicates traditional and contemporary society alike, acknowledging the literary possibilities that the latter opened for her that were "not possible in the rural space where Mgqwetho herself was physically assaulted by knobkierries" for her forthright speech.[72]

Yet even as the "loss of traditional values in the city" enabled Mgqwetho "to take up the title and position of imbongi through the medium of newspapers, a space and position denied her in the rural space because of her gender," the extent to which she speaks through a variety of assumed personae, often while writing under a nom de plume, suggests that the relationship between the woman poet and her readership was also complicated and possibly fraught.[73] Faced with social codes that prevented her from playing a public role in literature and politics, Mgqwetho adopted various strategies, including the technique of writing from the perspective of assumed voices that she uses to amplify her own arguments and concerns: "At times, she speaks in the stentorian and largely male voice of the praise poet/prophet admonishing corrupt and ineffective leadership and delivering jeremiads against those in authority. At times, she adopts the position of the male/female diviner and healer, offering her poems as prognostications and diagnoses."[74] Thus, even as "Mgqwetho advocates for the return to traditional African values," she also notes "the advantages of moving [out] of the traditional rural setting into the city."[75]

For Mgqwetho, shifting gender roles are both emblematic and metaphorical of broader social shifts and upheavals going on around her. For example, in "Ingxoxo yo Mginwa ku Magqoboka!" ("A Red debates with Christians") she berates Christianity from the perspective of an adherent of amaXhosa tradition.

> Zip' intombi zenu Izwi liyintoni
>   Zigqibe lomhlaba zifuna
>   ukwenda
> Ziqeshe zindlwana zishweshe utuli
>   Zibet' onomtatsi kwa
>   Tulandivile!

> Where are your daughters? What do you say?
>   They crossed the land in search of marriage,
> shamelessly shacked up with live-in lovers,
>   cavorted in dances with young men in New Clare.

Onina balila amehlo azidudu 　Kushiywa lusapo lumka bekangele Beyala belila bengenakuviwa 　Zintombi zemfundo nonyana bemfundo!	With eyes of porridge their mothers 　bemoan their absent children, who left them standing, advising blank air and pleading in vain 　with sons and daughters who've all been to school.[76]

Later, she directly connects female vulnerability to dispossession and injustice in "'Ub'inqo'! We-Afrika!!" ("Africa's petticoat"), wherein the dropping of petticoats signifies rape.

Mazitete! Nembongi mhla kwaw' inyembezi Zo "Mb'inqo" we Afrika sincede Mhlekazi Owawupilisa umpefumlo wo Hlanga Lwezizwe Zintsundu ngapantsi kwe Langa. . . . . Wawa! Ngenyani "Umb'inqo" we Afrika Kwane Bhaibhile isongwa isomb'uluka Apo zikon' inkosi zase mlungwini Ezi ne bhaibhile ezingo mb'axambini.	Let poets speak of the day of tears for Africa's petticoat—please, Sir— which restored the soul of the land of every Black nation under the sun. . . . . Truly, Africa's petticoat's dropped! The bible slips from our hands and slams shut; in that world of white lords and masters the bible speaks with forked tongue.[77]

The stanzas are unambiguous in their condemnation of the bible and the white lords and masters who wield it for their own gain. Missionaries were as much forerunners of dispossession as they were spiritual emissaries, and Mgqwetho suffers no illusions about the ulterior motives of whites, whatever their clothing and spiritual inclinations. In South Africa, particularly in Eastern Cape province and among the amaXhosa that are the focus of this study, missionaries played a large part in colonization and were perhaps more responsible than any other group for undertaking a complete conversion and revolution of traditional African life.[78] V. Y. Mudimbe describes at length how Christianity and its discourse operated as key features of the spread of European empires in Africa: "With equal enthusiasm, [the missionary] served as an agent of a political empire, a representative of civilization and an envoy of God. There is no essential contradiction between these roles. All of them implied the same purpose: the conversion of African minds and space."[79] In consolidating their power, missionaries used discursive approaches: "Derision of so-called primitive religions and their gods, refutation and demonstration to convince the evolving Africans, and imposition of rules and orthodoxy and conformity for converts."[80]

For Mgqwetho, who accepted Christianity but did not hesitate to point out the failings and inconsistencies of its leaders, Christianity provided a guiding moral framework but also spurred her fiery and rebellious verses. Crucial to the development of printed isiXhosa literature, Christianity also paved the way by introducing both printing technologies and orthography for the language. The decade in which Mgqwetho wrote marked a breakthrough for isiXhosa literature in which it began to break definitively from its missionary roots: "The slow groundswell of books published in the first twenty years of the century crested after 1920, when major works of poetry, fiction, drama, biography and folklore appeared."[81] African-language newspapers, which had begun to appear in the mid-nineteenth century, grew into a major vehicle for the publication of isiXhosa literature and extended the rich literary heritage established by nineteenth-century missionary presses. Newspapers played a significant role in the development of literary genres and styles and provided a forum for vibrant debate among the black intelligentsia.

It is noteworthy that Mgqwetho chose *Umteteli waBantu* (*Mouthpiece of the People*) as her principal venue after the publication of her first two poems in *Abantu Batho*. Established by the Chamber of Mines and the Native Recruiting Corporation in the wake of the mine strike of 1920 and published weekly until 1956, *Umteteli waBantu* was designed to counter the more radical newspaper, *Abantu Batho* (*The People*).[82] Established in 1912, "chiefly as an official mouthpiece of the newly established South African Native National Congress (SANNC)," *Abantu Batho* was published in English, SeSotho, isiZulu, isiXhosa, and SeTswana, making it the most widely read black newspaper in South Africa until 1931.[83] The paper commented on a variety of political issues and current affairs, including the inequality and exploitation of black workers in general and in particular their resistance during the 1918 municipal workers' bucket strike, the 1919 pass protests, and the 1920 African miners' strike.[84] It also took a particular interest in women's rights during these years, and its "reporting on women workers and the formation of the National League of Bantu Women (NLBW) illustrates editors' relatively progressive views on gender and class.⁸⁵ Yet the increasingly radical views of the paper upset both mine owners and conservative members of SANNC who opposed the growing Communist presence in the pages of *Abantu Batho* as well as within their own organization. The response, *Umteteli waBantu*, aimed to appeal to moderate blacks on the Witwatersrand and in its recruiting areas, competing with *Abantu Batho* not only for the same readership but also for many of the same contributors, whom they offered higher pay for their services.⁸⁶ *Umteteli*'s editorial policy, as expressed in its 30 August 1924 issue, stated, "We are charged to preach racial amity, to foster a spirit of give and take, to promote the will to co-operate, to emphasize the obligations of black and white to themselves and to each other, and generally to create an atmosphere in which peace and goodwill might thrive."⁸⁷ These editorial efforts resulted in "a major contribution to Xhosa literature"; over the twenty-five years in which it was published, "its pages were filled with creative writing of the highest order."⁸⁸

Jeff Opland speculates that Mgqwetho's transfer of allegiances may have been prompted by her disillusionment with SANNC leaders.⁸⁹ It is also possible that she was drawn to *Umteteli* through her friendship with Charlotte Maxeke, the editor's wife. In any case, for much of the period in which their publication overlapped, tensions between the papers simmered, with Mgqwetho's poetry adding heat. For example, her poem "Imbongikazi No 'Abantu-Batho'" ("The woman poet and *Abantu-Batho*"), attacked *Abantu Batho* and its editor both for criticizing *Umteteli* and for suggesting that it was *Abantu Batho* that had brought her to the Rand from her rural home.⁹⁰

Hawulele! Hule!	Hawulele! Hule!
Wena "Abantu-Batho"	*Abantu-Batho*,
Wawuba uyakusala	you thought you'd retain
Negama lobugosa.	the title of guardian.
Umteteli wa Bantu	*Umteteli wa Bantu*
Kudala akubonayo	saw right through you:
Uyimvaba engenawo namanzi	you're a sack without water
Eyode izale onojubalalana.	left to breed tadpoles.
. . . .	. . . .
Akuyazi wena Mvabaza	Mvabaza, you're blind
Nendalo ka Tixo	to God's creation,
Naku nam soundenza	wanting me woman poet
Imbong'kazi ka "Abantu Batho"	of your *Abantu-Batho*.

Uyavula wena weza	You brag that you brought
Nembongikazi e Ngqushwa	the woman poet from Peddi
Ukuba mayizokukwenzela	to earn your bread
Isonka e Rautini	in Johannesburg!
Sakubona	That'll be the day![91]

Sarah Mkhonza points out that through such poems, "Mgqwetho helps us to see how the papers created a dialogue on African issues . . . , enlivening debates via interactions of editors and contributors."[92]

These debates took place alongside rising political struggles that included the evolving presence of the ANC and the tightening and enforcement of imposed racial divisions. Mgqwetho responds to these conditions throughout her poetry and urges her compatriots to do likewise. For instance, in "Ukutula! Ikwakukuvuma!" ("Silence implies consent") Mgqwetho displays the traditional spirited energy of an imbongi rousing her audience to action over the state of the country, beginning by urging them to speak out and bring an end to compliant silence.

Taru! Mhleli ngesituba sezi Mbongi!	Editor, thanks for the poets' column, we can't sit silent, the country's rotten:
Asinakutula umhlab' ubolile	
Xa ndikubonisa ubume bomhlaba	if I exposed the state of the country
Angabhekabheka onk'amagqoboka.	the Christians' jaws would drop.
Ukutula! Ikwakukuvuma	Silence implies consent!
Xa ungatandi ukuhlala ujanyelwa	White eyes sear us on entering a church,
Ungapendula kwabezinye imvaba	
Akulunganga ukukonza unomkanya	but we're free to worship someplace else:
	It's no fun to pray looking over your shoulder.
Lemiteto idlula eka Moses	The laws outnumber those of Moses!
Lihasa kuwe eliza ngokutula	They dish out your portion if you sit silent:
Litupa lengwe lanyatel'esangweni	
Kuba ngokutula! Bati uyavuma!	It's the tracks of a leopard across your yard.
	If you sit silent they say you agree.[93]

Notably, even as she acknowledges the pain of dispossession and the undisciplined power of whites to wreak havoc on her people and her country, Mgqwetho does not allow her people to escape responsibility for the state of their nation. In many poems she gives voice to the heartbreak of her dispossessed people yet holds them responsible for the squabbling that keeps them in pain. In the opening stanzas of "Isizwe! Esingavaniyo! Nesingavelaniyo! Siyadwatywa Zezinye!!" ("Strangers strip a squabbling nation"), she writes,

Vusa! Inimba yakumakowenu	Induce birth pangs in your people,
Yakulo Ngubenc'uka kwezakowenu	as in Ngubencuka's time;
Utete ngelidala ngelika Hintsa	speak as of old in Hintsa's voice.
Amagama enkosi ayandipazamisa	(The names of kings confuse me.)
Shu! Hay' into imbi ukufa kwe Sizwe	Shu! The death of a nation's painful!
Obuzabuzayo ubuza nto nina	Why seek the why and the wherefore?
Siluhlantlalala olungenabani	We're just a dispossessed rabble,
Into zokudwatywa zicangalaliswe.	fit to be stripped for thrashing.[94]

Here she calls on great ancestral chiefs to inspire in their people the courage for rebirth from what she paints as a dying nation in which "people are crushed by their burdens" and eaten by their own envy. Yet in the third stanza, she seems to lose faith in the ancestors' willingness or ability to assist, writing, "Taru Afrika! Mfi ziyabizana / Abantu bako ngumhlamb' onganandili" (Mercy, Africa, you're dead to the pleas / of the ravaged flock of your people). In a later poem, "Singu-Ndabamlonyeni!" ("We're the topic of talk"), she denounces the oppressive presence of whites in South Africa, yet quietly chastises her people for their short-sightedness and naïveté in failing to see the true colors of the intruders:

Kanti nene nene beza kutshutshisa	The simple truth is they came to oppress,[95]
Nge bhaibhile zabo beza kunyelisa	they came to blaspheme with their bibles,
Safika sonke tina mzi ka Ngqika	and all of us in Ngqika's House
Sangayiboni nalo ntsimbi yomxaka.	failed to suspect their armbands of iron.[96]

At the same time, the poem goes on to describe how the early relationship between whites and the amaXhosa was not straightforward; given the spiritual and material largesse of the whites and the learning they continue to offer, the ongoing conflict and turmoil of the relationship is understandable:

Asivi ngandaba sibona ngamehlo
Azi batini bona abanamehlo
Izwe selimfusa ayawa amag'ora
Izwe lobawo namhla lizingxondora.

There is no hearsay, we actually saw it.
What do the far-sighted make of all this?
Our country's benighted, our heroes fall,
In the land of our fathers lie rough mounds today.

Baduda benetemba lezi Bhalo
Lahlani pantsi eyenu imibhalo
Namhlanje sesifana nezimumu
Izwe lo bawo ligquma zinkanunu.

They danced with their faith in the scriptures:
"Discard your striped woolen blankets."
Today we resemble mutes.
In the land of our fathers the canons roar.

Mhla bafika kwakuyole de kwancama
Namawonga akowetu sawancama
Sakubona nalemfundo beze nayo
Ndifungu Ndlambe no bawo 'ndizalayo.

The day they arrived there was joy without measure.
We freely abandoned our majesty on seeing the learning they brought,
I swear by Ndlambe and my father who sired me.[97]

In these and other passages Mgqwetho links land, dispossession, and spirituality in a seamless emotive flow. While she does so using the forms and devices of oral izibongo—rhythm, alliteration, exclamatory address—her poetry also conforms to formal elements of written poetry, including regular stanzas, regularly indented lines, and, in later poems, rhyme. Thus even within the formal construction of the written texts, African and occidental traditions are actively engaged with one another, destabilizing one another, writing and rewriting the story of colonial encounter and its environmental legacy.

EmaXhoseni Pasts and Futures

During eighty years of frontier wars against Afrikaner and British settlers, the amaXhosa fought for much larger stakes than the ownership and control of territory. The struggle was also for the right to continue to live in close kinship with the landscape and the animals and spirits they shared it with and for the right to maintain the independent lifeways that the land sustained. In precolonial emaXhoseni, the cattle with whom the amaXhosa people lived so intimately were an extension of land and independence, an integral part of a triumvirate in which the breakdown of any one element spelled the subsequent loss of the others. This was witnessed following the disastrous cattle-killing event that resulted in loss of land and the collapse of independent nationhood. The catastrophe was a decisive blow to precolonial amaXhosa society, and it further advanced a massive cultural shift that had begun with the arrival of missionaries nearly a century earlier. As people migrated or took up employment in colonial industries to survive, the cattle-killing became another in a series of violent processes that wrenched people from their ancestral lands.

Fifty years later Nontsizi Mgqwetho emerged as an utterly unique figure in South African letters; no other woman before or since has produced a similar literary output in isiXhosa. She certainly lived a bravely unconventional life for a woman of her era and exercised her ability to speak despite the various risks that such speech involved. Even more striking is the extent to which Mgqwetho engaged in a vigorous critique of the society that she saw taking shape around her. Her poetry speaks to and about the discord that she saw increasingly defining South African society. Divided conditions pitted rural against urban, white against black, Christian against Red in newly imposed dichotomies that were redefining social life and environmental relationships in an industrializing South Africa. Within this world both nature and women were treated as "free goods," while new sexual divisions of labor devalued women's work and role in society even as they offered new freedoms.[98] As a rural woman by birth who wrote from her urban home on the Rand, Mgqwetho speaks from a social segment that typically remains silent and silenced, prevented from public speech and sequestered in rural environments far from literary media. She brings to South African literature a perspective and voice that fearlessly challenged the emerging political and spiritual systems that constructed women and adherents of traditional practices as secondary citizens and that actively built the structural conditions to keep them in that place.

3 / *Black Mamba* and the Durban/Rural Nexus

> *You moving forest of Africa!*
> *When I arrived the children were all crying.*
> *These were the workers, industrial workers,*
> *discussing the problems in industrial work in Africa.*
> *I saw one of them consoling others,*
> *wiping their tears from their eyes.*
> *I saw workers, because in his eyes too the tears flowed.*
> *Worker, what's that cry "Maye" about?*
> *You're crying, but who's hassling you?*
> *Escape into that forest, the black forest that the employers saw and then ran*
>   *for safety.*
> *The workers saw it too: "It belongs to us," they said.*
> *"Let's take refuge in it to be safe from our hunters."*
> *Deep in the forest they hid themselves, and when they came out they were*
>   *free from fear.*
>
> —ALFRED THEMBA QABULA

So opens "Praise Poem to FOSATU," performed by Alfred Themba Qabula during his first public appearance at a rally of the newly formed Federation of South African Trade Unions in Durban in 1984.[1] Qabula, a migrant laborer and shop steward from the rural Transkei Bantustan, spent most of his working life as a forklift operator in the Dunlop tire factory in Durban. His boyhood was a story of hunger, violence, and insecurity familiar to millions of rural South Africans who grew up in the 1960s in the impoverished countryside of what is now Eastern Cape province. Yet as he took the stage that day, roaring out his impassioned, impromptu lines before an audience of several thousand, Qabula became exceptional. Over the next decade, as a playwright, poet, performer, and organizer, he grew into a leading member of what was to become one of the most dynamic cultural movements in the country.

Qabula was part of a vibrant working-class culture that arose from the South African labor movement of the 1970s and 80s. Drawing on traditional literary forms and motifs, the "worker poets" became a prominent voice of antiapartheid resistance. Performed during union meetings and community gatherings before audiences of thousands, their poems gave voice to the grim experiences of black laborers.[2] As union membership surged throughout the 1980s, iimbongi played a pivotal role in articulating the experiences of an invisible working class, educating its rank and file, galvanizing laborers into action, and promoting social cohesion in the pursuit of a common cause. In challenging the extractive theft inflicted on their communities and environments, the worker poets exemplify a version of environmentalism that resisted not only the exploitation of African labor under the apartheid regime but also the environmental injustice that this subjugation involved.

Resistance to white settlement and capitalist expansion was forceful and ongoing in South Africa from early colonial times onward, yet it was not until the Durban strike wave, student protests, and township uprisings of the early to mid-1970s that fragmented resistance developed into the sweeping, unified force that would eventually liberate the country. Following significant cultural shifts in the workplace and the removal of restrictions on union participation, South Africa's labor movement grew into one of the country's most significant instruments of rebellion and played a decisive role in the transition to democracy. The movement owed its success to the strength, tenacity, and organization of its participants as well as to the passion and dedication that the worker poets helped inspire.

In 1986 poets Alfred Temba Qabula, Nise Malange, and Mi S'dumo Hlatshwayo published *Black Mamba Rising: South African Worker Poets in Struggle*, a collection of their poems originally performed in isiZulu during the years of union activism leading up to the formation of the Congress of South African Trade Unions (COSATU) in 1985. In the months and years following its publication, *Black Mamba* quickly gained international recognition and drew attention to the newly formed Durban Workers' Cultural Local. This collective provided a venue for other laborers to perform and publish work that challenged the oppressive power dynamics of apartheid South Africa. By the late 1980s the labor uprising that the local was part of had begun to transform the country's political landscape. COSATU—which at the time of its formation became, with over half a million members, the country's largest trade union—continued to grow in force, swiftly becoming one of apartheid's most visible opponents.[3] In cooperation with the United Democratic Front (UDF), it helped launch a series of nationwide strikes and stayaways that, combined with a nationwide resistance policy of "ungovernability" and international labor solidarity, brought the country to a standstill and the government to the negotiating table. The cultural aspects of the labor movement and, in particular, its poets, were a notable part of the cultural reclamation that contributed to South Africa's transformation.[4]

This chapter begins with a brief overview and cursory discussion of the political history of South Africa from the establishment of apartheid in 1948 until its conclusion in 1990. It discusses the structural conditions prevalent in South Africa and the Eastern Cape during the latter half of the twentieth century as well the labor movement that arose in response to them. After setting the scene within which the labor movement and worker culture unfolded, I move into an analysis of the work of Alfred Qabula and, to a lesser extent, Nise Malange, both of whom became prominent cultural, political, and environmental figures within the South African labor movement through their cultural activism. By placing their work within the broader political ecology of late apartheid, I show that what have been considered by most critics as political texts are also important examples of South African ecopoetics that responded directly to issues of environmental justice and shifting ecological relationships. The writers and their poems speak to the cultural politics of the rapacious nature of South African industrialization, representing the racialized and attenuated body of the migrant worker, "a free peasant transported to an urban industrial setting," who responded to both realms.[5] In resisting racist processes of extraction and labor exploitation in apartheid South Africa, I argue that worker poets—like Nontsizi Mgqwetho, S. E. K. Mqhayi, and David Yali-Manisi before and alongside them—recognized and articulated the ties between capital and labor, landscape and dispossession. Most importantly, I show that through the skillful use of language and metaphor as well as the adaptation and deployment of traditional forms, the worker poets created oral texts with tremendous historical, cultural, and emotional resonance. Fine details of these texts emerge through close readings such as those included in these chapters, details that give the art its particularly affective power; this power, in turn, built the strength and voice of silenced and marginalized South African workers and unified their movement of mass resistance against the slow violence of race-based extraction in apartheid South Africa.

The Institution of Apartheid

In the wake of the 1948 election, Prime Minister Hendrik Verwoerd and his newly elected Nationalist Party government began implementing the apartheid policy on which their election campaign had been based. In particular, they developed a series of increasingly stringent policies to advance their agenda of complete and compulsory race-based, residential segregation. The Group Areas Act, which responded to the ongoing influx of rural blacks into urban areas, commenced in July 1950.⁶ In specifying where various racial populations could legally live, work, and own property, the act established black and colored township areas, leading to massive relocations from other parts of the urban landscape.⁷

A decade later, as racially ordered urban geographies became increasingly entrenched, the Promotion of Bantu Self-Government Act in 1959 expanded apartheid policies into the countryside, strengthening uneven rural geographies and the system of labor migration that had come to define South African society since the turn of the century. The act established a pseudonational "homeland" for each of eight different ethnic groups: North Sotho, South Sotho, Swazi, Tsonga, Tswana, Venda, Xhosa, and Zulu.⁸ The resultant ten "homeland" areas or "Bantustans" were fragmented into some 276 separate territories, of which only the Transkei was fortunate enough to constitute a large, contiguous land base.⁹ The Bantustans were to be governed without white intervention, gradually transitioning to the status of independent nation-states as their resident populations became more politically involved. Like the earlier land reserves they developed from, Bantustans were located in the least developed parts of the country—remote areas often unsuitable for agriculture and with no access to ports, no mineral rights, and no existing industry.¹⁰ With homeland designations drawn on ethnic bases, the Bantu Self-Government Act successfully deepened a simmering level of intertribal conflict that assisted the act's divide and rule approach.¹¹

Following the establishment of the homeland areas, deportations intensified from urban areas and "black spots" scattered throughout the country. These deportations continued for nearly three decades, uprooting an estimated 3.5 million people by the mid-1980s.¹² By 1990 the Bantustans, which accounted for only 14 percent of the South African land base, were home to half of its black population.¹³ Not only were these reserves too small to permit more than a handful of families to make their living there as independent farmers, they also allowed no room for population growth.¹⁴ This population density proved disastrous for the inhabitants of the reserves, who faced a growing crisis of poverty and malnutrition as the densely populated agricultural lands became increasingly eroded, overgrazed, and unproductive.¹⁵ These factors, combined with the outmigration of labor, gutted the productive capacity of reserve lands, and they remained neglected zones of reproductive labor, an externalized source of the laboring bodies necessary to sustain South Africa's rapidly industrializing economy.¹⁶ Govan Mbeki writes that "from the outset, the purpose of maintaining the reserves was to provide a source of cheap labor for white agriculture, mining and industry. On the one hand the reserves have served as mating camps for the production of migrant laborers, while on the other they have proved suitable dumping grounds for the physical wrecks whom industry discards."[17] South Africa's practices of racial segregation and economic polarization, enforced by systematic terror and violent repression of dissent, produced both unprecedented economic growth and drastic economic inequality.[18] Meanwhile, the geography of apartheid effectively veiled the ugly social and environmental consequences of economic growth by sequestering them in reserves and relocation sites often at a distant remove from national roads. Any ill effects were ascribed to the inferior culture and society of the subjugated race. Yet the underdevelopment endemic to Qabula's homeland and the rest of the South African countryside was clearly not the result of any inherent qualities of African culture. Instead, it was very much what Rob Nixon calls "an inflicted condition, the legacy of a very modern external plunder by far-off forces."[19] Maintained through South Africa's policies of racial segregation and separate development and enforced by systematic terror and violence, Transkeian poverty was the underbelly of industrialization, a direct result of the benefits of economic growth that were being enjoyed elsewhere.

As consumer prices rose and the ranks of the disenfranchised and unemployed grew, resistance became explosive. In 1960 revolts broke out in the rural Mpondoland territory in the northern Transkei. That same year the Pan-African Congress orchestrated pass law protests that culminated in the infamous Sharpeville massacre in which 69 people were killed and another 180 wounded when apartheid police fired a thousand rounds of ammunition into a crowd of peaceful protesters.[20] The police crackdowns that followed on the heels of these protests were vicious enough to impose an artificial peace that, over the decade to follow, swelled investor confidence and encouraged further economic growth.[21] Globally, only Japan shared the 6 percent average annual growth rate that South Africa sustained throughout the 1960s as it supplied 70 percent of the world's gold and saw its manufacturing sector expand by nearly 12 percent each year.[22] Yet far from mitigating South Africa's staggering economic inequalities, this growth merely deepened economic and racial polarizations and entrenched the country's geographies of injustice while doing little to set the country on stable economic footings. Unlike industrializing Asian countries that structured their economies around the mass-production and export of nondurable, labor-intensive consumer goods, South Africa did not find a way to absorb the willing laborers from either impoverished rural areas or the urban periphery.[23] On the contrary, the increasing mechanization of its industrial sectors produced diminishing labor requirements that swelled the ranks of the unemployed, who had no land base to sustain them. Extraction and export of primary commodities remained the principal source of foreign exchange for decades, accounting for the bulk of foreign-exchange earnings leading up to the country's transition to democracy.[24]

The Durban Strikes and the New Left

Expansion of the industrial sector during the 1960s and 70s was most pronounced in Durban and its peri-urban fringes. There, an influx of foreign capital quickly led to structural transformations of the workplace that occasioned a corresponding expansion of skilled labor and of the urban, industrial working class. Throughout the 1980s Greater Durban experienced "an annual flow of rural refugees estimated at one hundred thousand."[25] In particular, a massive influx of amaMpondo workers from Qabula's homeland swelled the populations of Durban's hostels and shack settlements.[26] By the end of the 1970s this new cadre of workers, many of whom sought the means to rebuild homesteads destroyed by government reprisals in the wake of the Mpondo revolts, made up more than a third of Durban's 650,000 workers.[27] Among the consequences of these adjustments was the intensification of competition for jobs and resources between the settled or permanent sections of the black urban working class and migrant workers. This would fuel animosities between these social layers and lead to open, violent conflict in the years ahead.[28]

The shift toward an increasingly educated, politically astute, and capably organized workforce brought profound political implications, beginning with the 1972 strike wave that started in Durban and quickly spread throughout Natal and on to industrial centers nationwide.[29] The strike was the largest since 1946, when the efforts of an earlier generation of union activists had been brutally suppressed. It began in Durban's Coronation Brick Factory and rapidly spread to other factories across the city until it involved over sixty thousand workers in nearly 150 different plants.[30] Black trade unions had been outlawed throughout most of the twentieth century, but in 1979, unable to stem a rising tide of resistance and aware of the value of unions in improving lines of communication between workers and companies, the state enacted new legislation legalizing them and workers joined by the thousands.

The structural changes of the era opened new roles for literature as ideological resistance and psychological liberation sparked by the black consciousness movement helped to propel oral poetry out of traditional spaces of the chief and king's court and into the realm of organized urban protest. The Durban strikes ushered in a new era of working-class cultural production that included the formation of the Durban Workers' Cultural Local in 1983. Unlike labor activism in capitalist countries of the global North, the union movement in South Africa was primarily "a poor people's movement" that "relied on a grassroots form of democracy and accountability."[31] In Durban the movement took the form of a proliferation of cultural activities: performances of oral literature, plays, and dance and the publication of poetry and other writing all "thrown into the melting pot to create a robust cultural contribution."[32] At a time of political transformation, these artists offered a firsthand representation of working-class experience, providing a voice for ordinary laborers and consolidating a sense of ownership and participation in trade unions and labor activism. Artists who hailed both from rural and urban areas spoke from the perspectives of urban dweller and migrant counterpart, allowing the movement to tackle misunderstandings and to help heal the cultural rifts imposed by apartheid capitalism.

In particular, izibongo increasingly became a form of resistance and social solidarity in the labor movements that grew into the driving opposition to apartheid.[33] Performed during union meetings and community gatherings, these poems articulated the everyday struggles of black laborers, providing a voice for ordinary workers and consolidating a sense of ownership and participation in trade unions. The literature demonstrated how the traditional cultural and political features and functions of oral poetry translated easily into a form of union activism, worker education, and apartheid resistance. Like iimbongi of the past, the labor poets inspired empathy and acts of bravery, exhorting people to realize their potential as active and engaged citizens.[34] As Nise Malange puts it, "Praise singing, it really makes people feel like we are in, we are going, because it raised solidarity and understanding. And I think the biggest thing is solidarity, that we're together with you. You know, if your praise singing is about us going into war, people will follow you and go and fight with you and that's what praise singing was all about."[35]

An awareness of the emotional power of poetry drove Qabula towards izibongo as a means of expressing the struggles and grievances shared by masses of workers. During his long, solitary shifts as a forklift driver, he passed the time composing songs that he later performed for audiences of thousands. In his own words,

> Poetry is the most powerful medium of expression in the cultural sphere for me today.... [It] tells about the sufferings and pleasures, the life experiences and future plans. I get inspiration from observing other people's experiences and my own direct experiences. My poetry has to preserve the history of the life of workers. Traditional oral poets tell the story of the king's virtues and wrong doings. From the poetry kings also learn to critique their own actions. My poetry is different. The history of workers is what my poetry is about, so that their experiences may be shared by our fellow comrades.[36]

While trade union culture drew on the izibongo tradition, it adapted the familiar form to fit new environmental circumstances. In the changing cultural landscape of the late twentieth-century workplace, subject matter shifted to emphasize the urban rather than the rural experience and to celebrate contemporary political leaders rather than traditional, hereditary leaders.[37] The revival of traditional forms offered a powerful mode to voice a shared experience of and resistance to structures of exploitation and repression. Yet much more than expressing mere resistance, the worker poets and their colleagues created a culture of learning, sharing, and mutual support. Despite the rising numbers of black workers who read daily newspapers, owned radios, and worked at professional jobs, the circulation of information among laborers was stymied by illiteracy—or at least a reluctance to engage with print materials.[38] Nise Malange emphasizes that workers' poetry and the workers' cultural movement played a key role in education:

> Because the whole thing with resistance poetry is to pass the message. It was not just for performance, it was to pass on the message. So, the workers' praise singers or the workers' cultural movement in Durban was established basically as part of popular education. It wasn't just to resist. It was also to educate the workers at the shop floor because remember those days the rate of illiteracy was very, very high and workers were not recognized, the trade unions were not recognized by employers. So [although] there were a lot of materials coming out in print form, there was little education happening on the shop floor. Those izibongo and poetry and theatre basically played a role in popular education. People always look at resistance but it was not, because you can't resist without knowledge. That's what we believed in. That the workers need to know what they are fighting for.... And that was the power of popular

education, whether through praise singing, whether through plays that we were doing. The focus was for people to be educated before they take arms. And I'm very proud of that, because most of those people . . . can articulate the struggle. It's people that, even now, when they talk, they talk from knowledge.[39]

Hope Is a Black Forest

A number of critics have written about Alfred Qabula and the works he produced, particularly during the 1970s and 80s as he became a visible cultural force.[40] A high-profile public poet, his writings and performances helped define popular understandings of the labor movement as well as the movement's aesthetic.[41] In the wake of the Durban strikes, he wrote and produced "The Dunlop Play," which critics have identified as "one of the first attempts to awaken worker consciousness" in South Africa.[42] In a stroke of inspiration, he placed a performance by an imbongi within the play and wrote his first isibongo for the character. Following the play's success, Qabula moved into active production and performance in the izibongo genre. As the new union legislation of 1979 opened the floodgates of the union movement, Qabula adopted the isibongo form to applaud the cooperation and leadership of laborers and unions. His poems, performed for crowds of several thousand, brought "mass audiences excitedly again and again to their feet in full-throated response," adding to the shifting consciousness of the working class and lending strength to their movement.[43]

Born in 1942 to a migrant laborer and a subsistence farmer in Mpondoland, the northern region of what would later become the Transkei Bantustan, Qabula personified the migrant laborer experience. In his autobiography, *A Working Life: Cruel Beyond Belief,* Qabula explains the methods employed by white capitalists to impose the system on his family and describes their effects.

> Then came capitalists demanding labor for the mines and tax collectors wanting cash. My father's father refused to work on the mines and became a transport rider to raise cash to pay his taxes: with his ox-wagon he footed the countryside from farm to farm, from the Transkei to Natal, from the Orange Free State to the Cape and back, carrying grain and other products. But he was destroyed by the arrival of the railways. He became a herbalist and consistently refused to go out and work for a wage. He sent my father and

his brothers out to work on the mines or in the sugar fields. From then on migrancy invaded our homes.[44]

Cruelly low wages prevented migrant workers from earning enough either to break the cycle of dependency or to provide adequately for families at home; instead they remained uprooted and estranged from their communities as they oscillated between reserve and workplace. The pattern was devastating to family life. As Qabula recounts: "My father was a miner at Egoli [Johannesburg]. He worked underground, as a machine-handler. He was a very strict man, had a short temper and loved his drink. Like many other men, he would cough out to his family the same bad treatment he received at work and on the streets of South Africa.... That is how they used to be: he used to explode on us and hold us responsible for his harsh life, of which we knew nothing."[45] Qabula's family, like many others, knew little about industrial urban life but plenty about the poverty, hunger, and violence of the rural reserves. Growing up in the destitution of the northern Transkei, his autobiography betrays the lasting trauma of a continual state of near starvation: it contains repeated references to food, including anecdotes in which he steals eggs and potatoes and learns to survive on foods gathered from the forest. He confesses, "You move through your childhood years feeling constantly hungry, so you move like a locust."[46]

Like his father, Qabula stepped into the role of migrant laborer as a young adult, taking up a life of perpetual migration between rural and urban spaces along with hundreds of thousands of his contemporaries. This massive collective movement blurred the boundaries and mingled workers' consciousness of the two realms such that rural sensibilities remained a key aspect of the cultural and environmental significance of the labor movement and its literature. The constant movement of workers merged elements of urban and rural, traditional and industrial into a unified sociocultural landscape. The rural, its traditions, and its natural environments remained present and relevant to the urban movement, informing its metaphors and cultural understandings.

Qabula's urban poetry is infused with images of his homeland, "a harsh and beautiful land—a land of unending green hills and valleys but also a land of poverty, of broken homesteads, of disease and malnutrition."[47] "Praise Poem to FOSATU," for example, speaks to the general experience of black working life as well as to the particular experience of Mpondo migrant workers. With the lines "Escape into that forest . . ." and "Deep in the forest they hid themselves . . . ," Qabula describes the forests that provided cover for the amaMpondo resistance of 1960, striking a strong emotional chord with the sizeable Mpondo faction of his audiences.[48] Yet in his explanation of the emotional resonance of forests in his autobiography, it is clear that while referencing a particular amaMpondo experience of forests, Qabula also draws on broader experiences shared with other migrant workers of other cultural groups who shared rural ties.

> But there in my head: those forests . . . They still lingered on in my memory—the only refuge from my father's beatings, my hunting ground which used to provide me with all kinds of prey, before I was turned into prey for others, the hunted. . . . The forest was its own universe full of wild fruit and dangers: mambas and crawling creatures of all kinds. Always a source of refuge for the homeless and the frightened, I remembered how during the Mpondo resistance it housed the Congress fugitives. It hid away teachers and commoners, it covered their tracks. . . . It was a retreat from the wilderness of the world outside: the world of beatings and torture and interrogations; the so-called normal world marked with murderous lists of names. . . . When MAWU got re-entry at Dunlop I knew the march through the forests had restarted.

The forest of Qabula's poetry and autobiography is common throughout the Transkei region. As a space both real and metaphorical, it is densely populated with meaning and memory as well as with animals, spirits, and humans seeking refuge from an angry and unjust world. Known to Anglophone botanists as Albany Thicket and to British colonialists as Fish River Bush, ethnobotanists Michelle Cocks and Tony Dold describe the Transkeian forest ecosystem as a "relatively impenetrable, woody, semi-succulent, thorny vegetation of an average height of 2–3 meters."[49] Impenetrability is a particularly salient feature of Albany Thicket that contributes to its cultural significance to isiXhosa-speaking peoples. As botanist Charles Bunbury noted in 1838,

> Hill and dale alike are covered with impenetrable thickets as dense as the undergrowth of a Brazilian forest and much more thorny. I never saw, in any other part of the world, anything resembling the Fish River Bush; nor, I should think, does there exist a tract so difficult to penetrate or to clear. The vegetation is so succulent that fire has no effect on it even in the driest weather, and at the same time so strong and rigid, and so excessively dense, that there is no getting through it without cutting your way at every step, unless in

the paths made by wild beasts. Yet the [amaXhosa] make their way through with wonderful skill and activity.[50]

The bush, impenetrable and impervious to fire, provided a secure source of cover for amaXhosa resistance throughout colonial times, notably during the War of Mlanjeni (1850–53), when British troops attempted unsuccessfully to flush out amaXhosa warriors by burning the thicket.[51] During the Mpondo revolts, it provided important cover for resistance fighters and people fleeing the violence of police reprisals.[52] The forest also offers a spiritual refuge for amaXhosa and amaMpondo peoples: inhabited by ancestral spirits, forests are a source of pride, comfort, and protection that is both physical and spiritual, revealed in such common expressions as *uThixo ulihlathi lam* (God is my forest).[53] Referring both to forests and to mother hens, Qabula highlights the guardianship quality of the trade unions and their function as *ihlathi lokuzimela* (forest of hiding), a term of great pride and respect for mothers who act as protectors and providers for their families.[54] Thus, in a context characterized by ties between migrant urban workers and the environments of their rural homelands, the forest of Qabula's poems is a powerful layered metaphor. The poem provides a clear example of the power of common ecological understandings to evoke deep emotions that contribute shared cultural understandings, and as such it rallied the urban resistance.

Yet Qabula's audience was also a fractured multiethnic and multilingual collection of migrant and urban laborers from throughout South Africa and beyond. In his poem "Africa," first performed for the opening of the Clairwood Trade Union and Cultural Center in October 1985, Qabula directs his lines to the various ethnicities of his audience that would find unity and commonality in "Africa," in contrast to the ethnically specific genealogical content created by traditional iimbongi, which would be potentially divisive. In the poem, a long ode to the natural splendor of the continent as a whole, Qabula alternately praises the beauty of the landscape, gives thanks to the Creator, and acknowledges how both have shaped and strengthened him. In the final third of the poem, the tone shifts to condemnation, not only of those who would defile this beauty but also of the people of the landscape who are failing to step forward to protect it.

> From inside you treasures are taken
> From your face, fruit, food and water.
> Africa of peace—you are beautiful

> But, in your face now
> We see the railway tracks
> The highways, the buildings, and factories
> The structures . . .
> They fought battles scrambling over you
> We hear
> The trains, the motor cars and machinery
> The bombs going off, the sound of gunshot
> . . . .
>
> Youth—
> Echo the sounds, the songs
> And dances
> Of the plants, the birds, the bees
> And animals
> You can make Africa flourish in its pride
> Sing, praise and thank the lord
> For molding us and placing us
> in Africa[55]

In these lines violence is explicitly linked to the exploitation of landscape: industrialization and the plunder of natural beauty go hand in hand with gunshots and bombs. Meanwhile, his invocations of both beauty and obligation call on his audience to find the courage to face their oppressors through love of homeland and its beauty that it is their responsibility to safeguard.

Qabula's performances also draw affective power from descriptions of shared experience of migrancy itself. The beseeching, elegiac tone of "Migrant's Lament—A Song" conveys the hurt associated with both the worker's alienation and the economic reality that produced it.

> If I have wronged you Lord forgive me
> All my cattle were dead
> My goats and sheep were dead
> . . . .
>
> I left my wife and children
> To look for work alone[56]

Here again Qabula strikes emotional chords at multiple levels. Ari Sitas emphasizes that Qabula not only captures a common migrant experience of alienation but also directly acknowledges that for amaMpondo and others, "cattle, sheep and goats were really dead. . . . There was nothing metaphoric about the content."[57] The passage also strongly evokes a situation that Mashudu Mashige calls "yet another ugly face of the apartheid reality" in which "the black family is rent asunder because the political environment does not allow for its continued normal existence."[58] In these lines the exclusion of rural women and families from the urban realm and the resulting separation of worker and family are clearly sources of enormous grief.

Just as Nise Malange describes, Qabula's poetry performs a vital educational and unifying function. For the sizeable urban amaZulu contingent of his audience, who hailed from Durban and viewed the influx of amaMpondo and amaXhosa workers with suspicion, it helped impart the particular challenges that their migrant colleagues faced. With the line "I didn't have a 'Special,'" Qabula draws attention to the "special" pass that rural laborers needed in order to apply for work outside of their homeland reserve. It reminds his listeners of the government's policy of enforced segregation and its divide-and-conquer approaches that drew artificial lines not only between rural and urban territories but also between people and ethnicities where the territories overlapped. Nise Malange points out that the matter involved both migration from rural to urban areas and migration between urban areas: "As people that were coming from the Cape we needed to get a 'Special.' So for people here, because they didn't have to do that, you have to educate them about some of these problems."[59]

In a similar vein, Qabula describes the process of mounting a stage play to communicate the experiences of workers: "We performed this play to make our wives and children aware of the conditions of the workplace and the disrespectful way in which we were treated. They had the impression that we were well-treated at work, well fed and earned a lot of money which we spent on girl friends."[60] The familial divisions produced by the migrant labor system imposed an almost unbearable level of interpersonal suspicion and strife, and the cultural movement played an important role in healing rifts within families and between rural and urban residents. "Migrant's Lament—A Song" reveals the effects of an industrial system in which the family unit and even the body itself had rapidly shifted from being an embedded part of the natural environment to becoming what David Harvey calls "a site of political-economic contestation" that acted as a disciplined "appendage of capital in both the workplace and the consumption sphere."[61] Capital's tendency to violate and damage "the integrity of the laboring body" and to do so "on an uneven geographical basis" was a palpable reality for Qabula.[62] Describing the Dunlop tire factory in his autobiography, he rails: "That place is hell: all the workers there are pitch-black from the black dust and powder that pollutes the place. I was pained by the way people were exposed to such harmful powders."[63] In another passage, he berates the company for its callous treatment of a colleague "liked for his dedication to Dunlop" who became less productive in his old age and was eventually fired: "From that time onwards I hated the Dunlop factory. It used people very hard and then, when they had no strength to produce more, dumped them like rubbish. I realized that I would eventually be in the same position as Mr. Makhathini."[64] Laboring in an industrial system organized around a deeply entrenched color bar, Qabula's literary work exhibits a keen awareness of the tight interrelationships between exploitation, environmental injustice, and human derogation imposed by apartheid capitalism. As an environmental writer, he places the subjugation of bodies and families as well as their landscapes and communities at the heart of his environmentalism.

In the case of Qabula and others, the effectiveness of the poet as a political activist and voice of radical democracy is evidenced by active suppression. Under apartheid, the political threat that the imbongi represented led to silencing and censorship in a variety of forms, including physical threats. As Qabula rose in prominence, friends and family members began to receive unwelcome visitors "looking for that poet: me. . . . From then there were many more visits, which made me decide to leave home. I have been uprooted since then."[65] As part of a persecuted class of artists and intellectuals, he joined other prominent African writers who saw themselves as witnesses, participants in a tradition of truth and testimony that drew on the power of words to make things happen.[66] Voicing this sentiment, Qabula states, "Poetry is more powerful than other forms of media like newspapers. If poetry was not so important Mzwakhe Mbuli's works would not have been banned. Poetry is straight and to the point. It stabs the heart of the enemy whilst it articulates precisely the experiences of [the] worker."[67]

Perhaps it was the experience of persecution that led Qabula back to the forests of his mind in a later poem. "The Black Forest of Africa" returns to the rich symbolism of the Transkeian forests that have now become darker, threatening. No longer an unequivocal place of safety, the forest shelters not only the persecuted but also the enemy.

> We never take it seriously,
> Not knowing it's the center of all nature,

> Security, happiness, all these are there,
> Life, death, suffering, all are there.
>
> In times of war, the forest,
> In times of sickness, the forest,
> In times of happiness, the forest,
> Honey, fruits, . . . there is no hunger in the forest,
> Cold water, deep in the forest,
> Even enemies like it,
> They say: "We will wait for dusk,
> We will enter without being seen,
> We will kill them and no one will know
> Who killed them."[68]

If there are honey and fruits in the forest, they are enjoyed by the fugitive and his enemies alike. As the center of *all* nature, the forest in this poem is no longer simply a place of safety and refuge but harbors death and suffering as well as offering life-giving fruits. While the forest is steadfast in times of war, sickness, and happiness, it is also implicated in much more serious acts: murderers as well as refugees seek out the forest and the cover it provides for their crimes. Unlike Qabula's hopeful poems of earlier years, "The Black Forest of Africa" concludes on a bleak note. If the forest of his earlier poems was a moving force of good, here its ambiguities and lethal indifference are revealed. The forest and the people who take shelter there, it seems, cannot always be trusted.

Politics of Language and Form

As the renown of the worker poets spread, demand grew for back issues of worker newspapers in which their poems had been published.[69] Seeing an opportunity to reach a broader audience, the Workers' Cultural Local decided in 1984 to publish a collection of the poems.[70] *Black Mamba Rising: South African Worker Poets in Struggle* is a slender, seventy-five-page volume featuring brief biographies of its three contributors and a selection of their poetry. The book was published entirely in English translation; the original isiZulu poems were published separately in an effort to make the book affordable for working-class readers.[71] When one reads the English edition, it is clear that much of the impact and vitality of the performances is lost. The transcription and translation of the poems themselves weaken their power, as does their removal from their urgent cultural and political setting via the two-dimensional medium of the printed word. Presented in an uncomplicated diction, the poems' formal elements often work against the content; thus it is understandable that the English edition drew criticism. Despite the praise that *Black Mamba* garnered, a number of critics argued that the poetry was mere sloganeering—conceptually shallow and linguistically unsophisticated. A fierce debate broke out among intellectuals (none of them black) regarding the literary value of the work. For example, Brenda Cooper criticizes the poetry for its "one-dimensional triumphalism," claiming that "much of the poetry is flawed by the lack of a sustained and rigorous poetic language."[72] Lionel Abrahams rejects Jeremy Cronin's "patronizingly high praise" of "passages of very minor achievement," arguing that the uncritical acclaim does black artists more harm than good.[73] Nadine Gordimer offers the surprisingly ill-informed view that "now, beyond the opportunities to acquire knowledge of modern science, technology and administration, there is asserted the masses' right to enjoy the self-realization of literature."[74] Her stance seems to ignore the fact that "the masses" have produced literature, largely ignored by elite audiences, for as long as there has been language to do so. Farouk Asvat displays his obvious irritation at the eagerness of some white intellectuals to heap praise on the worker poets, complaining about "the usual perpetuation of the great white myth that whatever originates from the masses in this country is of no significance unless it gets the authoritative stamp from whites."[75] He goes on to cite important yet uncelebrated black writers of the 1960s and 70s who faced persecution, censorship, and even, in the case of Nkutsweu Matsau, criminal conviction for practicing their art.[76] From Asvat's perspective, the major novelty of worker poetry is the excitement and attention it has aroused among white audiences, which he claims is misguided based on the simplistic, sloganeering nature of the poetry.

Each of these criticisms derives from a certain set of literary, political, and cultural understandings of the context in which worker poetry was produced, yet all betray a lack of understanding of the multidimensional nature of the work. Ari Sitas, editor of *Black Mamba* and perhaps the commentator most closely tied to the politics and production of worker poetry, is more circumspect in both his criticism and his praise. He is also clearly much more cognizant of the complexities of performed verse:

> One notes that oral performances are impressive in their magniloquence and communal wisdom whether they are lengthy narratives or short proverbs. These performances furthermore use words as sounds, or better, events of sound imbued with power.

At the same time, a word in such performances may set off a chain of associations which the performer will follow into a cul-de-sac unless skilled in his craft.... Qabula's performances resemble the tradition of oral poetry but are informed by a broader set of cultural experiences. One witnesses a form that has undergone dramatic changes.[77]

The amaXhosa society from which Qabula's literature arises is complex and the poetry dense with cultural allusions and a literary aesthetic that other commentators do not discuss. Their oversights on certain points signal that a closer reading of the text and an examination of the relationship between performance and print, rhythm and translation is long overdue.

The VHS recording of Qabula in performance lent to me by Professor Russell Kaschula reveals a disarmingly humble character.[78] Tall, slender, and mustached and wearing a large pair of 1980s-style glasses, he is far from the strident militant I expected to see. Instead he cuts an almost endearing figure in a black tunic trimmed with a fringe of colorful rags, a striped tie to symbolize capitalist overlords, and white trousers torn into fringes to the knees representing the impoverished state of workers. He displays none of the hard-hitting self-assurance I've seen in other iimbongi; although he shouts, he does not break into the imbongi's grating, guttural roar. His words are clearly spoken, and his pace is balanced, interspersed with pauses; occasionally he appears to be collecting his thoughts. Performing in isiZulu, his second language (and mutually intelligible with isiXhosa), it is likely that he speaks with the accent particular to his Mpondoland roots. At one point he breaks into laughter along with the crowd as a small child climbs onto the stage to join him and is carried off by a member of the stage crew. Later the boy reappears, gazing out at the audience from Qabula's side to join the latter in performing a shuffling dance to the ululations of the crowd. Qabula's popular appeal is obvious: this is not an awe-inspiring radical but a man of the people.

These performative aspects of Qabula's poetry are lost in its conversion to print, but much more importantly, the English translations obliterate much of the artistry of the original lines. This is clear when a translated text is juxtaposed with the isiZulu transcription.[79] Appendix A in this volume includes a transcription of the FOSATU poem in isiZulu alongside a translation that closely resembles the version in *Black Mamba* (although I have made some minor adjustments to the punctuation for clarity).

Qabula's original oral poem clocks in at over two hundred lines.[80] The poem that appears in *Black Mamba* and subsequent anthologies is a splinter of the original, pared down presumably to suit a modern English aesthetic and, likely, to reduce the time and labor involved in converting an oral work to a printed one and to minimize the cost of the marketed volume. The juxtaposition of two versions clearly illustrates how much is lost in translation. In the isiZulu version, the lines in the opening stanza are tight and rhythmic, building through regular rhythm and assonant repetition. In this example, the stressed syllables are indicated with \ and the unstressed syllables with ∪.

\∪∪\∪	∪∪\∪∪∪\∪
Nguye wavela!	It is he who has appeared!
\∪\∪\∪∪\∪	∪\\∪∪∪∪\∪
Basho bonke bathi wavela!	They all said that he had appeared!
\∪\∪\∪∪\∪\∪\∪∪	\\∪\∪∪\∪∪
Wena hlathi elihambayo laseAfrika.	You moving forest of Africa.

I am not an isiZulu speaker, and the scansion here is no doubt imperfect. What it illustrates is that in the original language, although not all the stressed syllables have equal emphasis, the opening lines have a clear, regular rhythm strongly marked by stressed and unstressed syllables. On the other hand, where the stresses fall in the English lines is not at all obvious. The second line contains a series of six single-syllable words; since the stress could fall on almost any of these, the result is a stammering and uncertain cadence. This comparison shows how the translation fundamentally alters the speech rhythms in the written lines, transforming the opening line of the original isiZulu poem from a tidy spondee and iamb to a stuttering collection of monosyllables in English. Not only rhythms are altered: sounds too are rendered entirely differently, and the affective quality of the words is transformed. In the fourth line, the smooth, alliterative *l*s and open vowels of isiZulu are evocative of the lamentation they describe; these effects are lost entirely in the English. Further down in the poem, the beautifully alliterative iambs of "Bangena kulelihlathi baphuma," is awkwardly rendered as "Deep in the forest they hid themselves, and then came out." The distinction between "Sifukamele nathi" and "Sikhukhumeze nathi" is not translated.

This example illustrates that the two poems—isiZulu and English—are in essence different texts, presenting different sounds, rhythms, forms, meanings, and emotional registers. Although choices in the construction and presentation of the transcribed and translated text can seek to re-create the language of the original, no print version can re-create the resonant meanings present in the original piece. If a literary work is a piece of writing in which, to quote Terry Eagleton, "*what* is said is taken in terms of *how* it is said," then it is necessary to acknowledge that literary criticism of a printed English translation differs in fundamental ways from literary criticism of an original-language text, whether printed or performed.[81] The differences between the transcribed translation echo the changes to the genre that Sitas comments on above. Just as Nontsizi Mgqwetho, S. E. K. Mqhayi, and other poets before Qabula navigated the transition from oral performance to print, here Qabula draws a traditional form from his rural life into his life in industrial Durban. In the process of translating a traditional form into performances meaningful for his audiences and of recording transcriptions of those performances to be turned into translations meaningful for readers, meaning itself becomes slippery.

Nightshift Mothers

Born in Cape Town in 1960, Nise Malange was among the youngest of the labor poets and the most prominent of the few women involved in the workers' cultural movement. She developed an interest in labor politics at an early age, drawing inspiration from her uncle, Reverend Marawu, who had served time on Robben Island for his political activism.[82] Malange became involved in the trade union movement after her arrival in Durban in 1982, and by 1983 she was active as a playwright, poet, and songwriter with the group that became the COSATU cultural unit. Throughout much of the 1980s, she worked seven days a week as a union organizer and was a vocal proponent of workers' rights.[83]

As an isiXhosa-speaking migrant from the Western Cape, Malange found herself on the outside of urban black society in Durban. Her gender in particular set her apart in a labor and cultural movement defined and directed by men. The working class in South Africa has always been oppressed, yet within this class women faced the double burden of wage labor and labor in the home. Generally unable to find work in male-dominated industries, they were confined to poorly remunerated service work that resulted in their social isolation and inability to organize with other workers. Many women could only find employment as domestic workers, which often required them to live at the homes of their employers, where they were subject to further abuse.[84] Malange expresses these frustrations in her poem "Nightshift Mother."

> Left with a double load
> At home
> My children left uncared
> Anxiety
> At work
> My boss insists we should
> Be grateful for the opportunities
> He gives women to be exploited.
> . . . .
> And I work wandering on my knees,
> Through these deserted and desolate spaces,
> The group of us lost in these vast buildings,
> Forgotten and neglected
> Exploited as you sleep[85]

The cleaning work performed by black women was not only brutally demeaning and physically punishing (the speaker spends her nights shuffling around her workplace on her knees) but also dangerous. Women who finished their shifts after midnight would often struggle to find somewhere safe to sleep because of the dangers associated with late-night travel home to the townships, which were, according to apartheid spatial organization, invariably at a significant remove from the white spaces where women worked.[86]

These workplace arrangements may offer a partial explanation for the absence of women in the workers' cultural movement. A further explanation lies in Ingrid de Kok's forceful statement that "South Africa is so deeply phallocentric, it seems to me, both in its present capitalistic and racist mode, and in the practices of its progressive opposition, that these dismissals need constant confronting."[87] Women's exclusion from union activism and cultural activities and their invisibility in broader public and political commentary had significant consequences. As wages of domestic workers fell by 16 percent between 1973 and 1980, there was little opportunity to lead collective action for better conditions. And with women bearing the primary responsibility for ensuring the wellbeing of their households, it was children who bore the brunt of women's overwork, low pay, anxiety, and absence from the household—all of which left their marks on the generation to follow.[88]

Despite Malange's contributions as a writer and activist, she remains marginal or absent in most critical work about the movements of which she was part. As an example, the Congress of South African Writers

(COSAW), a group committed to redressing the imbalances of apartheid, proclaimed its January 1990 issue of *Writers' Notebook* to have a "Focus on Women," however the issue opened with an eleven-page tribute to Alfred Qabula and his poetry. The "Focus on Women" was limited to a few pages at the back of the issue that included only a single poem by Malange.[89] This glaring imbalance ignored feminist mobilization and the formation of the Natal Women's Forum within COSAW that "passed a resolution to work towards 50% representation on all committees and to form a Forum that would focus on encouraging women writers."[90]

As a woman Malange belonged to a demographic group more often relegated to rural hinterlands than to the urban laboring environment. Writing poetry from this perspective, Malange tackled the intersectionality of apartheid capitalism, making visible the gender impacts of the migrant labor system and calling for the cultural transformation of patriarchy. Although Malange is the third contributor to *Black Mamba*, she is allocated only the final six pages within the collection as compared to the forty-one pages shared by her two male colleagues. Yet she offers a closing note that is strong and compassionate, her poetry emphasizing the interrelationships between labor and the domestic realm and offering praises to May Day and workers lost to the struggle. In "I, the Unemployed," she speaks plainly and bluntly of women's experiences in paid employment and in unremunerated reproductive labor in the reserves, emphasizing both the social value and economic necessity of paid employment.

> I spit at the sun
> Shining on me
> Blazing everyday
> I am waiting for the rain to come
> And I cannot plough this beautiful piece of earth.
> Here I am: unemployed
> I
> the unemployed
> I am here but invisible.
> Preacher man pray for the rain to come.
>
> White collars
> in your chrome and brown arm-chairs
> Please brighten up this thinning light.
> . . . .
> My kids are dying—
> Malnutrition, kwashiorkor

> There is nothing growing here
> And the animals have died.[91]

The poem poignantly depicts the social and environmental conditions of a rural landscape and traditional society pillaged for capital growth elsewhere. Despite her urban origins, Malange has an intimate knowledge of the lifeways of these rural settings; as a youth she was sent to the homeland areas to reconnect with her heritage. As she describes in "A Time of Madness," not only were the rural areas plagued with malnutrition and illness, they also lacked the tranquility of earlier times.

> And lightning struck us in 1976
> The year where all the madness started.
> The madness started for me in the Transkei
> Where I was leading a different life in the bundu[92]
> Collecting wood and after school tending the land
> Feeling superior to the people because I came from CTA[93]
> But I enjoyed the milk straight from the cows
> And the life among the sheep and goats
> And people ploughing fields
>
> I looked forward to this on my arrival but also forward
> To a life without policemen
> Without thugs and harassment
> And I enjoyed collecting cowdung[94]
> Instead of using cobra floor polish from the shops
> And I was delighted to know that I could make my own samp
> And wandering in the forests to bring wood to light the fires[95]

As an urbanite, Malange looks to the rural Transkei as a realm of peace and tranquility. Indeed, for a period she enjoys the subsistence life of the village, where she lives in intimate relationship with the forest and with cattle, who supply both nourishment and the raw materials needed for a tidy, well-kept home. Yet this bucolic peace does not last. With violence erupting around her in the Transkei, Malange returns to Cape Town, where she is met by further violence. In the second half of the poem, she describes the events and their lasting social effects.

> Then Soweto happened
> And the madness started
> . . . .
> And whatever they did not destroy the soldiers finished,

And we hurled petrol bombs,
And they sliced with their pangas,
And there was blood too much blood,
And our parents were being killed coming from work,
Still sweated from the day's toil
That I am trying to banish from my memory,
Only to forget,
Only to remember that the wounds must not open again,
Because they have scarred our minds,
We are mentally ill,
We are the mad generation,
Born in the eruption of madness,
Raised when madness struck.[96]

This sense of "madness" has stayed with her for the ensuing decades. As an activist and counselor for victims of violence during the township unrest of the 1980s and 90s, Malange is painfully aware of the intergenerational trauma the events inflicted and the need for ongoing healing. Her current literary and activist work is deeply engaged with the liberation and trade movements and with the roles women play within these movements; their oppression within the patriarchal domains of home, workplace, and social organizations; and their general absence from cultural production. Of the trade movement, she observes, "The presence of women has been sporadic, rather than regular and strong. Few women have participated in the creative workshops and performances or in writing poetry." The absence of women in performance culture effectively excludes them from a realm that would enable them to, in Malange's words, "realize their creative potential and extend their self-confidence as participants in the struggle for cultural transformation."[97]

Yet despite the oppressively patriarchal culture of 1980s South Africa, Malange, like Nontsizi Mgqwetho before her, was aware of the opportunities it offered that would not have been available in earlier times:

> Traditional culture and the law have played a big role in the oppression of women because for a long time, women were regarded as minors who cannot make decisions—even in the absence of their menfolk. In traditional culture women were seen as objects who have to bring up the kids and ululate whilst the praise poet is praising the Chief or Induna.
>
> Many women will remember the storytelling (*intsomi*) which was told during the night and in the dark. If they told the stories

during the day, it was said that they will grow horns. As kids we were made to believe that.[98]

In raising her voice Malange stood up not only against the racist oppressors of the apartheid regime but also against the sexist oppression of her own people and their claims that women's literature "is not powerful enough, [is] too simple and straightforward etc."[99] Throughout her cultural activism she calls on women to "come together and write about their problems, [and] empower and encourage other women to write and document their stories."[100] Through such speech women could find mutual strength to address and change patriarchal attitudes and end women's oppression in both apartheid and black South African society.

In the years following independence, Qabula found himself sidelined and then forgotten as the newly liberated country "was taken over by a world of cellphones and briefcases." Retreating to his rural home, he continued to write, his poems now steeped in the pain of disillusionment. Nise Malange describes his anger in the years following what had seemed the labor movement's success:

> Some of Qabula's poetry deals a lot with that pain of neglect. You know from COSATU, from the ANC and from the silencing of the voices of the workers. . . . If you look at all the research, the impact of what we did in the 80s, and what the workers did in 1973, and the beneficiaries today, that's what Qabula was talking about. That we fought, we made a step-ladder. People walk up to get on top and we're left down there to die, you know. And where are these people that we fought with? Have they forgotten? Remember that you can fall from there, and know that no one is gonna catch you.[101]

In 2002 Qabula suffered a stroke and died shortly after. In his tribute, fellow poet and activist Ari Sitas also remarked on Qabula's withdrawal and sense of betrayal in the years preceding his death.

> He was deeply disappointed that revolution was taken over by a world of cellphones and briefcases. As he discovered that his talents as an oral person were lost in the winds of change, these disturbing poems preceded his self-imposed exile. Truly, none of us was spared in these poems. "The Long Road" is a criticism of all of us on our road to wealth and power, climbing over his back with spiked shoes. His "Of Land, Bones and Money" is one of the more profound expressions of our negotiated settlement—reminding

us of the "restless dead" and that "seasons of drought have no rainbows."[102]

In the years before his death, as the world of engines, industry, and noise expanded, Qabula found his own measure of peace in the hills of his homeland.

> My ancestors ploughed this land and trailed these hills with cow-dung. They did so from way back, as far as the memory reaches in the clan of Miya; in the lines of Muja, of Sibewu, of Manqadanda, of Eluhluwini, of Sijekula, of Siyalankulandela, of Manciba and of Henqwa. For two centuries their praise-names and their cattle echoed around these valleys.[103]

Despite his regrets, Qabula's later poetry revealed an abiding faith in God and humanity. If his Transkeian landscape was to be rendered a dumping ground for South Africa's capitalists, so be it. There was beauty to be found there and, in spite of the poverty and neglect—or perhaps because of it—a prevailing human dignity and kindness.

> At the dumping ground
> and we do not exploit
> we do not cheat profits out of each other
> we have slipped through their grip
> leaving their cheeks blown-up with anger
> and we are growing
> We are responding
> and someone is calling
> He is calling on us
> to work hard as daylight is coming
> it has been a very long sunset
> and a very long night
> We are to sleep and listen to the voice in our dreams
> do not fear
> The one who is beginning to call
> is standing beside you
> with gifts and with infinite talents
> Work on![104]

4 / Versions of Silence

> *There is no simple formula for the relationship of art to justice. But I do know that art—in my own case the art of poetry—means nothing if it simply decorates the dinner table of power which holds it hostage.*
> —ADRIENNE RICH

In 1990 state president and National Party leader F. W. de Klerk lifted the thirty-year ban on the African National Congress and, as political exiles returned to their homes, Nelson Mandela walked out of a twenty-seven-year imprisonment onto the home stretch to freedom. Four years later, as Mandela took the podium at his presidential inauguration, an exceptional story of struggle and hope reached its celebratory conclusion. Common people had overturned a brutally unjust social order and instated a democratic government with the power to bring equality, prosperity, and progress to a country that had suffered centuries of oppressive racial violence.

Of course, the story of South Africa does not end there. Despite significant gains in the early years of the new administration, twenty-five years of black majority rule has not led to a shared prosperity. Rather, the net result of several centuries of institutionalized inequality has continued to be, unsurprisingly, geographic and economic asymmetry. Counter to popular anticipations, South Africa has largely failed to transform its mineral wealth and industrial prowess into lasting sources of prosperity and economic security for the majority of its citizens.[1] Instead, the country's geography and institutions continue to reflect its long history of exclusion and uneven development under white rule.

In "Praise Poem to FOSATU," Qabula remarks,

> But to our dismay,
> After we had appointed them, we placed them on the
> Top of the mountain,

and they turned against us.
They brought impimpis into our midst to inflict[2]
Sufferings upon us.
Some of us, those who were clever, were shot down
To the dust with bullets[3]

While this passage may indeed have described the tumultuous nature of union politics in the early 1980s, it is eerily prophetic of subsequent events. On 16 August 2012, thirty-four people were killed and another eighty or more injured when police opened fire on striking platinum miners and their allies near the town of Marikana.[4] The massacre triggered a nationwide wave of strikes for the remainder of the year, leading some commentators to call it a historical moment equivalent to the massacres at Sharpeville and Soweto in 1960 and 1976.[5] Although mainstream media coverage of the event promoted a story of the South African police pitted against irrational and violent protesters, alternate narratives emphasize police collaboration with Lonmin (the British-owned company that operates the mines) and describe a shift in the role of unions and union leaders from protectors to corrupt and violent oppressors of people peacefully demanding change.[6]

Qabula to some extent forewarned of the disillusionment and violence that would follow independence if the instruments of power merely passed from one set of hands to another without the reconfiguration of the underlying structures and institutions of apartheid capitalism. His lines highlight the difficulty of achieving true liberation, as those who find their way into newly vacated positions of power are often quick to adopt the use of force to solidify their position and create a new system of exploitation.[7] In the struggle for independence, not only leaders must change but also the systems, structures, and mindsets that granted them political legitimacy.

Qabula is not the only one to raise his voice in concern over the dynamics of South Africa's transition to democracy. Despite a resistance movement that was "bravely militant, resolutely socialist, and waged with the support of progressive nationalists around the world," the nascent democratic state was no match for the force of the neoliberal ethos that had come to define the global political economy in the preceding decades.[8] Since then, as crime and corruption have risen and the gulf between a prosperous middle class and an impoverished majority yawns ever wider, hope and celebration have soured into disillusionment and a general sense of betrayal. In this climate of discontent, large-scale public protest has become a defining feature of the political landscape as popular sentiment finds voice in shack uprisings, labor unrest, and student protests that question the very meaning of democracy and liberation.[9] Over the past two decades civil protests have increasingly come to reflect a widespread and growing recognition that South Africa's liberation is incomplete and that the transition to democracy alone has been insufficient to amend historical imbalances.[10] Just as in the apartheid era, South Africa's social struggles are ideological as well as political.[11] Far beyond contesting material conditions and service provisions, contemporary activists call for decolonization of the social and political structures that perpetuate these deficiencies and for restructuring of the language, narratives, and ideologies that prop them up.[12]

In the climate of extreme censorship and police brutality that defined apartheid South Africa, poets were a visible and powerful cultural force whose role as freedom fighters garnered them banning orders, police violence, detention, and death threats.[13] Drawing on a traditional practice based on speaking truth to power, poets performing in the izibongo style inserted themselves into an ideological struggle against racism and dispossession that had been ongoing since colonial times.[14] In the late apartheid period and the years shortly after it, scholars emphasized the significance of poets and oral performance to the resistance movement, focusing in particular on the emergence of iimbongi from the traditional realm of chiefs and kings into a contemporary scene of trade union rallies, liberation protests, and presidential addresses.[15] Although it is clear that iimbongi have played a valuable role in social and political commentary and the development of South African modernity through the nineteenth and twentieth centuries, my research suggests a more nuanced picture of their significance and role in a decolonizing, postapartheid South Africa.

Political oppressions continue in the New South Africa, albeit in transmuted forms. Several iimbongi I spoke with remarked on a contemporary culture tainted by a pervasive climate of political tension and expressed a reluctance to raise their voices on certain topics for fear of reprisals. Instead, their words are circumscribed by the nature of public performance venues, their need to derive an income from their work, and the unwillingness of patrons to endure public criticism, no matter how artful. Ironically, their comments suggest that iimbongi have bowed to this sense of oppression even as South Africa as a whole has established itself as a country of vocal protest and mass demonstration, where over the past twenty years courageous bands of shack dwellers, mine workers, and students have raised dissatisfied voices, placing their jobs, relationships, and bodily integrity on the line in the course of resolutely demanding change. Whether iimbongi have also taken a stand in these demonstrations is beyond the scope of my research, but anecdotal evidence suggests that performance art has not been a major feature of South African political dissent in recent years. Despite the absence of formal censorship laws that were so much a part of the apartheid regime, it appears that independence has ushered in a new era in which iimbongi no longer function as the fiery political commentators and visible social agitators so celebrated in the past. Indeed, the current circumstances could be seen to cast doubt both on the scholarly claims of their past political import and on the political relevance of the imbongi in contemporary society.

On the other hand, in the years following independence the young imbongi Zolani Mkiva quickly became a widely recognized figurehead of black strength and identity thanks to high-profile opportunities to perform alongside Nelson Mandela. Mandela's efforts to integrate African customs into democratic society reflected a new constitution that officially recognized the authority of traditional, hereditary leaders and perhaps marked the start of a new ethos that placed African values and concerns first. However, Mandela and leaders since have been inconsistent in their embrace of cultural traditions and ideals, trotting them out to curry political support (for example, Mandela's strategic deployment of iimbongi and President Jacob Zuma's rhetorical flourishes with regards to traditional gender relations) while failing to provide sufficient financial or political support for the full-fledged development of African arts and languages. Meanwhile, individual iimbongi are part of a diverse tribe ranging from humble poets with an altruistic concern for society to astute showmen seeking career opportunities in a lean and individualistic marketplace where public success—or lack thereof—is not necessarily a reflection of poetic talent. Whichever position they speak from, it is not obvious that iimbongi fulfill their previous role of giving voice to popular grievances or that they can be counted on to advance a progressive agenda. Instead, as a left-talking liberation movement has walked off to the right, it may be that iimbongi have also followed the new opportunities that democracy has given rise to. As they say, money talks.

This chapter explores the contemporary political role of the amaXhosa iimbongi within the postcolonial, postapartheid cultural arrangements of contemporary South Africa and looks at how they figure in the vocal popular struggles that have shaped its social and political landscapes. I begin with an examination of my interviews with practicing iimbongi and their perspectives on the issue of censorship in the political landscape of contemporary South Africa. I then turn my attention to Mkiva, poet laureate to the late Nelson Mandela and one of the most prominent iimbongi practicing today, using his work and criticism of his work as a means of discussing the difficult topic of commercialization of the izibongo genre. Building on these discussions of political censorship and commercialization, I then analyze the transcription of an isibongo performed at the State of the Nation Address in 2016. In my discussion I show how the poem is limited by censorship and commodification yet nevertheless works within these constraints to engage in a veiled yet potent political critique. Finally, I turn my attention to the general absence of women iimbongi, linking this to social factors that, as in the past, continue to erase the presence of women and inhibit their voices at every level of society.

Given these factors and the current constraints on the izibongo craft, I argue that the primary role of iimbongi has shifted; much of their contemporary power lies less in their political acumen than in their ability to satisfy a hunger for cultural connection, to resist the Western hegemony that threatens to define the South African identity, and to infuse a specifically African identity and worldview into mainstream culture and politics. In this respect, their voices retain their transformative power in a tumultuous period of decolonization and change.

Figures of Speech?

In his autobiography Nelson Mandela comments on the particular power of the imbongi, recollecting his sensations in the late 1930s on witnessing the arrival of the great poet S. E. K. Mqhayi during his studies at Healdtown, a Methodist college in Fort Beaufort, not far from Makhanda: "The sight of a black man in tribal dress coming through that door was electrifying. It is hard to explain the impact it had on us. It seemed to turn the universe upside down."[16] He goes on to describe Mqhayi's performance, which included a denunciation of white domination of black South African society. Mandela remarks, "I could hardly believe my ears. His boldness in speaking of such delicate matters in the presence of Dr. Wellington and other whites seemed utterly astonishing to us. Yet at the same time, it aroused and motivated us, and began to alter my perception of men like Dr. Wellington, whom I had automatically considered my benefactor."[17]

During his fifty-year career as a journalist, historian, and imbongi, the great poet Samuel Edward Krune Mqhayi foretold of South Africa's coming liberation. His performance that day at Healdtown awakened a new sense of nationalistic pride in Mandela, who recognized from that moment that black subservience and disempowerment had been fundamental features of South African society since the arrival of Europeans. Mandela's account suggests that the nature of white supremacy in South Africa—a cultural norm thoroughly embedded in public consciousness—was often difficult to perceive, let alone question, without a critical intervention such as that offered by Mqhayi. The process of generating similar awakenings in others and producing the critical consciousness necessary for a political transition took decades and required many cultural interventions, including the black consciousness movement led by Steve Biko in the 1970s, the rise of black newspapers and radio programs that accompanied the urbanization of black South African culture through the 1960s and 70s, and the anticolonial and antiapartheid verse written and performed by generations of iimbongi.[18]

To highlight the importance of African arts, culture, and heritage in the New South Africa, Nelson Mandela offered Zolani Mkiva a prominent platform at the first democratic presidential inauguration ceremony in 1994, placing the young man's performance at the beginning of the program. In doing so, Mandela clearly understood the emotional power of the imbongi among the amaXhosa, if not all black South Africans. As well as signaling Mandela's intention to recalibrate a culturally skewed society, the inclusion of an imbongi at this auspicious event can also be understood as an astute political move designed to confirm the triumph of the ANC, inspire confidence in Mandela as a leader, and distract citizens from the party's political dealings by promoting the image of an African cultural renaissance.

Despite Mandela's impressive achievements, his role in promoting cultural and political expression is equivocal; he knew firsthand the power of iimbongi to affect public consciousness and, as the political tide ebbed and eddied in the final decade of the twentieth century, he may also have had a hand in silencing them. On 25 February 1990, newly released from Robben Island and confronted with some of the most brutal violence South Africa had yet seen, Mandela addressed a crowd of some hundred thousand followers in Durban: "My message to those of you involved in this battle of brother against brother is this: take your guns, your knives, and your pangas, and throw them into the sea. Close down the death factories. End this war now!"[19] One of Mandela's best-known speeches, it denounces the prolonged and deadly clashes between the amaZulu Inkatha Freedom Party (IFP) and the ANC (primarily amaXhosa) that threatened to plunge the country into a full-blown civil war.[20] Yet for poet and activist Nise Malange, who had risen to prominence as a performer and educator during the trade union movement of the 1980s, the speech marked a turning point for freedom of speech and political criticism. During our conversation in late 2015, Malange explained how the subtext of Mandela's speech made it clear that, like physical violence, criticism of the new black leaders violated the new spirit of peace and solidarity:

> The other side of [that speech] was for us as praise singers no longer [to] sing against Buthelezi, about Botha, . . . because there were a lot of people that were doing it. . . . Nothing that would be "anti" any of the leaders. So that was the kind of reconciliation that was imposed on people. That created a quiet moment because you're told by the leader that now you're not supposed to be protesting, you're not supposed to be saying all these resistant things, you know. For the sake of peace.[21]

Mandela's heavy emphasis on unity and peace may have stemmed from the ANC's policy of suppressing dissent and criticism within the ranks of party members to prevent divisions from arising within the movement.[22] The policy intensified under the subsequent Mbeki administration, when it became an established aspect of the political culture. As William Gumede describes, political figures in the New South Africa faced demands "for absolute loyalty to the cause," while "in wider society those with dissenting views often faced ridicule, marginalisation and attacks on their integrity."[23] The result has been the stifling of commentary, innovation, and public debate.[24] While Mandela's approach helped prevent the country from sliding into civil war in the years immediately before and after apartheid, the tone has weighed on poets and intellectuals alike, casting a pall over Malange's work as a social critic and liberation activist. Years later, despite worsening economic and political conditions and many vocal and often violent protests, an overbearing climate of censorship continues to stifle her work.

> There's a lot of capitalism that has been entrenched within the trade union movement. . . . There's no way that you can sit there and get workers to think and be critical of the union leadership today, because all [the union leaders] see would be that these people want to criticize us and it is wrong to do that. . . . The field is not as fertile as in the past, and I'm sure all the workers out there will still yearn for that. They probably write and put it in their drawer for the next life, because that's what I do. That's what I do. I just write and put

things there and read for reflection and ask questions: . . . Is this
the kind of freedom that we're fighting for? You know? And it's the
same question now—it's even worse. This is what we fought for?
Because that's what we're asking ourselves all the time. Do we have
to go into exile in order to be able to write?[25]

Malange and presumably other iimbongi experienced this silencing at a
crucial moment in the country's political history. As the balance of power
shifted from the white minority to a new black political elite, the radical
movements of the past that might have called for redress were stifled by
a new hegemony that on one hand promised change while on the other
removed possibilities for such change to occur.[26]

The Root of Acquiescence

Bound up in the issues of censorship and political exploitation of iimbongi is the question of commercialization. In a democratic and neoliberal South Africa, the moral imperative of toppling apartheid has passed, but the desperate need to make a living remains. In contemporary South Africa, iimbongi may have their own agents and may charge significant amounts of money for a performance.[27] This complicates their traditional role: even as their calling demands forthrightness, economic and political realities require them to watch their words. In Malange's opinion, the new commercial culture empties poems of their content and drains them of political power: "The poetry that is happening today doesn't address the issues. I think that the power izibongo had in the past—I don't think it plays the same role as it did in the past because it's not driven by people. It's commercialized. There's [an] imbongi for the president and a person who gets paid to follow up. So the impact and the cultural role and the political role, they're lost within commercialization of the culture."[28] On the other hand, Mandlenkosi Dyakala, a young Makhanda-based imbongi, denies that this is the case. Dyakala, who grew up in the rural community of Salem, a half hour from Makhanda, understands his artistic practice as both a literary and a spiritual calling, similar to that of a traditional healer, and he has immense respect for the tradition he is part of. During an interview in English and isiXhosa in early 2016, he explained to me that iimbongi cannot be commercialized because it is impossible to coerce an imbongi to say particular things. Instead, they respond to an inner conviction and commitment to conveying a message; they cannot be bought.

> Dyakala: You can't just tell imbongi don't say this, say this. No. You can't just say, "You see, imbongi, I need you to praise here but just say this and this." You can't just say that to imbongi. It's imbongi who decides: "No, I have to speak in this way. I have to speak in that way at this time."
>
> McGiffin: So, they know they can't tell the imbongi what to say.
>
> Dyakala: No, they can't tell imbongi what to say. Even if you are going to pay me. Just take your money! If there's a mayor, if he's corrupt, I should tell him so, even if the municipality is going to pay me. So, I should tell the mayor that the things that you're doing are not good for the community. The community is suffering because there's a corruption in the municipality so please, fix those things to the community. So even if they're going to pay just... keep their money if they don't want to pay me. As long as I've expressed what I feel.[29]

Yet as the interview progressed, it became clear that the situation is in fact more complex. With assistance from an interpreter, Dyakala explained:

> Interpreter: So, what's happening, currently there's changes because it's hard for them to express themselves most of the time. Now, if I express my true poetry, my true appraisal, then it might lead to a point where some of the people that I'm praising will feel offended and then mouth me around to other people that I must not be called upon to do a certain praise in a certain ceremony. Because now,... even though I know the mayor is corrupt—the imbongi's supposed to say that if he wants to, but if he says that, there's the possibility that he will never be called again.
>
> McGiffin: That's what I was wondering in terms of the payment, for example. Whether they would say no, we're not paying this guy. We'll get the other one who says what we want him to say.
>
> Dyakala: Yes! Yes.... So, as he says, now [the imbongi] has to adjust his words. Some things, he can feel that he wants to say them, but he has to hold them. But as imbongi he has the right to say those things but then it's kind of hard these days, through politics. Because politics are an issue these days. Politics they enter anywhere at this time.
>
> McGiffin: So, you find you have to censor—
>
> Dyakala: Yes.
>
> McGiffin: —what you're saying.
>
> Dyakala: Yes.

McGiffin: And that's something that didn't happen in the past?
Dyakala: No. No.

Similarly, Yakobi Sixham, an imbongi based in the township of Zwelitsha, which adjoins the city of King William's Town, commented on changes to the tradition, including commercialization, that have not only prevented iimbongi from expressing themselves freely but have also affected the very content and tenor of their thinking.

> Iimbongi long ago praised animals that belonged to the royal palace and they received nothing in exchange. They would just praise the chief and leave when they had finished. Then times changed. Now iimbongi are invited to praise at weddings, political rallies, and community events; they benefit. They've become commercialized, unlike the way it used to be. I used to stand and praise and then leave. Now it has changed to become something I can live off, that's how it has changed. That has even changed attitudes of iimbongi—times have changed and the way they see things has changed too. If you are the one who always invites me to your ceremonies, *it means that I should see things the way you see them* so that I can eat. Even though I see you that you are not doing right, that you are misleading people, I don't say anything about it. Yes, I need to eat, my sister.[30]

During her pioneering work in the early 1970s on African oral literature, Ruth Finnegan found that even at that time, iimbongi often received compensation from patrons and royalty that could be seen to compromise their objectivity.[31] Yet there is a difference between traditional rewards and contemporary commercialization of the genre that becomes evident when deeper aspects of the imbongi's calling are considered—a difference reflected in the divergent experiences of rural and township iimbongi. Thokozani Ntshuntsha is a young teacher in Willowvale who leads a youth performance troupe in addition to pursuing his own calling as an imbongi. When we spoke in a schoolyard in early December 2015, Ntshuntsha described the vivid childhood dreams that portended the emergence of his calling as an imbongi:

> Ntshuntsha: And I was so amazed of the dreams. So, what I'm saying is that the imbongi, although you cannot believe what I'm saying, that is what is happening to them. You understand? The way these things come, the words come. No matter you're going to close your mouth, thinking that the words won't come out, they come. They come. It will come, it will come, it will come.

And the only way to take those words for you is just to record. You understand?

McGiffin: I see. So, you can't repeat it again.

Ntshuntsha: You cannot. You cannot. No, no. You cannot.

McGiffin: Ok.

Ntshuntsha: It happens. I don't know.

McGiffin: So how did you know, at what point in your life, that you were an imbongi? That you had these words that needed to come out?

Ntshuntsha: People.

McGiffin: People were telling you?

Ntshuntsha: [affirming] People. Because you'll be going here and there because of inviting you. And people will tell you that you are— This is not normal.[32]

Ntshuntsha did not choose to be an imbongi; the talent within him was called forth by people who recognized his abnormal facility for language and sought him out. During performances such as Ntshuntsha's, imbongi and audience alike are often rendered nearly powerless in the face of a sudden flow of words that can be neither staunched nor interrupted. At the same time, the understanding between imbongi and patron includes the possibility that the imbongi might not perform at all:

> Once I told someone that when you are calling the imbongi to come and make praises, make sure that even when you're paying your man, na?, maybe the imbongi cannot come through, maybe he will come through. You understand? If it's coming from emotions and those ancestors or other things. Because imbongi does not know what to say until the voices, the emotions can come to talk. Understand? It's like that.

In Ntshuntsha's context, an imbongi can neither be told what to say nor be held responsible for remaining silent. Thus, the words that do come gain additional power through the fact that their arrival has never been guaranteed. In being true to their calling, iimbongi cannot fabricate a message that does not exist. Furthermore, as Ntshuntsha alluded above, not anyone can be an imbongi; the practice requires not just a special talent but a particular gift.

McGiffin: So, for example, do you see people who aren't necessarily iimbongi but these praises come to them so they just start praising, like you were saying the cows, the trees. Anyone can do that?

> Ntshuntsha: Not anyone. That's why I'm saying that it's like a blessing.
> McGiffin: A blessing?
> Ntshuntsha: Because . . . A long time ago, we as Xhosas when I read some books were respecting poets, which is iimbongi, were respecting them so much. The reason is that even if there will be a war you find iimbongi coming, saying where, talking with people. Talking with people about what is going to happen. Before the thing happens. You understand? . . . Even the king. There is not any king that is not having an imbongi. The reason is, I think, maybe smart, because I was asking even the King Zwelonke. I was asking him, why do you wait before imbongi stops? Why don't you speak while . . . You understand? They respect iimbongi. Even the presidents. They respect iimbongi. They will wait for the imbongi to talk and talk and talk and sit down. Because they know that even through what they are going to say, maybe there is something that they can get from this imbongi, before they can talk with the people. And sometimes, [iimbongi] can tell you that maybe you must be aware of something that can happen, now. Maybe people are not happy about you. Because the poet, as I said before, can speak everything. No matter you like, no matter you don't like it. You understand? Because it's something that comes from the heart, you understand?
> McGiffin: Ok, so even if they are saying things that the— They might say bad things about the king?
> Ntshuntsha: The king must listen.
> McGiffin: He has to stay silent?
> Ntshuntsha: He's silent!

Ntshuntsha's statements suggest that what has been characterized by Western scholars as the imbongi's "poetic license" to criticize figures of authority with impunity is actually a complex set of understandings regarding the nature and power of words and their provenance, the imbongi's obligation to utter them, and the danger of failing either in speaking or listening. Yet despite the public and political respect for the tradition that persists into the present, the situation is complicated here, too:

> McGiffin: So, they invite you to come to events and things?
> Ntshuntsha: To events . . . But now it's like business. It's not like before. . . . You'll find that now the poet will be put on the program. But before, the poet, you would not put the poet on the

> program. He's just like someone who's disturbing your occasion. You understand? So the only thing that you can do when you invite imbongi is just tell people that I invited imbongi, he is around. Don't be afraid! Because sometimes [he'll] stop, stop and do those things.
>
> McGiffin: So, it's not like, at 3 o'clock the imbongi is going to perform.
>
> Ntshuntsha: No, no, argh! You're wasting your time!

Ntshuntsha's words suggest that in the rural Transkei, respect for tradition encourages the continued acceptance of the power and primacy of the spoken word and of the mysterious source of the messages the imbongi brings. There is an inherent willfulness not necessarily to iimbongi themselves but to the spirit or spirits that compel them to speak. There is also a magnificence to the spoken words that transcends a mere literary or political practice. The understanding of the iimbongi and their verse as a medium of communication with ancestral shades may have enabled a greater freedom of expression than what is possible in Western contexts with their specific notions of time and social conduct that tend to frown on lengthy or unexpected orations. The unpredictable practice that Ntshuntsha describes contravenes Western expectations of performing artists. Thus, as iimbongi have moved out of traditional realms and into a modern secular society unschooled or uninterested in the roots of the genre and its larger meanings, so too has their ability to criticize and provoke been eroded. Ntshuntsha's closing lines above reveal the tension of a tradition in transition. In some contexts iimbongi still retain an element of control over the timing of their performances and their content and duration—traditions that Ntshuntsha would like to see continue. Yet public understandings and expectations of the tradition have clearly shifted. As the presence of iimbongi at gatherings increasingly becomes a business transaction, iimbongi find themselves placed between acts on a program, squeezed by the expectations of clients and audiences who want a good performance, a punctual performance, and a performance that does not exceed five minutes.

Iimbongi in the Political Economy: Zolani Mkiva

The tension that exists between the tradition of the imbongi as an outspoken political figure and the various constraints on their practice only increases as iimbongi move beyond community gatherings and onto the main stage of national politics. The contemporary imbongi Zolani Mkiva began his career as apartheid ended, taking the podium to praise newly elected President Nelson Mandela on the day of his inauguration in 1994. From these auspicious beginnings, Mkiva regularly accompanied Mandela at public appearances to become perhaps the nation's best-known imbongi. His high-profile public persona breathed new spirit into the art form and helped it gain widespread recognition, particularly among an enthusiastic following of young iimbongi across the Eastern Cape.

Mkiva's fame is no doubt assisted by his marketing savvy. Recordings of his performances are available on YouTube and iTunes; on his personal website he offers an impressive list of public appearances and offers online purchases of his albums and his personal brand of merchandise.[33] Perhaps most significantly, Mkiva's commercial performances include not only an address at Nelson Mandela's funeral but an advertisement for the South African First National Bank, official sponsor of the 2010 FIFA World Cup.

This commercial success has also earned him detractors. In particular, poet and scholar Raphael d'Abdon is dismissive of Mkiva's poetry, claiming that it fails artistically and creatively even as it succeeds commercially.[34] In d'Abdon's appraisal, "Mkiva is an astute entrepreneur who utilizes izibongo as a device to gain the favor of well-targeted, affluent audiences, thus contributing to a hazardous commodification and commercialization of post-apartheid poetry."[35] Furthermore, d'Abdon claims that Mkiva exploits "the noble art of izibongo as an instrument to make money" via "his subservient attitude towards the questionable leaders of the political and economic-financial establishment of this country (and beyond)."[36] D'Abdon's critique of Mkiva's poetry is rigorous and in certain respects rings true. Lackluster couplets such as "I do not have a dog nose / But I can smell and distinguish between carbon-monoxide and oxygen" certainly support the claim that Mkiva's success is not based on an ear for poetry alone.[37]

From d'Abdon's perspective it would seem that, like the ANC party itself, Mkiva has sold out, packaging easily consumed verses for sale in the commercial world. Yet it is also true that Mkiva is using his position to insist that the commercial world include Africans. At the end of 2015 I paid a visit to Mkiva at his ancestral home in the village of Bholotwa, near Willowvale in the Mbashe municipality. A community elder had died the day before, and we sat talking in the midst of preparations for the funeral: one team of men had slaughtered a cow in the kraal outside and were in the process of butchering it; another group was busily erecting a tent in the yard in front of the house. Members of the Mkiva family are traditional leaders of three communities surrounding their home, which is a majestic structure relative to the surrounding rural homesteads and is suitable for hosting the crowds that were already beginning to gather. Here Mkiva explained to me some of his political and cultural philosophy.

> Mkiva: The winning formula for us as Africans will only be when we do everything that we do in an African way. And it does not close the door from taking the best from the West. Take the best from the West and infuse it in your own arrangement. And you mustn't be peripheral when you talk about that. We're not saying we must go back to wearing skins. If these clothes that we are wearing, they are from the West, good enough. Congratulations to the West, we are wearing your clothes. But the content of our character is what I'm talking about. The thinking patterns is what I'm talking about. I don't have to export my brain to Britain in order to think about how to survive in Africa. No. . . . I use a lot of technology. I am brutally exploiting technology in order to enhance that which belongs to me. I am the first imbongi to put everything on iTunes. I've got my renditions on iStores and iTunes, which I think is good. I must put it on Instagram, I must put it on Facebook, everything. All these instruments, I must use them. It's Western instruments, but I'm putting in the content, which is African, to reeducate and educate society.
>
> McGiffin: You don't see it as exploiting the tradition or commercializing it?
>
> Mkiva: No. Because it's not a commercial subject. It's a subject that I'm putting out there for society and they put on search engines so people are able to get that which they want.
>
> McGiffin: So, you're merging the different cultures?
>
> Mkiva: Absolutely. We must do that. We must do that. You know, I am a strong believer in African culture. I agree that one of the weaknesses of our culture is not to write down things. Or record things. Now if you are not writing you must at least record because writing is also a form of recording. But audio recording and visual recording are also forms of recording. I've done a lot of recording in terms of audio, it's very key. So, I say I criticize my culture for not moving quickly in terms of recording. We need to digitize the things that we have. Otherwise they will be

overtaken by events given that emotion that is happening at a media level.

McGiffin: Right, so you use Western tools to boost up the traditional culture and keep that alive.

Mkiva: Yes, to preserve it as well. It's very critical for me.[38]

Mkiva's ideological stance is at odds with the South African hegemony that has embraced colonial institutions and languages as the organizing principles of a liberated nation, despite official commitments to multilingualism and ethnic pluralism.[39] In contrast, Mkiva argues for a reconfiguration of institutions and cultural policies to align more closely with African traditions and worldviews. During an interview with Duncan Brown, Mkiva emphasized the agency and power inherent to the act of creating and the spin-off effects of African cultural production: "Culture is our own creation, it is a true design of life. And if we need redesign of life, it's going to be done by us."[40]

Mkiva promotes his cultural and decolonial politics—which include emphatic support for free speech, African language education, and the validity of African justice systems—through the Mkiva Humanitarian Foundation, which "helps the rural people on a number of issues relating to education, development of arts and culture, welfare and education."[41] Little information on the foundation's activities is available online apart from scattered references to the Mkiva Humanitarian Awards, established in 1999 "in memory of Richard Mkiva, a community activist and fighter for the rights of rural communities who was poisoned in 1959 by colonial forces."[42] The 2013 recipients of the award included former Ghanaian president J. J. Rawlings, whom Mkiva crowned Global Champion for People's Freedom. Rawlings's acceptance speech, delivered at the Butterworth campus of Walter Sisulu University, denounced the abuse of power at global and national scales and called on leaders to fight against predatory capitalism in South Africa and elsewhere:

> My dear brothers and sisters, let us not allow the monster of unbridled and corrupted capitalism and political power to dominate us and create a new form of political insensitivity under which people who fought with us to create an equal and just society use their new-found wealth and political power to lord it over the people and exploit their vulnerability. We owe it to those whose blood was spilled to compel our leadership at national, party, and local level to protect national interests and ensure that the wealth of our countries is not hijacked.[43]

Ironically, despite this egalitarian rhetoric, Flight Lieutenant Jerry John Rawlings is a strongman who twice overthrew the Ghanaian government and held power for twenty years. Following his second coup d'état in 1981, Rawlings suspended the Ghanaian constitution and outlawed political parties. As the economy faltered in the wake of these measures, he adopted a range of neoliberal economic measures, including privatizing various state-run enterprises, dropping subsidies, and devaluing the currency to promote exports.[44] Mkiva's public endorsement of a political figure with such a checkered, antidemocratic past certainly calls into question which political leanings inform Mkiva's poetry and rural development initiatives.

Despite these issues, Mkiva is an important figure in South Africa who offers a vision of decolonization in which "Africanness" is mainstream, featuring social institutions built around African aesthetics, cultural identities, and values. For Mkiva, who oscillates between Johannesburg and his ancestral home in Bholotwa, adopting modern modes of cultural reproduction and distribution does not compromise the integrity of traditional art forms. On the contrary, the redesign of life in South Africa must engage with mainstream culture on African terms. Mkiva asserts the equal authority and validity of African identity and tradition in a world that has alternately appropriated and maligned them. As the first imbongi to perform at high-profile, televised events viewed by millions of South Africans, Mkiva not only demonstrated a means of bringing African culture to the fore in a newly democratic nation, he has used this platform to articulate his decolonial politics of African autonomy, linguistic and cultural independence, and economic and legal sovereignty.

I had traveled to Bholotwa in the company of a community arts worker trained at Walter Sisulu University and a friend who works as a civil engineer. Both in their mid-twenties, they had been raised in the rural countryside near Willowvale but had also pursued studies and careers in nearby East London. Our trip home involved a heated debate over Mkiva's politics, which they disagreed with in various ways. They were not supportive of Mkiva's ideas about African language education: they felt that English clearly opened the door to economic opportunities, while being obliged to study yet another language in school (particularly one that they deemed unhelpful from an economic perspective) would place an unacceptable burden on students. Mkiva's ideas about prosecuting traditional leaders through the traditional legal system were new to them, and they regarded them as equally preposterous. It seemed that for these members of the younger generation, at least, language and heritage are inextricable aspects of their identity and yet are also experienced as hindrances in achieving the illusory promises of the New South Africa. It also seemed that Mkiva's messages offered them plenty of food for thought.

Stage of the Nation

In the contemporary political economy of South Africa, iimbongi are victims of silencing and perpetrators of silencing as well. As President Jacob Zuma rose to deliver his address during Nelson Mandela's funeral, he was met with the loud derision of a vocal populace disgruntled with the latest revelations related to Zuma's exorbitant expenditures of public funds on his private residence at Nkandla.[45] Zolani Mkiva stepped up to the microphone ahead of Zuma, shushing the crowd before going on to deliver an isibongo devoid of criticism for either the current or the past administration.[46] Through these actions Mkiva turned his back on the imbongi's celebrated role of giving voice to public sentiment and speaking truth to power; instead he silenced the public on behalf of power itself. His motives, he explains, were to save face for South Africa at an internationally televised event and to separate a contemporary political fiasco from the memorial for a revered international hero.

> Mkiva: During the memorial service of Nelson Mandela, at the FNB stadium, . . . President Zuma was about to talk and the master of ceremonies had already announced that the president is about to deliver a keynote address. And then the people started making noise booing the president in the memorial service. Who was wrong? Was it the president? Was it the people? What was the occasion? The occasion was in memory of Nelson Mandela. So, if you've got an issue with the president, don't raise that issue in the memorial service of Nelson Mandela. So, the people were wrong. So, an imbongi came and put the people down, and then the president spoke.
> McGiffin: He said this is not the time and place?
> Mkiva: Not in so many words. He just came in and said, "Settle down. The president of the country is about to deliver a eulogy in memory of Nelson Mandela, our beloved president." That's why I'm saying not in so many words. You don't have to say "You can't do what you are doing." You just say "Settle down. The president is about to deliver a eulogy in front of the international community. Settle down." And people settled down.

The incident shows that iimbongi continue to play an influential political role in South Africa, albeit one very different from the role that has been celebrated by scholars. The new avenues of expression they have found do not sit well with some observers. James Matthews, a poet who was jailed repeatedly during the apartheid years for the content of his activist writings, comments, "What further distresses me is that some poets have allowed themselves to become praise singers for a political party. Their verses that sustained people in their rage against apartheid's abomination are now structured into sycophantic symphonies lauding the new political elite. They have become unmindful of their poetic role performed in the revolution. Will they now place their verses on the altar of political expediency?"[47]

A prominent public position is held by the imbongi who performs at the annual State of the Nation Address (SONA). The poet changes from one year to the next, reflecting the cultural and linguistic diversity of the country. First delivered at the opening of the new parliament in 1994, SONA is a speech that presents current political and socioeconomic concerns given by the president of the Republic of South Africa to the two houses of parliament, the National Assembly (NA) and the National Council of Provinces (NCOP).[48] On 11 February 2016, as the speaker of the NA, the chairperson of the NCOP, and the president filed into the packed house of parliament to the applause of the standing members, the singular voice of an amaZulu imbongi accompanied their arrival.[49] Using the recording of the televised performance available online, Dumisa Mpupha, an imbongi and translator from Makhanda, prepared a transcription and preliminary translation of the performance and provided an in-person interpretation. The full transcription and translation of the poem are included in appendix B.

In the recording, the SONA imbongi is a young man, perhaps in his twenties. He wears a leopard skin over his shoulders, another around his waist, leopard-skin armbands and a fuchsia ostrich plume in his leopard-skin headband. He carries a broad, flat assegai with which he gestures for effect throughout his performance.[50] As he speaks, the assembled members of parliament remain standing and cheer intermittently in response to his words. The imbongi is poised and self-assured yet modest; although he gestures and speaks strongly, emphasizing particular words, he does not shout or draw attention to himself through elaborate postures or vocalizations. Neither does he make eye contact with anyone in the crowd during his two-minute oration. While the poet's presence at the occasion illustrates the cultural and ceremonial importance of the imbongi, the calculated brevity and innocuousness of his performance would also seem to indicate that, in this context at least, the imbongi is symbolic—his performance is drained of meaningful political commentary.

The imbongi's poem centers on President Jacob Gedleyihlekisa Zuma, who served as deputy president of South Africa under Thabo Mbeki from 1999 to 2005 and was president of South Africa from 2009 to 2018.[51] A member of the ANC since 1959, Zuma joined the armed militant group Umkhonto we Sizwe in 1962 before being arrested in 1963 and sentenced to a ten-year prison term on Robben Island. Following his release in 1973, Zuma became one of the lead implementers of the ANC underground structures until he had to flee the country in 1975. For the next decade he continued to serve as a principal organizer for the ANC while in exile in Swaziland, Mozambique, and Zambia.[52] In 1990, when the ban on the ANC was lifted, Zuma returned to South Africa and joined other ANC leaders in negotiating South Africa's transition to democracy.

From the time of his return to South Africa, Jacob Zuma's political career was fraught with legal battles. In 2005 his financial adviser and funder, Schabir Shaik, was convicted of charges that included bribing Zuma, then deputy president to President Thabo Mbeki. Fired by Mbeki in 2005, Zuma returned to defeat the incumbent Mbeki in the ANC leadership race in 2007 after his case was thrown out of court.[53] After defeating Mbeki, he was once again charged with corruption and fraud, along with "additional charges of money laundering, racketeering, and tax evasion"— charges that were ultimately dismissed due to a legal technicality.[54] From at least 2015 until his resignation in February 2018, Zuma's presidency teetered on the brink of dissolution. He survived an impeachment motion leveled against him by the district attorney in late 2015, ignored repeated calls to step down, and, following a corrupt scheme to oust Finance Minister Pravin Gordhan on trumped-up charges in 2016, was the subject of the largest popular demonstration since 1994.[55]

Jacob Zuma is amaZulu, as is his imbongi. Thus, the SONA poem delivered in 2016 arises from a linguistic and cultural tradition with its own poetic conventions. Despite some differences, isiXhosa izibongo and isiZulu *izimbongi* have much in common. Both are forms of panegyric poetry that celebrate ancestors and current rulers and recount historical events. Ruth Finnegan emphasizes the adulatory aspect of the poetry that gives it "profound political significance as a means of political propaganda, pressure, or communication."[56] The SONA poem conforms to panegyric conventions, displaying several features that link it directly to the political context in which it was performed. Overall, the poem is ebullient, celebrating a president who is both magnanimous and wise and is able to overcome adversity that includes the treachery and disloyalty of those around him. Yet even as the imbongi praises Zuma's courage, learning, and leadership, there is a backhanded quality to this praise. Take, for example, the lines

Bethiwa okaZum'unecala	They said Zuma is guilty.
Icalokutyholwa ngosopolitik'epalamente	Charges were brought by politicians in parliament,
Amany'amacala etyholwa ziimanty'enkantolo	Other charges were brought by judges in court.
UGedlehlekisa, abanye bemkhamfula	Gedlehlekisa, others disrespected him,
Umazul'az'ayithole	He who walks around until he finds it.
Nanamhlanjena ziyathakaza izizwe zonke	Even today nations are excited,
Uvula bevalile	He opens where it is closed.
Umgoq'abawuvale phakath'epalamente	They conspired against him in parliament,
Bethi ke asoyiphind'ibus'eka Msholozi	Saying Msholozi will never lead again
Nanamhlanj'iyangena	And today he enters.⁵⁷

Here the poet reminds his audience that Zuma's past is mired in lawsuits and controversy, that he is not universally beloved, and that he has been condemned and conspired against by his colleagues. While the poet's intention is ostensibly to praise Zuma for his courage and strength in overcoming these difficulties, he also places details of Zuma's troubled past into the minds of his listeners without disputing them—a subtle form of criticism that shrewdly undermines Zuma's power, authority, and credibility in the eyes of his listeners. The same is true of the lines

Ngob'enkhulul'amaAfrik'onke	Because he liberated you, all Africans,
Umdon'omile phezu kweNkandla	A wild tree standing up on Nkandla.
Haye bawulabalabela	Goodness they play around!
Unomfundi woqobo abethi akafundile	The learned said he's uneducated:
Ngiyo baphikisa ngiyoze ngife	I'll disagree with them till I die.
Ufundil'okaMsholoz'ufundisiwe	The son of Msholozi is learned,
Kungafakaz'unina khulu	His grandmother can bear witness.

Here the imbongi reminds his audience of the Nkandla scandal of which Zuma stands accused and then tops that observation with the statement that, unlike his University of Sussex–educated predecessor, President Thabo Mbeki, Zuma has no formal education. In this matter, "the learned" are ranged against him and only his grandmother can attest to his learning, a pronouncement that, while reflecting the value of traditional learning and ostensibly deferring to the wisdom of elders, hardly seems a compliment, particularly in the patriarchal context in which it occurs.

At the same time, throughout the poem the imbongi emphasizes the impunity that surrounds Zuma: despite his lack of formal schooling; despite a high-profile rape trial; despite the 783 criminal charges of fraud, corruption, and racketeering filed against him; despite being found guilty of unconstitutional conduct in benefitting unfairly from state expenditures on his private residence, Zuma proved unimpeachable.[58] For years he remained head of state despite the best attempts of his rivals and irate South African citizens to unseat him; he was a figure of unparalleled and unassailable power and authority. Thus, the imbongi underlines not only Zuma's status as the leading symbol of dominance and masculinity in the country but also the awesome and incontestable power of the ANC.

Dumisa Mpupha felt that the poem was clearly prepared beforehand rather than composed spontaneously, claiming that in articulating only safe topics it displayed evidence of careful restraint. The poem lauds Zuma in a celebratory spirit, by and large steering clear of anything that might provoke derision or contention. Interestingly, when I suggested to Mpupha that the imbongi seemed to have sold out, he heartily disagreed, explaining that the SONA imbongi was surely an ANC member and as such his poem unequivocally praising its leader merely displayed party loyalty. Russell Kaschula is very correct in pointing out that "Southern African imbongi often walk a tight-rope between propaganda and criticism" and that their work may serve to legitimize the questionable words and deeds of people in positions of power.[59]

It may also be true that in mentioning Nkandla, education, and lawsuits, the imbongi is reminding Zuma of those shortcomings that stand out in the minds of his supporters and adversaries. As one interview participant explained, "The praise singers are actually giving advice or counsel to politicians in terms of how they should behave when they deal with people. So then it's up to that politician to heed the call of that advice. So it actually depends on the particular politician, but it's common that the praise singer will then counsel and warn the politician in terms of conduct, how they conduct themselves as leaders."[60] That is, despite the isibongo's lack of obvious criticism, the imbongi may be subtly preparing Zuma for an address to a potentially hostile audience, carefully coding public sentiment in messages that are clear to Zuma. This, after all, is the imbongi's job, as Dyakala and his interpreter pointed out:

> Interpreter: Maybe he's just making sure that he's representing the people. To the leaders. Expressing how the people feel and then showing that to the leaders. So that's his main importance when it comes to praising.
> McGiffin: So, as an imbongi, if you see the mayor, for example some mayor is corrupt, and you want to say that but you can't say that in a straight way, can you use your language to—
> Dyakala: Yes.
> McGiffin: —come around—
> Dyakala: [affirming] Around.
> McGiffin: OK.
> Dyakala: Which is very important, even the comment that this guy's having a talent of saying things. Because even if I know he's corrupt, I can't just say that "you are corrupt." I need to find a way to tell the mayor that [he is] corrupt. But at the end of the poem he should understand that he is corrupt but in a good way.
> McGiffin: Yes, so you're maybe entertaining—
> Dyakala: Yes, entertaining, yes, yes.
> McGiffin: Making it light, just finding some way . . .
> Dyakala: Yes, yes. That's very important. That's very important.

Through their speech, iimbongi transmit a message that a particular subject at an event must receive. Their poetic gift lies in their ability to weave this message into a tapestry of image, metaphor, and praise such that only the intended recipient may fully comprehend it. At least, this is how the role of the imbongi has traditionally been understood. But as various participants pointed out to me, everything is different these days.

A Forceful Suppression of Voice

The political power of the imbongi is further dulled by one of the most glaring shortcomings of contemporary practice. While various participants commented that contemporary iimbongi can be either gender, the practitioners I was able to find and speak with were exclusively male. Among younger practitioners, I was able to find one female poet, a high school student, who eschewed the traditional style in favor of written and performed poetry in English and Afrikaans about "things we experience daily and things that people can relate to." Her comments suggest that performances by male iimbongi performing in the traditional style are not representative of the interests and concerns of her or her peers and that there is little room in the practices of traditional performance to accommodate her style and voice.

Traditionally the practice of oral izibongo was strictly limited to men; the subject matter of their izibongo centers on patriarchal lineages and the achievements of male leaders—aspects of the tradition that appear to be foundational to and uncontested within contemporary practice. Yet this form of praise is a practice of erasure as much as celebration. The ancestral names and celebrated deeds uttered by iimbongi are those of the *forefathers* who occupy positions of authority and recognition, while the women attached to them remain unnamed and obscure, a practice of exclusion that obliterates thousands of people and their lives and achievements from spoken genealogies and, by implication, from cultural memory. Within the traditional culture from which izibongo arose, the possibilities for women's and men's lives are restricted by the dictates of custom and tradition, yet women shoulder particular burdens. Within their family of birth, which they are destined to leave after their marriage, and within their husband's family, which they enter as adults, women are denied rights of movement and speech that are available to their brothers and husbands, contributing to a situation in which they are unable to achieve the full familial belonging that their male counterparts enjoy.[61]

Gender oppression is a continuum that ranges from having one's speech and accomplishments unacknowledged to being categorically erased from genealogies to having one's voice and bodily sovereignty actively and violently suppressed. In South Africa a prominent and terrifying culture of sexual violence restricts women's freedom of movement and sense of safety, brutally impairing their sense of autonomy. This physically enforced form of censorship contributes to the ongoing exclusion of women from political and cultural realms and reinforces the unjust distribution of wealth and wellbeing across gender lines. Women remain particularly vulnerable among at-risk groups and particularly subject to sexual violence when they find themselves—as they too often do—in relationships on which they are economically or socially dependent.

Researchers investigating South Africa's problem of rampant sexual violence point to significant gender power imbalances, widespread poverty, and a general societal tolerance of rape and violence as being among its principal causal factors.[62] Yet as we have seen, much of the present malaise has its roots in a racist and exploitative system that involved the ongoing deformation of familial and social structures. The migrant labor system—and its affiliated structures of segregation, dispossession, forced removals, and tightly regulated habitation and movement—that forms the foundation of the South African economy, and indeed the South African state, was thoroughly violent. Like other forms of unevenness all too present in South Africa, violence is unequally distributed as well. Yet rather than seeking redress and protection for the most vulnerable members of society, political systems and discursive practices throughout much of South Africa's history have enabled continued violence against them. It should come as no surprise that the intergenerational effects of this violence continue to be disproportionately suffered by the most vulnerable—and the most silenced—members of a troubled society.

While much sexual assault occurs in the most intimate of settings, it does not occur in a vacuum.[63] In South Africa, as elsewhere, the culture of rape is excused or even endorsed at the highest levels; Jacob Zuma himself stood trial for rape in 2006, three years before being elected to the presidency. He infamously remarked that "in Zulu culture you cannot leave a woman if she is ready. To deny her sex, that would have been tantamount to rape." The claim sparked public outrage, as did his assertions that his accuser, a woman dubbed Khwezi to protect her identity, was obviously in a state of arousal because she was wearing a knee-length *khanga,* a simple garment commonly worn by women throughout the African continent.[64] The comments also derailed the work of scholars and activists who have contested the colonial discourse that constructs sexual violence as a particularly black or Third World problem rather than investigating the patriarchal nature of South Africa—indeed, Western society—as a whole.[65]

Zuma's contemptible defense revealed a corrupt and heartless political culture fashioned around oppression, inequality, the exploitation of vulnerability, and an objectification of women and a sense of entitlement to their bodies. His subsequent leadership set a tone of general acceptance of sexual violence throughout the country. Of the rape trial that concluded with Zuma's acquittal, journalist Lisa Vetten reports, "Whereas some limited gains have been made in relation to aspects of the law on rape, the decision in the *State vs Zuma 2006* reclaims legal ground from feminist interventions by upholding and valorising conservative and exclusionary ideologies around rape, sexuality and gender relations."[66]

The prevalence of rape in South Africa, legitimized by the president himself, is seen as a means by which men strive to maintain authority and control through the intimidation of women, an issue that becomes particularly pronounced in instances where men face the potential loss of power.[67] The fear and stigma that women experience as a result of the normalization of gender-based violence makes the problem of sexual violence difficult to understand in absolute terms because so few women are able to speak about it. For instance, one recent report found that in Gauteng province only 3.9 percent of women who had experienced gender-based violence filed police reports, and only one in twenty-five rapes was reported to police.[68] Although 2015–16 saw a 3.2 percent decrease in sexual offenses, the Institute for Security Studies has voiced grave concern at this apparent decline, stating that it suggests a decreased rate of reporting rather than a decreased level of offenses.[69] The drastic level of underreporting further underscores the crisis of women's silence, reflecting a combination of women's fear of speaking out and their awareness that they are unlikely to be taken seriously if they do. It also indicates a culture in which "women have such low expectations of genuine sexual negotiation in relationships that being forced to have sex when men (husbands, boyfriends or often would-be lovers) want it, or provide it as a unit of exchange, is seen as 'normal.'"[70]

The system of patriarchal control in South Africa includes forms of violence up to and including murder—whether of the woman or her children. At the national level, this was played out in the lengthy and high-profile case of Oscar Pistorius, who was originally convicted of culpable homicide for gunning down his girlfriend, Reena Steenkamp, before being convicted of murder on appeal. The country's history of and present experience of violence permeate society, and repercussions of the country's traumatic past include violent acts perpetrated by damaged individuals who have never had the opportunity to heal:

> Malange: They've never had any therapy, they've never talked about it, they've never had any trauma counseling. And those people are the ones that kill their partners. I mean we have the highest, highest rate today in this country of domestic and culpable homicide. Somebody that just phones the wife and says, "I'm killing your children now, listen to them on the phone" and stab the children and—
>
> McGiffin: Oh, my goodness! When did that happen?
>
> Malange: It happens all the time. It happened . . . The last case happened last year, just towards August, September. August

is woman's month. August, September, October, November because that's when there's activism against women and children abuse you see the highest rate.⁷¹

South Africa's rape epidemic not only reflects the dismal social and economic status of women in the country, it is also evidence of and reinforcement of their silence: violence against women spikes when women dare to speak out. The situation points to a profound need to heal the pain of past trauma that recirculates through communities, moving from one generation to the next.

The imbongi is certainly not a static social figure. For instance, in 2015 the SONA imbongi was a woman. Yet my research suggests that this valued social institution remains primarily reserved for men. While iimbongi are not responsible for South Africa's culture of patriarchy and sexual violence, it may not be a stretch to say that in failing to help cultivate a safe and welcoming platform for women and in neglecting to encourage women's participation in this traditionally masculine genre, iimbongi are complicit in a broader culture of silencing that enables gender-based violence to go unchallenged. Denied the spaces to raise their voices, women articulate their right to bodily integrity and freedom from violence in the silent spaces available to them. Four women who demonstrated during Zuma's announcement of municipal election results at an election center in Pretoria in 2016 interrupted the president's speech with a silent reminder of their presence and his past. Standing in a row in front of the stage, the women held placards reading, "Khanga," "Remember Khwezi," "I am 1 in 3," and "Ten years later," aiming to "pierce the silence around rape through a silent protest."⁷² Simimakele Dlakavu, one of the women involved, remarked, "This is another black feminist protest strategy—of silence."⁷³

In contemporary South Africa Nelson Mandela is a complicated figure, alternately venerated as a saint, respected as a deeply noble human being, and lambasted as a sellout. As Mandela's imbongi laureate—high profile, commercial, modern—Zolani Mkiva has attracted his own share of criticism, yet he has succeeded in asserting the beauty and validity of a culture, language, and heritage that, after centuries of disparagement by the ruling classes, is finally finding its footing in the cultural mainstream. In his own words,

> I would say that in the new dispensation of South Africa, I have had the singular honor and privilege of foregrounding the role of

Fig. 2. #RememberKhwezi protestors during Zuma's speech as municipal election votes are announced. (Photo by Herman Verwey; used by permission)

iimbongi in South African society. Not only foregrounding it but mainstreaming it, such that each and every key event that occurs in the country has an imbongi. Whether it's at a local level, provincial level, or national level, you will see them. . . . That if you open your legislature, if you make a provincial statement as a premier, make sure that in events like those iimbongi is mainstream. This is part and parcel of restoration and it has worked wonders. So today if the president is going to be delivering a State of the Nation Address I can assure you that there will be an imbongi in that event. There's no question about it. . . . So, it's a revival of the tradition and it's also striking a balance between Western forms and our African forms. So, I'm saying in this day and age it's very relevant and it plays wonders in terms of the path of transforming the landscape of our country. Imbongi has become a national instrument in the transformation of the heritage landscape of South Africa.[74]

In contemporary South Africa, with its economic preoccupations and political muzzlings, the poetry and role of iimbongi have changed. Mkiva has demonstrated this through his genre-bending work that embraces commercial culture and Western technologies. His contemporaries—the anonymous amaZulu imbongi at the State of the Nation Address, Yakobi

Sixham, Mandlenkosi Dyakala—face similar challenges when it comes to adapting their ancient art form to the demands of the contemporary world. Faced with often conflicting allegiances to family, community, political party, tradition, and poetic calling, they increasingly seek paid gigs and embrace new modes of distribution—all factors that affect their ability to comment on or criticize the political establishment. Yet it also seems that the tradition has changed selectively, embracing particular aspects of modernity while accepting outdated forms of gender oppression.

What is the role of the imbongi in contemporary South Africa? The question is much larger than the politics of commercialization or censorship. To pose the question is to inquire into the nature of the political, economic, and cultural relationships among South Africans generally and between Western and African societies in the modern nation of South Africa in particular. Whether an imbongi is able to criticize power is perhaps less important than the questions of how power and voice are exercised more broadly, how shifting forms of oppression are made manifest in postapartheid South Africa, and whether the relationship between forms of power allows the full expression of the tradition the imbongi represents. Which worldviews are visible in contemporary South African society? Which are credible? Which are given airtime and allowed to speak the languages of their choice? Appraising the existing balance opens the further question of what sort of balance South Africans want. Current conditions in the country—which is rocked by student protests, political scandal, and sexual violence and where much of the population lives in continual fear of violent crime—suggest deep and divisive imbalances. The place of the iimbongi in this flux is uncertain, but, given the opportunity, they will undoubtedly have much to say.

5 / Literature, Iimbongi, and Ideologies of Development

> *The greatest problem we have on this continent is a deficit of imagination. We focus too much on feeding the belly, on the politics of the belly. We don't focus enough on the poetics of the belly. Because sometimes it's poetry that allows us to wake up the following day and say yes to existence.*
> —BIBI BAKARE-YUSUF, FOUNDER OF CASSAVA REPUBLIC PRESS

Twenty years of democracy have done little to alter the uneven development embedded in South African geography and society by its segregationist history. Instead, the country's long-anticipated transition to democracy ushered in a new era of neoliberal capitalism that has further deepened economic and social divisions and intensified crime and civil unrest.[1] In cities and towns throughout the Eastern Cape, residential areas formerly reserved for whites remain unaffordable for the vast majority of blacks. These neighborhoods feature tree-lined streets and large, well-appointed houses with expansive gardens ringed by security fences. Meanwhile, in the outlying black townships at the peripheries of formerly white settlements, small, poorly constructed houses are densely packed on denuded land that stands in sunbaked contrast to the lush greenery of treed town sites. In these disenfranchised areas, purposely located at a remove from services and amenities, disruptions in water and electrical services are common; garbage disposal is irregular or nonexistent; sewage oozes across the streets; and the dogs, cows, and donkeys roaming the boulevards graze on windblown trash. People's movements and daily activities are tightly circumscribed not only by the availability of public transit (or lack thereof) and the long distances that they are often compelled to commute, but also by safety and security concerns, which vary from moderate to acute by zone, season, and time of day.[2] The environmental realities of contemporary townships coupled with their traumatic history of violent oppression have resulted in poverty-stricken zones of social exclusion where crimes of all varieties are a daily norm. Environmental conditions have also proven a major contributor to further health problems and social ills. Elevated rates of tuberculosis are linked not only to substandard housing but also to the length of time people spend crowded in poorly ventilated commuter vehicles.[3] Residents of informal settlements in particular disproportionately suffer from a range of physical and mental illnesses linked to poor water and air quality, overcrowding, and lack of sanitation.[4] In rural areas people continue to struggle against the legacies of dispossession, the forced removals and relocations of some 3.5 million people, and a notorious migrant labor system that extracts young, able-bodied men to fuel distant, white-owned industries.[5] In both rural and peri-urban areas, poor health outcomes and epidemic levels of violent crime and rape point to the dangerous implications of inequality and marginalization.[6]

In the face of such circumstances, literature would not seem to be a development priority and has not been treated as such by either the apartheid or postapartheid administrations. Yet literature is a valuable, if often underappreciated, means of redressing social imbalances and divisions; it played a notable role in apartheid resistance in South Africa and could offer an equally valuable resource for addressing contemporary challenges.[7] The United Nations Human Development Index (UNHDI) offers a measure of development that emphasizes three key elements of human wellbeing and capabilities: leading a long and healthy life, being knowledgeable, and having a decent standard of living.[8] Among its leading indicators are education and literacy, which are clearly necessary components of a knowledgeable and inclusive society. While the UNHDI suggests that the South African population is reasonably well-educated and literate (it gives the adult literacy rate as 94.3 percent), the accuracy of such figures is contested by scholars who cite highly uneven educational quality across the country and ambiguities associated with survey methods and literacy measures.[9]

The UNHDI offers no metric to measure access to literature; neither does it offer indices pertaining to the content of that literature, its authors, or the language it is written in, making it difficult to determine whether the majority of the population benefits from the country's printed literary works. Meanwhile, the inequalities associated with literacy and education are emphasized by contemporary writers who point to unequal access to cultural goods: "The South African literary landscape is physically based in the cities, and in the white suburbs. That's where the publishers are. That's where the bookstores are. I grew up in a township and I grew up in a village. There are no bookstores there. Here, you've got all the literary activity; there, you've got absolutely none."[10] In South Africa the geography of bookstores, libraries, and publishing houses reflects the postapartheid landscape in general. Much like access to clean and healthy environments, access to many cultural goods is skewed to favor the middle and upper classes while the perspectives, life experiences, and languages of the poor majority remain marginal and undervalued.

Given the primacy of colonial languages and their attendant ideologies, there is also a danger that discussions of literacy in development prioritize secular Western norms of print media and printed literary forms.[11] This orientation risks marginalizing or erasing the rich literary history that South African peoples are heir to.[12] Traditional oral literary genres—whether poetry, fiction, or theatre—are vibrant and complex art forms that more accurately reflect the social, cultural, and spiritual realities of the communities that produce them than do literatures produced by mainstream or international publishing houses.[13] As well as speaking directly to the marginalized majority mainly responsible for producing it, oral literature is a living component of the cultural heritage of South Africa whose value and artistry are often overshadowed by the printed word. In making literature widely available in vernacular languages to people who lack access to books, oral literature has an important and underappreciated potential to contribute to learning and social development in rural and urban contexts alike. Traditional literary forms may also be tightly conjoined with African spiritual understandings, giving this literature added layers of meaning and resonance for audiences. This is certainly true of performances by iimbongi, whose oral poetry holds profound spiritual significance and offers a rich potential for social awareness and healing.

In speaking with practicing iimbongi and members of their audiences, I found that despite the massive political and social upheaval that has defined South Africa over the past half century, the oral literary practice of iimbongi and the spiritual aspect of their izibongo genre remain alive and well in rural communities of the Eastern Cape and, to a lesser extent, in township communities as well. Iimbongi are not numerous, but a widespread respect for these figures and their literary tradition exists among the general public in the Eastern Cape. In my interviews with community members in Willowvale and Makhanda, participants were nearly unanimous in their approval of and support for the tradition, which they considered very important to their communities and their cultural identity. Participants felt that iimbongi encourage mutual support among community members, remind people of the beauty of their language and heritage, act as spiritual healers, and serve as upstanding role models for the youth in their communities.

In this chapter I draw on fieldwork I conducted in several Eastern Cape communities to examine the spiritual significance of iimbongi and their literature in social development and decolonization in contemporary South Africa. I argue that the ongoing practice of spiritually rich literature has a profound effect on audiences, contributing directly to people's psychic and emotional wellbeing and to the social development of their communities. In particular, I argue that in giving voice to marginalized languages, experiences, and spiritual understandings, the imbongi's literature affirms black agency, creativity, autonomy, and vision, helping to effect grassroots development that addresses community priorities and considers a full spectrum of human endeavor and wellbeing. Finally, I draw on interviews with community members to show how, despite the limitations imposed by current political and economic conditions, contemporary iimbongi play a vital social and cultural role. By acting as spiritual healers and by invigorating pride in African language and heritage, iimbongi have much to offer communities struggling through the difficult debris of a post-apartheid society.

Spirituality, Literature, and Development in the Eastern Cape

Poetry, particularly performed poetry, is an art form whose affective power lies not only in the meaning of its content but also in the emotional force of its rhythm and form. Poetic devices—rhythm and meter, metaphor and allegory, parallelism, alliteration, and richly detailed vocabulary—are not merely matters of aesthetics; in performance poetry, especially, these features are material undertakings that produce physical and emotional effects in their audiences.[14] Scholars are increasingly finding that emotional engagement with issues of oppression and injustice are fundamental to social movements and collective action.[15] Anna Barford notes, "Emotions are central to how people are positioned in relation to a topic or situation. Being emotionally engaged may amplify attitudes and provide an impetus for action. In contrast, denial of something being morally problematic may mean not feeling disturbed."[16]

People living in difficult circumstances in rural and township settings undoubtedly have plenty of emotions related to the challenges they face. Where the imbongi's talent lies is in the ability to identify and give voice to collective sentiment, allowing people to see and hear it expressed, to reimagine themselves in relation to "historical and potential identities," and to respond accordingly.[17] As literary performers, iimbongi have the power to move and inspire audiences through their skillful and eloquent use of the isiXhosa language and through the particular message that their oratory contains. The imbongi's words are events, part of a long tradition that recognizes the power and magic that reside in the spoken word.[18]

The political importance of the genre is well documented, as is its role in representing social conditions and complexities.[19] Less commonly acknowledged is the power vested in the poetry by the imbongi's spiritual vocation. Like all creative arts, the imbongi's literature flows from an unknown source. Iimbongi are held by many to be inspired by an umoya or *thwasa*, a holy or ancestral spirit, and their spontaneous compositions are said to be both visionary and capable of making things happen.[20] With their spiritually significant messages, iimbongi are closely related to the amagqirha (singular, *igqirha*), who are traditional healers, diviners, and herbalists. These various aspects and associations of iimbongi's poetry combine to give their words an energizing and transformative power.[21] The potentials and capacities of the imbongi's literature can help catalyze social development originating in and driven by communities themselves.

Development approaches in South Africa since 1994 have been complex and multifaceted, beginning with the ANC's emphasis on social provision under its Reconstruction and Development Programme (RDP) followed by a much-criticized shift to the right with its Growth, Employment and Redistribution program unrolled in 1996.[22] The UN sustainable development goals (SDGs) adopted in 2015 as part of the 2030 development agenda aim to "end all forms of poverty, fight inequalities and tackle climate change, while ensuring that no one is left behind."[23] The SDGs go further than their forerunners, the millennium development goals, in calling on all countries "to promote prosperity while protecting the planet" and in recognizing that "ending poverty must go hand-in-hand with strategies that build economic growth and addresses a range of social needs including education, health, social protection, and job opportunities, while tackling climate change and environmental protection."[24]

Despite the emphasis on sustainability in these laudable and well-rounded goals, development approaches that prioritize economic growth and the provision of goods and services often overlook human development outcomes that are intangible, difficult to measure, or assumed to follow in the wake of economic wellbeing.[25] Ilan Kapoor discusses this trend at length, describing how development approaches tend to view culture as "a 'luxury' to be indulged only by wealthy, post-materialist societies." This implies that "development policy needs to prioritize economic growth and, based on the West's industrialization experiences, recommend strategies that help fulfil people's material needs first." Developing countries should "put aside" culture "until such time as [they] can pay for it."[26] The presumption that economic growth is a necessary precondition for the cultivation of other aspects of human wellbeing is particular to an ideology that views culture and spirituality as subsidiaries to material needs rather than as vital aspects of human existence that are central to public life.

While "development" is far from uniform or monolithic, there are well-known shortcomings in development interventions that emanate from the economic orientations of the West. Policies that impose market deregulation and restrictions on government spending risk concentrating wealth in the ruling classes, resulting in the sort of economic polarization that is particularly evident in South Africa.[27] A development approach focused on economic growth can therefore be self-defeating, since, as Gilbert Rist puts it, "poverty is not a disease of capitalism of which it might one day be cured, but on the contrary stimulates accumulation and therefore represents a sign of good health within the existing system."[28] Meanwhile, signs of health and strength within communities may be erased by a development discourse that emphasizes lack, constructing under-resourced societies as "perverse, abnormal and passive" with limited cultural and artistic complexity relative to the accomplished West.[29] Development policy is not culturally neutral. Rather, it involves systems of language and representation throughout the process of policy formulation, and its managerial practices are aimed at improving living conditions in accordance with the norms and values of the industrialized West. Development practitioners may lack training or interest in the fields of literature, philosophy, history, or art. Yet to produce holistic advancements in human wellbeing, rural, nonindustrial, and otherwise "underdeveloped" societies must be respected for the complex organisms that they are, which means recognizing their wealth of humanistic learning and practices that are at least as well developed and as central to public life as those in the West. For all of these reasons, Graham Huggan and Helen Tiffin call for a critical examination of development theory and practice, noting that "postcolonial critics and, especially, postcolonial *writers* have made a valuable contribution to ongoing debates about social and economic development in many regions of the formerly colonised world."[30]

Iimbongi present a radical rebuttal to the discursive practices of Western society and the development models that emanate from them. Over the past two centuries (the period for which documentation is available) iimbongi have actively engaged with traditional leadership and colonial politics, voicing a sustained, emphatic critique of dispossession, segregation, corruption, and the racial and economic injustices that have impinged so catastrophically on the development prospects of African peoples. In the contemporary context, iimbongi continue to assert the value of African lifeways and cultures. Thus, even when they do not directly dispute Western hegemonies and imperialist practices, they destabilize these ideologies and help shift the discursive space by actively asserting alternatives. Speaking from the margins, iimbongi articulate a radical and nonassimilationist politics that places African literature and spirituality front and center, asserting the wisdom and power of some of society's most marginal classes. Unlike many westerners, iimbongi have no doubts about the cultural sophistication of their South African audiences, whom they know to be appreciative of the complex and densely metaphorical genre of izibongo. They simultaneously demonstrate and exercise the critical intelligence of their listeners, calling on people to remember and cherish African heritage and language and to undertake those development initiatives that are relevant to listeners' own lives and situations. Through their poetry, iimbongi challenge the pernicious notion that rural, poor, or otherwise marginal peoples are without literature or have suffered the loss of their cultures and traditions. On the contrary: iimbongi and their enthusiastic audiences proudly uphold cultural practices, literatures, and spiritualities that are very much alive, despite their marginalization and erasure since colonial times.

Iimbongi in Contemporary Society: Responses from the Communities

From late 2015 to early 2016 I interviewed fifty isiXhosa-speaking people about their views on iimbongi. Twenty-five participants lived in the rural areas surrounding the town of Willowvale in the Mbashe municipality; another twenty-five lived in the township adjoining the small city of Makhanda (formerly Grahamstown). My research area spanned all three of the pre-1994 constituencies that now form the Eastern Cape, which includes Cape Province and the former Ciskei and Transkei Bantustan areas. Research in these former Bantustans was particularly revealing; although these jurisdictions represent examples of reviled apartheid policies, they were also zones of cultural and political resistance that successfully challenged attempts to erase amaXhosa culture and practices.[31] Participants within each subset were chosen purposively to reflect the demographics of their respective communities, and each subset included, insofar as possible, a balanced blend of ages, genders, and professions. Interviews were conducted in either English or isiXhosa according to the participant's preference; the responses included in this section were transcribed from various interviews conducted in English.

In speaking with practicing iimbongi and members of their audiences and in analyzing transcriptions of performances of izibongo, I found that despite the enormous political and social upheaval that has defined South Africa throughout its modern history, the tradition of the iimbongi and the ritual aspect of izibongo remain alive and well throughout the Eastern Cape. In the interviews conducted in the rural villages around Willowvale, I was immediately struck by the participants' ubiquitous knowledge of the imbongi tradition and their shared sense of its importance to their communities and cultural identity. Participants felt that iimbongi encourage mutual support among community members, remind people of the beauty of their language and heritage, act as spiritual healers, and serve as upstanding role models for the youth in their communities. Asked whether the role of the imbongi remains an important tradition, participants were unanimous: "Kakhulu!" (very important). Praise of the

Fig. 3. Rural areas near the town of Willowvale. (Photo by the author)

Fig. 4. Joza Township at the outskirts of Grahamstown. (Photo by the author)

iimbongi was emphatic: "We love iimbongi," people said; "Iimbongi make us happy." At the same time, various research participants conceded that iimbongi were uncommon and opportunities to see them perform were rare. Several participants, while appreciative of the tradition, had only attended performances by iimbongi a few times in their lives.

In the township responses were more subdued. Numerous participants were ambivalent about the tradition, while others voiced a strong sense of identification with it. Most participants spoke of having seen iimbongi on television (for example, during Nelson Mandela's funeral or while watching the annual SONA). However, several participants had seen iimbongi only on television and never in live performance. As in the rural areas, participants in the township felt that iimbongi were generally scarce and that there were few opportunities to see them perform. However, as in the rural setting, an appreciation of the role of the imbongi was nearly universal among those familiar with the tradition. Many people expressed a desire for more opportunities to see live performances by iimbongi and felt that these opportunities would be beneficial for their communities.

Despite the emphasis on the imbongi's political role in much scholarship on the topic, most participants did not consider this an important aspect of the art form. In the rural Transkei, with its enduring kingdoms and chieftainships, people associated iimbongi with traditional leadership, yet it is notable that they did not consider this affiliation "political." Instead, they distinguished between an imbongi's role in traditional, hereditary leadership and the incorporation of iimbongi into the realm of Western-style party politics. Township participants mentioned that the iimbongi they saw performing at televised political events, such as Nelson Mandela's inauguration and funeral or the SONA, were paid by politicians to "cultivate an atmosphere" to help sway the audience and advance the political agenda of their patrons. Yet participants also expressed a general appreciation for these performances. Zolani Mkiva was widely known by those I interviewed, who seemed to regard him as a combination of celebrity and folk hero. It was clear from the responses that iimbongi are much more to people than mere television celebrities or political puppets. The presence of iimbongi at televised events was culturally significant, but even more significant was the opportunity to view performances of iimbongi in person, which had a greater effect on audiences. As one participant explained:

> Sometimes when there's some rallies and stuff like that they are invited. And they comment on what is happening in South Africa but they can pinpoint some stuff which government is doing. And that message is now spread easily because it's coming from mouth to the ears. In front of what someone is saying, delivered straight to the live audience. So I can think that can play a very, very important role. Because if you can hear something from the radio or from TV, there's some chances that you might forgot. But then when you get it from the horse's mouth, then you picturize that person, that costume that he was wearing, that event. Then you build it into yourself and you can pinpoint some items or some message.

Overall, the interviews confirmed that a widespread awareness of and respect for the imbongi tradition exists among the general isiXhosa-speaking public in the province. My findings differ from those of past scholars who have written extensively on the content, style, and structure of the izibongo genre and have emphasized its role in social commentary and political critique.[32] However, I did not find the same emphasis in today's very different political context. Although the tradition is diverse and changing, on the whole the participants that I spoke with emphasized and valued the spiritual aspects of iimbongi, pointing out their connection to amagqirha, spiritual healers in the amaXhosa tradition.

Much has been written on amagqirha and associated spiritual beliefs.[33] Yet apart from Jeff Opland's *Xhosa Oral Poetry*, I have found no research that offers a substantial discussion of the relationship between the vocations of the imbongi and igqirha, despite the fact that iimbongi, amagqirha, and community members with whom I spoke noted the connection and discussed its importance. This scholarly omission may be due in part to a perception that "izibongo has lost its ritual connotation."[34] However, I found that this perception does not accurately reflect community sentiment in my research areas. In honoring ancestral obligations, iimbongi play a healing and empowering role in communities, much like amagqirha, and offer a route to improved wellbeing through the active affirmation of the culture they represent.

Poets as Prophets and Healers

Within the shifting culture of the Eastern Cape, shaped and informed as it is by both Western and indigenous influences, the tradition of the imbongi is neither static nor uniform. While iimbongi are often conceived of as spiritual figures, I found that spiritual understandings of iimbongi varied widely from one context to the next and from one individual to another. Most participants recognized iimbongi as gifted individuals who "have got a message" and whose talent for language enables them to convey that message through spontaneous and deeply affecting oral performances at public gatherings ranging from meetings to funerals to royal ceremonies. As Fundiswa, a twenty-eight-year-old woman in Willowvale, expressed it,

> Imbongi, Emily, it's a calling. You have to understand it like that. Not just anyone can be imbongi. It is a calling, it's a gift. . . . .How they do it, Emily, maybe there is a ceremony somewhere and then they feel something when they're there, they feel—I don't know how they feel, but there is a feeling that they feel, and then they just burst out and say those things. Maybe there's a celebration, maybe there's a wedding then they just burst up and then they're calling those names, I don't know how to call them. But it's not something you can go to school and study for. . . . It is something you are gifted, you are skilled to do. And the way the way they use the words, if they pick up Q then they only use Q for like maybe ten words with Q. Like q-q-q-q. You see those words. So it is a skill. It comes with passion. You don't just do it.
>
> There are a lot of different types of iimbongis. There is imbongi zomthonyama, there is imbongi yosiba. The umthonyama is the one that just blasts out, and then the one of usiba, imbongi yosiba,

is the one who writes down. So, there are two different, two different types.³⁵

A forty-six-year-old man from the Joza township who was particularly knowledgeable about the tradition offered an insightful summation:

> Imbongi, I think it's someone who's been sent by the ancestors, if I may say so. To pass the message, the prophet, you know. They're kind of gifted. [There are] different kinds of iimbongi. There is imbongi zomthonyama, which is an imbongi that was appointed by the ancestors who does not write his or her message but it just comes spiritually. And when it's ready to burst, even if there's a ritual, then he or she can just come up and say things. That's imbongi zomthonyama.

Like most others, these participants distinguished between two types of iimbongi: iimbongi zomthonyama are spiritually motivated and compose their oral poems spontaneously according to custom; iimbongi zosiba, on the other hand, write their poetry according to Western convention during periods of quiet or solitary reflection. Contemporary performers, who often use rap, hip-hop, or slam poetry styles, may combine oral and written methods and may adopt the title of imbongi. However, while writers and hip-hop performers may have a respected knack for language, and while there is certainly fluidity among genres, iimbongi zomthonyama are considered by many to be gifted and even prophetic public orators thanks to their connections to ancestral or holy spirits—characteristics that are not necessarily seen to be shared with performers in more contemporary styles. Rather than writing or memorizing poems ahead of time, iimbongi zomthonyama burst forth with a message that they deliver in verse composed on the spot. Their spontaneous poems are event-specific, often highlighting the genealogies, features, and accomplishments of key figures present.³⁶

The spiritual aspect of these performers is reflected in the "zomthonyama" appellation. Historically, cattle enclosures (*kraals*) are particularly sacred spaces for amaXhosa peoples, and elaborate patterns of behavior governed human interactions with them. "Umthonyama" refers to the sacred center of the kraal under which the household patriarch is buried, making the kraal the abode of the patriarch and his ancestors as well as of the living cattle who are closely associated with them.³⁷ Ritual sacrifices performed in this kraal traditionally involve reciting genealogies and clan poems that Opland describes as "the medium of communication with the ancestors." The slaughtered beast itself provides a further channel of communication; its bellow affirms the presence of the ancestors, while its movement between life and death during the ceremony links the world of the living with that of the ancestral shades.[38]

Iimbongi also spoke about this feature of their art, which is linked both to the spontaneous composition of the verse and to the communal aspect of its content, which expresses ties to lineage, homeland, clan, and community. As previous scholars have reported, contemporary izibongo draw on the genealogies, features, and accomplishments of key figures present at an event.[39] Whether or not iimbongi are requested to perform ahead of time, their poems are specific to the particular occasions at which they are performed, and their words may form part of the sacred meaning of the event. In Thokozani Ntshuntsha's words, "You cannot just be imbongi, because imbongi is not a writer like a poet. It's just someone who is having his own, no not own, but the ancestors, I can say, that are talking with him, understand?"[40] Here Ntshuntsha takes care to clarify that the imbongi does not own the words he speaks but rather is in conversation with the unseen forces around him.

Similarly, Makhanda imbongi Dumisa Mpupha stated,

> For me [an imbongi is] someone who is being inspired by the spirit to say something or to advise people about something. . . . Most of us as iimbongi will see things before people can see them. Myself, I would say that iimbongi are the sons and daughters of the amagqirha. Because of the way they speak or because of the way they utter their lyrics, they resemble the amagqirha. Because the . . . amagqirha, they take inspiration from the place that the iimbongi take theirs. The spirit is more or less the same between the amagqirhas and the iimbongi.[41]

This prophetic aspect of iimbongi is seen as part of their vocation and as evidence of their prophetic ability that is inextricable from their poetic talent. Ntshuntsha remarked, "I remember there is a poet that is called Mqhayi, in South Africa. S. E. K. Mqhayi was a good imbongi because many things that he has said they happened. You understand? They happened."[42]

Other participants familiar with the imbongi tradition also commented on the importance of the prophetic aspect of iimbongi, such as one man who remarked, "And what they're saying, especially the one from the ancestors, he can foresee things from away, kind of a prophet, and warn if there is something bad or a misfortune that is coming your way." Others echoed the connection between iimbongi and traditional healers: "They're kind of igqirhas, you know. Because igqirhas they can come and just sing, sing, sing. When that spirit comes, it can just tell you something without expecting something from you."

Understandings of the Imbongi's Role and Message

Like amagqirha, iimbongi zomthonyama were recognized by many participants as having talent as a result of the spiritual calling common to the *amathwasa* (singular, *ithwasa*): that is, people who are called by the ancestors to perform a guiding and healing function in their communities. Individuals called to serve as amagqirha generally recognize their calling by the appearance of certain conditions symptomatic of *ukuthwasa*, a term that means "to emerge or become new, as of the moon."[43]

Ukuthwasa commonly manifests as a litany of mysterious and untreatable afflictions that arise along with vivid dreams that may include images of ancestors or symbolic animals.[44] A person afflicted in this way has been visited by ancestral or other spirits that interfere with mental and physical processes, making the candidate sensitive to the ancestral call.[45] Accepting this call leads to a lengthy initiation in which the initiate moves through a period of severe physical and psychic distress or disarray under the guidance of a fully initiated mentor, who facilitates the spiritual transformation and the emergence of the new personality. This *inthwaso* process (literally, "spiritual emergence") culminates in the consecration of the new diviner through the ritual slaughter of a goat or a cow. Once an igqirha is fully initiated, he or she is relieved of their afflictions and is henceforth able to maintain close communication with ancestral spirits in order to "provide for the spiritual wellbeing of the community."[46] The physical and psychological wellbeing of diviners thus depends on their ability to recognize and accept their vocation and to progress through the various stages necessary to become fully inducted into it.[47]

A similar process may be experienced by iimbongi who begin their practice upon finding themselves called to ukuthwasa. As with amagqirha, a network of associations links iimbongi to the ancestors; the special skill of both diviners and iimbongi lies in their ability to perceive and articulate these hidden connections, which is part of their healing arts.[48] As messengers chosen by the ancestors, the amathwasa have a spiritual vocation and an obligation to both receive and transmit information between the earthly and spiritual realms. In this capacity iimbongi serve their communities as literary intellectuals and prophetic visionaries able to perceive aspects of reality that the average person cannot.

Even iimbongi practicing in the zomthonyama style certainly may choose not to emphasize or participate in the spiritual or ritual connotations of their practice. Many iimbongi enjoy literature and performance and find that they have a talent for these arts. In addition, many iimbongi and their audiences are devout Christians who, in accepting the ritual significance of the practice, are forced to reconcile two systems of belief. Although some Christian sects in South Africa have incorporated traditional beliefs into the religion, others insist on closer adherence to particular readings of the scriptures, which can lead to spiritual conflict for those who feel the pull of ukuthwasa while holding Christian beliefs. Several iimbongi I spoke with stated that their talent was God-given in a Christian sense; another devoutly Christian imbongi explained that although his talent was a result of ukuthwasa, the vocation must be a result of God's wishes. These Christian iimbongi, acting in the service of God, prayed to God for inspiration and guidance, yet accepted their talent and its demands on their lives.

The imbongi's acknowledged affiliation with the amathwasa confers certain privileges. As messengers chosen by the ancestors, the amathwasa have a spiritual vocation and obligation to receive and transmit information between the earthly and spiritual realms. In this capacity, iimbongi serve their communities both as literary intellectuals and as prophetic visionaries. Mongameli Mabona notes: "Authority and power is, in Xhosa traditional society, held and exercised in fealty to the ancestors. Both the chief and the diviner in the exercise of their duties profess allegiance to the ancestors. . . . Chiefs hold authority from the ancestors by right of lineage, whereas diviners obtain their legitimacy through a special vocation."[49] Like diviners, the ancestral vocation of iimbongi endows them with particular rights to speech. Regardless of whether an imbongi's oratory has been prearranged or not, it remains a respected part of the proceedings at public events.

The compulsion to speak often exists as a physical force within iimbongi that must be respected. Dumisa Mpupha, for example, reported that iimbongi prevented from speaking have been known to collapse. Thokozani Ntshuntsha related that he hears voices in his body that tell him what to say. Later in our conversation he explained this experience.

Ntshuntsha: You'll find that some other poets, you'll find that these ones are just like sick because this message is supposed to be delivered to the people. Because you cannot *stop* them. You cannot stop them. Someone can just, maybe if on the stage can just jump. Understand?

McGiffin: He'll find a way to communicate the message.
Ntshuntsha: [affirming] Communicate the message. Try to talk with the people. No matter you give them the mic, no matter you don't give them the mic.[50]

As in former times, iimbongi perform at public gatherings and official functions where they may spontaneously interrupt the proceedings with their impromptu verse. Although this practice is less common in modern society, where meetings and gatherings are increasingly conducted according to Western notions of time and punctuality, several participants maintained that iimbongi are moved by forces beyond themselves and have license to speak out; the audience is compelled to listen. Regardless of whether an imbongi's oratory has been prearranged or not, it remains a respected part of the proceedings at public events. In accordance with the spiritual tradition in which ancestors are invited to be present at gatherings of a lineage or clan through ritual and oratory, the imbongi both invokes and attends to this ancestral presence.[51] As one participant expressed it, "If the initiation ceremony is performed by a certain clan, for example the Jorha clan, then the imbongi will talk about the Jorha clan, the history of that family line, that lineage, creating that atmosphere. Because there's a strong belief in Xhosa that wherever they perform, any traditional ceremonies, the ancestors are here. So, introducing them properly and using imbongi is the accepted way in Xhosa."

Healing Poetic Practice and Community Wellbeing

The imbongi's spiritual function was demonstrated during an invitational event I attended in December 2015 at King Zwelonke's Great Place at Nqadu, a few kilometers from Willowvale in the Mbashe municipality. The event—the launch of a holiday season antidrinking campaign by the Eastern Cape Liquor Board—was attended by around two hundred people from the region and involved a series of speeches and performances by traditional leaders, government officials, dance troupes, and representatives from the liquor board and South Africa breweries. Official speeches alternated with music, dance, and spoken-word performances, making for a lively, interesting, and fairly informal event that lasted about three hours and concluded with an ample lunch.

According to custom, the amaXhosa king was the final speaker on the program. As he rose to the podium, Thukela Poswayo, the imbongi designated to perform before him, took the microphone and stood on the grass below the stage, facing the king directly. Poswayo's performance began mildly, but over the course of five minutes the volume and emphasis of his speech built to a crescendo that finished rousingly to the applause and ululations of the gathered crowd. Lacking the trappings common to other iimbongi (porcupine quills, skins, assegai, and so on), Poswayo cut a modest figure in a simple button-down shirt, black dress pants, and polished shoes. He was empty-handed and wore no skins, beads, or head covering, and his delivery lacked the booming, guttural roar common to many iimbongi. Standing almost motionless throughout his poem, his performance style was minimalist. Yet this very simplicity clearly conveyed a sense of gathered strength and composure. Overall, he gave an impression of challenging or provoking the king, riling him to a more vigorous or impassioned address. As the excerpt below clearly shows, Poswayo's poem is confident and eloquent, calling on the king to show leadership in both speech and action, to act boldly and generously to help heal a damaged nation, and, through words and deeds, to inspire others to do likewise.

Ewe kaloku ndibiza ngabom.	Yes, now I name them deliberately.
Ngoba kaloku ukuze kulunge	So that all may go well
Ndithi Zwelonke	I say Zwelonke;
Funeka ndiyibiz'imilambo ye Afrika.	I must name the rivers of Africa.
. . . .	. . . .
Thetha ke! Nasi isizwe sakokwenu	Speak then! Here is your nation.
Nang'amaGcaleka ka Khawuta.	Here are the Gcalekas of Khawuta.[52]
Nalusapho luka Zanzolo.	Here are the children of Zanzolo.
Nal'usapho luka Sarhili.	Here are the children of Sarhili.[53]
Thetha ke nalo	So speak to them.
Ngoba kaloku okwakh'ukuthetha	For certainly your words
Ngekhe kulambathe	Will not be in vain
Ngoba kaloku uThix'uMdali, uQamata	Just as God the creator, Qamata[54] Of our forefathers,
Woobawo mkhulu,	Pointed with his finger,
Wakhomba ngomnwe wakhe	Choosing a man to lead others,
Wakhomb'indoda'emayi khokel'amanye amadoda,	So to your voice he turns his ear.
Ke ngelakh 'ilizwi uyakubeka indlebe.	Listen well! And make things right for us.
Aphulaphule enze kulunge kokwethu.	

In these lines Poswayo invokes ancestral presences by speaking the names of Zanzolo and Sarhili, helping to ensure their "protective sympathy."[55] Throughout the performance he entreats the king to speak wisely and judiciously, to lead his people through the strength and inspiration of his words as much as through his actions. He acknowledges the hereditary authority of King Zwelonke, but he affirms the responsibility and obligations that inhere in the royal position, reminding his audience of the king's place within a broader lineage and as part of a social and spiritual assemblage to which he has significant responsibilities. The imbongi here is tasked with giving the king the courage to speak and to deliver a steadfast and inspiring message to the people. This calling to account is of particular importance within the context of democratic South Africa, where the new constitution has endowed traditional leadership with a set of powers that is often controversial.[56] In this poem the power of the king's speech is clearly profound: uQamata himself is keen to listen.

Unlike amagqirha, whose healing practice consists of private consultations with afflicted individuals, iimbongi are public performers whose role involves tapping into the collective sentiment of their audiences, both living and spiritual. They perform a public service with social responsibilities that include "healing people through words" and addressing community issues through their praising. Like Poswayo, Mandlenkosi Dyakala, a young imbongi who grew up in the rural community of Salem and now practices in Makhanda, understands the ritual aspect of his artistic practice and has immense respect for the tradition he is part of.

> Usually traditional healers, what they do is just heal you on the sickness that you have. But traditional praisers, their form of medicine is their mouth, their words. When they give out the words, what they say is a form of spirit, it's a form of uplifting someone. . . . Because he's using his voice to heal. What happens, for example, if there's a ceremony we're sitting there. We're just sitting, chilling, chatting. He just gets up—because he still just comes at any time—he gets up and then when he praises you will see some people coming with tears, because of what he's saying it goes through some other people's hearts. So, he's a form of healer but using his voice.[57]

Three hundred kilometers away in Willowvale, Thokozani Ntshuntsha expresses the same sentiment:

> We have a responsibility to heal people through words. We have that responsibility. We as iimbongi, although we deliver the mes-

sage to people, people must be aware that some of the words that are coming from us are not coming from us. They are coming from somewhere else. No matter it's God, but there's someone who's driving the poet to speak. You understand? . . . We're having that responsibility to take care of people.[58]

Within townships and rural environments alike, the need for healing is profound. Generations of South Africans have been traumatized by exclusion and deprivation, and the contemporary economic reality of mass poverty, unemployment, and meagre educational opportunities has wrought harrowing social damage.[59] Meanwhile, historical patterns of land appropriation, community displacement, and uneven development have left millions of South Africans living in degraded and polluted environments. These malignant conditions coupled with the enthusiastic public response to the healing properties of an imbongi's poetry indicate that greater attention to recognizing, encouraging, and cultivating literary talent is a worthwhile endeavor with far-reaching benefits.

The rural Transkei, torn by generations of familial upheaval and division, surely benefits from the unifying spirit of the imbongi. Yet rural and township areas alike suffer from a shortage of iimbongi to perform this healing work; the absence of these poets goes hand in hand with a shift away from traditions that had been common in rural areas in recent memory. The following exchange with Fundiswa, a twenty-eight-year-old woman in Willowvale, reveals a sense of regret that her community's traditions are not as present in her life as she would like, largely as a result of economic constraints, including poverty, isolation, and inadequate transport.

> McGiffin: And so, what is the role of the imbongi, in the community?
> Fundiswa: In such events, the role of imbongi in certain events is to make people laugh, is to enjoy the actual event, is to add—is to spice up the event, just to make it sparkly. If maybe people were dull and then there comes iimbongi doing their thing, and you're like this [asleep], you wake up and you enjoy the actual event. How they do it, it's very interesting. So, I can say, in the community they play a big role. They bring people together. . . . In the community, it's good. It's good to see the skill of a person being displayed in front of you and this person didn't even plan this. And then he just comes up and burst and says those words. And make people laugh. They play a big role.

McGiffin: Do you have a lot of iimbongi around?

Fundiswa: We do, Emily, we do have. Because . . . I don't want to say we don't have. The fact that we cannot see them is because we don't have much events, and it's because people they don't have that self-confidence to do such things. They become afraid. I think if they can be exposed to the idea of being iimbongi and become confident, then we will know who is iimbongi in our communities. Just that some of them they do have that but they don't want to express it. Because they are not exposed to the idea. We only know uZolani Mkiva, we only know a few of iimbongi. That's the thing about rural areas, we are not exposed to such things. That's why such talents we cannot identify in our communities. Otherwise we do have iimbongi.

McGiffin: Do you think it was different in the past? Has the tradition changed or were there more . . . ?

Fundiswa: It has changed a lot. It has changed a lot, Emily. Back in the day, if I remember correctly, here there was, at this time of the year, everyone in their garden they have vegetables, they have maize and there were all the traditional, what do you call, the ceremonies. . . . But now today because we're becoming modern, people they don't do those things anymore. So, I think maybe because of the time, it has lapsed or something, I don't know. But it's different nowadays. I don't know whether maybe the technology has taken over or what is happening. Or people they've forgotten where they are coming from. Because it can be like that. People have forgotten how we celebrated being in the rural area and how to make fun within ourselves. Everything has changed now. I think maybe the technology has taken over, and then we have been blind, because we have to remain ourselves even if the technology is becoming more, but we have to remain ourselves.

McGiffin: So, it sounds like the iimbongi kind of went hand in hand with the community events, and you see less events so you see less iimbongi. Both of those things would have brought people together more.

Fundiswa: Yes, yes, yes. It's few nowadays. It's very few.

McGiffin: Do you see that having an effect on the community?

Fundiswa: Everything has affected the community. Everything my dear. People, they don't know where to belong, they don't know how to adjust to such events. For instance, we've got crisis of drought. People, they don't know how to adjust on that one.

Bear in mind, if there's a drought in South Africa, the food, the cost, is gonna be high. Now, everyone must plough whatever works within the certain weather. For instance, potatoes they don't use much rain. Why don't we plough potatoes, so that we feed ourselves? The value of food is gonna be high, because of drought, so my point—what I'm trying to say is people, they fail to adjust in new circumstances, in new occasions. So, to go back to your question, I don't know how people think anymore. They are too dependent, not independent, they are too dependent on the government. They don't want to think. At all. They don't want to share their ideas.

According to Fundiswa, iimbongi, in adding a tone of humor and levity to community gatherings, instill in their audiences a sense of joy in being together and an enjoyment of one another and the occasion they are sharing. They are known to offer messages clad in figurative language that makes people think; thus their very presence catalyzes critical thought. The decline of community gatherings is coincident with a shortage of iimbongi who would promote a sense of unity and communal wellbeing. With fewer opportunities to come together, there are fewer opportunities to exchange ideas and share observations and insights on changing social and environmental conditions. This bodes ill for the community's long-term wellbeing, as its very cohesion and ability to adapt to change— particularly those pressing environmental changes that have significant impacts on people's welfare—is undermined. The unravelling of community cohesion threatens a loss of morale that the imbongi could also offer an antidote to. In Thokozani Ntsuntsha's words, "When someone has an imbongi coming with those words, you will quickly know about who you are and you will be proud of what you are. You'll be not doubting about yourself."

While the response of research participants to iimbongi and their performances was overwhelmingly positive, it would be simplistic to state that the tradition and its practice are always unequivocally good. As discussed above, oppressive political circumstances and a prevailing climate of censorship often prevent iimbongi from saying all that they would like to.[60] Worse, they may use their power to rouse people to action to enact xenophobia, gender oppression, and other regressive politics. While all iimbongi I spoke with clearly acted with the best of intentions and stressed the importance of prayer, spiritual purity, and the necessity of being an upstanding citizen who provides a role model in the community, these approaches are no guarantee of a liberal or egalitarian politics. Indeed, one imbongi I spoke with enthusiastically described how he used his platform to promote a view of the world that was alarmingly sexist and xenophobic. Given their widely acknowledged poetic license to speak their minds and the weight and spiritual power carried by their words, there is clearly a potential that iimbongi will advance a conservative social agenda—if not abuse their power outright.

These dangers aside, research participants repeatedly claimed that iimbongi perform an important healing role in their communities and voiced their belief in the value of the imbongi's performances to community upliftment, social cohesion, self-identity, and pride. In the fraught social environments of contemporary South African townships, "iimbongi give people hope," as one young man explained. In the words of a middle-aged man, "Iimbongi, they revive a spirit of *ubuntu*" (loosely, humanity). "They'll teach you many things," said a twenty-five-year-old woman. "How you can communicate with other people, how you can respect your culture, whether you are black or white, rich or poor. To respect who you are." A twenty-six-year-old man claimed that there are many iimbongi around the Makhanda area. Although he was not one of them, he liked to hear them—he "liked the sound." As he explained, "They heal us. Like when they talk isiXhosa, when they're rhyming their words, they bring us a knowledge that comes from them to us. And how they feel, their emotions."

This embodiment and expression of public emotion has a powerful effect on audiences. As Ndileka, a thirty-year old woman, explained:

> Some people they get inspired by iimbongi. They show those emotions in different ways. Sometimes people will actually applaud by some sort of cries out [i.e., ululations]. I'm sure you've heard that. And some people actually will really be inspired to continue the legacy of their ancestors in terms of performing traditional rituals and ceremonies. . . . They give a lot of applaud to the imbongi and some people do actually cry. It actually makes them too emotional sometimes when the imbongi speaks.[61]

She went on to describe the way the imbongi's emotionally-charged praises affected her:

> Ndileka: It's so overwhelming hey? Because we're all happy. We'll look up and say wow! And they will clap their hands, they will be happy, you understand? Because he's praising that someone. He's

praising you. Starting from your hair, the way your hair looks—nicely, in a Xhosa way. Starting from your face, the way you walk, the way you're touching things. It's so beautiful. Especially if you understand what the imbongi's saying.
McGiffin: And the language they use has an effect on people?
Ndileka: It does have because when they're speaking my language I feel like, wow! Because Xhosa's my mother tongue.... Like for instance, if you're saying you're walking, *uyahamba,* and then they will say "*uyanawuka,*" which is the same thing as uyahamba. You see? So that's what I'm saying, it's a deep Xhosa that we can say like, "Wow! My Xhosa is a beautiful language."

The beauty of the isiXhosa language is too seldom celebrated in a society dominated by English, whose use and mastery are bound up in issues of class and economic security. Despite the recognition of eleven official languages in South Africa's constitution, the oppression of African languages since the arrival of Europeans has actively discouraged native speakers of these languages from taking pride in their beauty and expressiveness, thwarting the development of vernacular literary cultures.[62] As one participant commented, the persistent emphasis on English, even in a liberated South Africa, has resulted in a lack of appreciation of African languages and their development: "Especially young people undermine their language. [They say,] 'Ah, English is better!'" Not only does the emphasis on English neglect the power and beauty of African languages, the precedence it is given has profound consequences for the cultural lives of black South Africans—consequences that have been recognized for generations. In 1986 Ngugi wa Thiong'o observed that in the ongoing struggle for autonomy and control over creative initiative on the African continent, "the choice of language and the use to which language is put is central to a people's definition of themselves in relation to their natural and social environment."[63] The preference for English, which continues to hold true today, inhibits the emergence of a literary culture among vernacular-language speakers and prevents connections between readers and writers. Russell Kaschula notes with concern that the ongoing oppression and trivialization of indigenous language literatures has resulted in the "lack of identification with the indigenous written word by speakers of African languages" such that "today, speakers of African languages themselves are loath to read literature written in indigenous languages."[64]

South African writer Thando Mqolonzana has voiced a similar belief that current conditions are the result of a literary system that remains quintessentially colonial. In 2015 his public refusal to attend either the Time of the Writer or Franschhoek literary festivals went viral. As he explained during one media interview:

> We are talking about a system here. . . . One which I chose to define as the colonial literary system. There has never been a deliberate decolonial project. These things of freedom and democracy are not decolonial in nature. So, we inherited a colonial literary system and did nothing about it for the past twenty years. I decided I was going to stop asking whiteness to take me more seriously to accommodate me better in their system, because that's not what we need. We need two things. One being to crush the colonial system completely, because there is no improving colonialism and then imagine new things that are not framed by notions of colonialism.[65]

During a visit to Makhanda in February 2016 for the annual Puku Storytelling Festival, renowned South African author Sindiwe Magona expressed a similar decolonial politics, citing the title of W. B. Rubusana's classic literary text *Zemk'inkomo magwalandini* (which translates loosely as "Defend your heritage" and literally as "There go your cattle, you cowards!"), as a battle cry. Referring to the willingness of black South Africans to neglect or abandon their linguistic and cultural heritage, Magona stated, "The cattle aren't even being taken as spoils: they're being driven away." In the New South Africa, the black majority government has proven anxious to embrace not only the neoliberal norms of Western political economy but also the West's hegemonic cultural institutions and expectations. Such an attitude is deeply associated with colonial and postcolonial spaces and perpetuates the cultural oppression of the colonial era.[66]

There are eleven official languages in South Africa, including Afrikaans, English, isiNdebele, Sesotho, siSwati, Tshivenda, xiTsonga, isiXhosa, and isiZulu, making the linguistic situation in the country far from simple. Yet rather than operating via a polyglot assemblage of African languages, government and administrative bodies and educational institutions from the primary level upward use the language of the colonial and apartheid masters. In promoting English and the cultural and political norms linked to it, the government has abandoned the ideological struggles of the past at yet another level, instead advancing the same consciousness and worldview that governed oppressive systems of the colonial era. With English valued over their mother tongues, people are squeezed into the psychic and cultural realm of the colonizer and the cultural, economic, and political ontologies embedded within the colonial language.

In celebrating the beauty and expressiveness of their mother tongue, iimbongi help their audiences resist the cultural and linguistic hegemony that exists in South Africa. Like any poet, iimbongi have the skill to make available to their audiences particular forms of the language that are seldom heard. As Ntshuntsha explains,

> Ntshuntsha: The way that we have of using words in these ways is not like the Xhosa. . . . Like for instance when you're greeting someone in Xhosa you're saying "Molo!" na? Just general Xhosa. But before it was not molo, you were saying "Bodani!" Which is the deep Xhosa, you understand. So there are words that are special that poets use.
> McGiffin: Like an old-fashioned language?
> Ntshuntsha: Old-fashioned kind of words. *Amaqhalo,* which is the metaphors. *Izaci,* which is figures of speech, whereby you cannot even understand sometimes the message, but the message goes straight to you.[67]

While traditional iimbongi generally perform in isiXhosa, the same is not true of performance poets more broadly, who often express the cultural hybridity of their contexts by mixing languages and performance forms. While such expressions of cultural hybridity are by no means lesser than the "deep Xhosa" of the traditional imbongi, there is value in the imbongi zomthonyama's linguistic offering. Historically, iimbongi were instrumental to the development of the isiXhosa language, and they continue to remind people of the beauty and complexity of its precolonial forms. A thirty-five-year-old woman living in the township commented:

> They're doing it in English now. If they could do it in their vernacular language, I think it would be . . . And again, I don't think they understand Xhosa like we do, hey? These young ones. Because you can take a Xhosa word but they won't understand. Uthini's this?[68] You understand. They don't know that Xhosa Xhosa Xhosa. Even if you can go to Transkei, the Xhosa from Transkei and from here is so different. Because I'm coming from Transkei. The time I came here, everybody was like wow! What are you saying? You're speaking Xhosa? But wow your Xhosa is so different! But as time goes on we adopt the Xhosa from this side and we're speaking like them now.

As this speaker points out, different dialects of isiXhosa are spoken from one region to another; township dialects can differ significantly from the dialect of rural areas even a short distance away. While Ntshuntsha may be comfortable using words and metaphors that his rural audience is unfamiliar with, the same is not true of all iimbongi. Dyakala, who grew up in a rural community only a half hour from Makhanda, explains:

> Dyakala: When I'm in a rural area, it's easy to understand me, on what I'm saying. But here in the township some people do not understand me. "What he's trying to say? Ohhh, he's trying to say this thing." So when I'm praising in my rural area, I know that the people in the community understand me very well. But here in the location I have to change words in a polite way, just get people to understand.
> McGiffin: In the rural areas do you use the deeper Xhosa?
> Dyakala: [affirming] The deeper Xhosa. Here in the township I can't just get to the deeper Xhosa because they will not understand what I'm saying.[69]

The iimbongi's "deep Xhosa" is archaic, poetic, and draws on a linguistic heritage that predates colonialism. Their rich and figurative language, their use of ancient and often unfamiliar words, their culturally resonant metaphors and historical subjects, their forthright and deeply personal and relevant messages all serve to elevate the marginalized language and identity of millions of people trapped in the painful reality of neoliberal, postapartheid space. In those spaces—dangerous, often dilapidated, and sidelined by the middle and upper classes of South African society—iimbongi offer a glimpse of the natural world and a reminder of human connectedness to it. With their words, says Zwelitsha imbongi Yakobi Sixham, they offer affirmation of beauty in the world around them and hope of a brighter future ahead:

> The way I see iimbongi, my sister, firstly, they are people who have visions and are very fond of nature. Everything in nature they love. If there are bushes maybe in December there are bushes with flowers, they like that. Including rivers, changing of seasons—people who are iimbongis like that. Iimbongis are people who are useful to the community because if something good is happening in the community, you'll hear the imbongi. The imbongi will not keep quiet when there's something which is not right happening in the community. Like for example, let me say the community is affected by xenophobia, the imbongi cannot just keep quiet. The imbongi is supposed to stand up and say no, this xenophobia is wrong. If

maybe there is a rainbow nation now in South Africa, imbongi is supposed to stand and say, "This is good."[70]

South Africa today is drastically different from what it was during earlier periods, and the role of the imbongi has necessarily shifted as well. Resistance movements are no longer oriented toward the specific enemy of the apartheid state but are instead directed at the much more slippery and pernicious demons of inequality, underdevelopment, and ongoing racism. Literary resistance is made more difficult by the climate of censorship that has prevailed in the postapartheid period, as discussed in chapter 4. Furthermore, economic and social shifts—particularly related to the declining overall importance of the mining sector and rapid technological change—have resulted in increased urbanization, less oscillation between rural and urban areas, and altered relationships between these realms. Within this matrix, the people I spoke with valued the cultural identity and language that iimbongi voice, their ability to entertain and liven an event, their connection to God and ancestors, and their ability to provoke reflection and critical thought.

Likewise, it is also clear that iimbongi, good intentions notwithstanding, can also give voice to adverse sentiments that simmer within communities, whether xenophobia, sexism, homophobia, or other conservative values. Iimbongi act as mediators between communities and authority figures, voicing public sentiment and concerns. Just as iimbongi in the employ of politicians and corporations may have difficulty seeing or expressing truths that countervail the party line, so too are community-based iimbongi immersed in a social culture that they risk uncritically propagating and perpetuating. In this, iimbongi are no different from other artists; they are individual humans who generally act conscientiously within the constraints of their own awareness and voice and are often responsive to the tastes and sensibilities of their audiences. Some iimbongi will be inclined to sell their talents; many others will accept financial sacrifices in service of curiosity, creativity, and the opportunity to explore the intricacies of human emotion and experience through their art.

My interviews suggested that iimbongi take their responsibilities seriously and tend not to be driven by self-interest but by their spiritual experiences and their desire to use their gifts to serve their communities. As spiritual figures accorded deep respect among their communities, iimbongi hold a unique and underappreciated potential to share knowledge and history with their audiences, and to inspire the pride, hope, and humanity that are requisite components of meaningful development and progressive social and political change. In addition, iimbongi and their art offer an example of an alternative means by which development practitioners can begin to access grassroots perspectives of the histories and priorities of disadvantaged communities. Thus, despite their current marginalization and scarcity, iimbongi remain a relevant and respected source of knowledge and cultural production that can help heal the lasting psychic trauma wrought by colonialism, apartheid, and contemporary crime and unrest.

These findings present a case for development policy to include greater consideration for creative arts and their expressions of cultural autonomy. "Alternative representational genres," such as izibongo, offer diverse perspectives and insights by illuminating broad historical, cultural, and environmental complexities that other research methodologies and associated literature may fail to capture.[71] Appreciation of the role of literature and the arts in scholarly knowledge production is growing, leading many researchers to embrace it as a way of gaining more nuanced understandings of social dynamics and suitable policy responses.[72] In South Africa's postcolonial, postapartheid, and decolonizing context, integrating traditional arts and culture into development scholarship is part of an ongoing process of recognizing African agency, positioning indigenous voices into their rightful place of authority, and deferring to the wisdom resident in communities themselves.

As iimbongi demonstrate, rural and nonindustrial societies possess complex, sophisticated, and well-developed artistic genres that, just as in Western cultures, reveal societal histories, values, and aesthetics. Through its invocation of ancestral shades as well as its emotive and energizing effects on audiences, the poetry has the power to make things happen. It also offers a means of enlivening the cultural, spiritual, intellectual, and emotional lives of people living in conditions of oppressive deprivation. While poetry may not remove these conditions immediately, it expresses an aspect of the human spirit too often overlooked by reductionist development discourse and practices that emphasize material needs to the neglect or even detriment of other human faculties. Thus, iimbongi and their literature can make a valuable contribution not only to knowledge for and about development but also to development practices that strive to enable people to live rich, healthy, and imaginative lives. Iimbongi animate African identities and languages for their audiences, they open spaces for discussion and decolonization, and, in a society so damaged by the horrors of its past and the environments of its present, their words offer the healing possibility of hope.

6 / Land Expropriation without Compensation and the Vocal Dispossessed

> *For a colonized people the most essential value, because the most concrete, is first and foremost the land. The land which will bring them bread and, above all, dignity.*
>
> —FRANTZ FANON

As the newly elected ANC government stepped into power in 1994, it found itself faced with the daunting task of dismantling several centuries of discriminatory policies and redressing their legacies. In particular, a long history of conflict, land seizures, and forced relocations had left the country with an extraordinarily unequal system of land tenure wherein over 65 percent of the South African land base was owned by less than fifty thousand white farmers.[1] The issue of land rights was therefore a key focus for the ANC government, which aimed to redistribute a third of white-owned farmlands to black citizens within the first twenty years of its tenure.[2]

The ordeals of dispossession and separate development left South African spirits battered, hence reforms to address unequal patterns of land tenure hold symbolic importance as well as offering a route to improved material conditions.[3] With much at stake, emotions run high where land is concerned, and land reform has remained one of the central issues on the postapartheid political agenda as well as one of the most difficult to resolve. Between 1994 and 2009 the land restitution program, which aimed to compensate claimants forcibly removed from land as a result of racial laws, met with reasonable success. Tens of thousands of claims against the state were resolved through compensation payments and by restitution or grants of over two million hectares of state land.[4]

A racially equitable distribution of privately owned rural lands has proven much more difficult to achieve. The justice and effectiveness of the government's land redistribution program have been limited by various failings, including disagreements over structural changes to the commercial agricultural sector, issues with land transfer and title, and the absence of effective redistributive mechanisms that truly benefit disenfranchised groups.[5] As a result, the vision of a reordered countryside that would establish the secure land rights of "a major smallholder class" of independent farmers and landowners remains elusive.[6] Most notably, policy has increasingly emphasized on market aspects of agricultural land—shifting from small grants to poor households in the early years to large grants in support of black agribusinesses during Thabo Mbeki's presidency and finally to a "willing buyer, willing seller" approach under Jacob Zuma. These shifts have biased the land reform process against poor and marginalized classes, the very people it was originally intended to benefit.[7] Furthermore, in privileging large, capital-intensive agribusinesses, the current approach raises real questions about long-term environmental sustainability, particularly as South Africa's water resources come under increasing pressure. Change is clearly needed if South Africa's land redistribution program is to establish true social justice and environmental sustainability that attends to many meanings, histories, and concerns.

This chapter wades cautiously into the increasingly stormy waters of the South African land reform debate, examining the complex and multilayered cultural politics surrounding dispossession as expressed through oral literature. Much has been written on land reform and on the various government failures to ensure that it either increases the nation's food supply or provides secure tenure for disenfranchised South Africans. The brief discussion presented here is not intended to simplify a knotty debate that involves complicated overlapping issues but rather to present aspects of that debate that are of particular relevance to this discussion. I join scholars calling for new approaches, and in this chapter I emphasize the potential of artists to spark fresh and empathetic thinking.[8] The chapter begins with a brief overview of some of the factors at play in land politics in South Africa and then offers close readings of historical and contemporary isiXhosa poetic texts. In my analysis I explore poetic articulations of alternative understandings of land that extend far beyond narrowly defined market relations to the rich matrix of relationships and responsibilities that land holds. As in chapter 5, I argue that the affective power of izibongo derives from details of the craft: an imbongi's choice of words and metaphor, the rhythm of the language, the performance style, and the layers of spiritual significance that inhere in the poetic tradition. I discuss how these details combine to create an expression of society, culture, spirituality, and politics that is stronger and more powerful than the words alone would suggest. In this way, iimbongi help tighten connections to landscape, kin, and heritage not only by informing people about their history, culture, and attendant responsibilities but also by enabling access to and expression of deeper emotions about these things.

Policy Changes and System Failures

Despite some limited successes over the course of two decades, South Africa's land redistribution program has been plagued with difficulties and has largely failed to significantly benefit the rural poor.[9] From early policies involving grants to poor households to enable the purchase of land for subsistence and small-scale farming, the ANC shifted to land negotiations based on market values, principally through a "willing buyer, willing seller" model.[10] As well as slowing the land reform process, this market orientation protects (primarily white) landowners at the expense of the disenfranchised majority. It also promotes a view of land reform as a market-driven procedure for the redistribution of a commodity, neglecting the symbolic elements involved in restitution and reconciliation.[11] Instead, as a market commodity, land has become "functionally and discursively disembedded from socio-political histories of dispossession" that ignore the social, historical, cultural, and spiritual aspects wrapped up in land tenure and increase "the social invisibility of marginalized people."[12] Since the willing buyer, willing seller model was implemented in 2011, "the state itself has become the purchaser of land, acquiring land for redistribution to beneficiaries [via lease] without transfer of title."[13]

The shortcomings in the current approach are exposed in a 2017 study by Ruth Hall and Thembela Kepe of eleven land reform projects in the Sarah Baartman District of the Eastern Cape. During field visits over a three-year period, they found that none of the intended beneficiaries in any of the case studies had secure tenure on the lands they inhabited. Noting that "this is possibly the opposite of the vision of secure long-term rights for black South Africans which was at the core of land reform as envisaged in the 1990s" the authors go on to comment that, "in a twist of Orwellian irony, the 'beneficiaries' may not benefit at all, but are allowed to be temporary squatters on land over which they have no rights."[14] Without clear and secure tenure status, farmers are unable to access credit and are often barred from making leasehold improvements, which thwarts their efforts to develop productive farming enterprises. This is particularly true given that policies have tended to favor the transfer of large, capital-intensive agribusinesses that come with requirements for high skill sets and funding. This leads to failings of the kind that Karol Boudreaux describes in an earlier study in which 29 percent of the projects reviewed by the Land Redistribution for Agricultural Development had failed and an additional 22 percent were declining and could soon become unproductive in the absence of agricultural support.[15] Both studies clearly raise pressing questions of public concern.

At the national level, land reform policy looks set to shift yet again. On 16 February 2018, the day after taking office as the president of South Africa following Jacob Zuma's resignation, Cyril Matamela Ramaphosa delivered the 2018 SONA. Citing rising levels of poverty and unemployment and ongoing economic disparities defined by race and gender, Ramaphosa listed numerous new government initiatives to address these, including, most notably, a renewed emphasis on land reform and redistribution:

> We will accelerate our land redistribution programme not only to redress a grave historical injustice, but also to bring more producers into the agricultural sector and to make more land available for cultivation. We will pursue a comprehensive approach that makes effective use of all the mechanisms at our disposal. Guided by the resolutions of the 54th National Conference of the governing party, this approach will include *the expropriation of land without compensation*. We are determined that expropriation without compensation should be implemented in a way that increases agricultural production, improves food security and ensures that the land is returned to those from whom it was taken under colonialism and apartheid. Government will undertake a process of consultation to determine the modalities of the implementation of this resolution.[16]

Less than two weeks later, Julius Malema, leader of the Economic Freedom Fighters (EFF) party, tabled a followup motion in parliament. Acknowledging the 1913 Land Act that confined the black South African population to 13 percent of the land base and recognizing the difficulties that have plagued the land reform process since 1994, the motion goes on to identify the problem "at the centre of the present crisis": namely, "section 25 of the Constitution, the 'property clause' which protects private property rights and requires the State to pay compensation when expropriating land in the public interest and for a public purpose."[17] The motion concludes by proposing the establishment of a parliamentary committee to review and amend Section 25. Of 324 sitting members of parliament, 241 voted in favor of the motion; 83 were opposed. On 5 December 2018, the National Council of Provinces "agreed that section 25 of the Constitution be amended to make expropriation of land without compensation more explicit."[18]

The EFF defines itself as "a radical and militant economic emancipation movement" that "draws inspiration from the broad Marxist-Leninist tradition and Fanonian schools of thought" and sees "expropriation of South Africa's land without compensation for equal redistribution in use" as the foremost of seven "pillars for economic emancipation."[19] The party's emphasis on expropriation without compensation is a bold stance that offers both a corrective for historical injustices and a controversial break with market-driven norms. Yet the position overlooks crucial, endemic problems in distribution and management of land that perpetuate poverty and insecure tenure. As Hall and Kepe show, despite the state's interventionist role it is doing little to reorganize class relations and is instead "becoming a significant player" in a land market that remains oriented toward wealthy interests.[20] Constitutional amendments to facilitate the nationalization of land will do little to address the ongoing poverty and inequality resulting from the government's maladroit management of land already in its care.

"Decentralized Despots" or Legitimate Leadership?

An added layer within this complex milieu is the lingering power of traditional leaders, particularly in rural areas of South Africa.[21] Despite its vexed status in a modern democratic nation, traditional governance remains integral to social, cultural, and political life throughout much of rural South Africa. Traditional leadership is specifically recognized in chapter 12 of the Constitution of the Republic of South Africa, which grants these leaders the authority to operate in accordance with customary law and to act as institutions at local levels on matters affecting local communities.[22] This constitutional enshrinement considerably increased the power of traditional leadership, a development that scholars have criticized, pointing to the dysfunctionality of the traditional leadership system as reinvented by the apartheid regime and its unsuitability in a liberal Western democracy in general; its retrogressive influence on land tenure arrangements have particularly been condemned.[23] As Sonwabile Mnwana notes, the negative effects of this increased power are out of step with the precolonial role of traditional leaders: "Distributive power over land doesn't rest exclusively with chiefs. There are multiple layers of power that rests in different social units, families (and individuals within them). . . . African land rights are acquired through membership to a group—a productive and social unit such as a family or clan. Once allocated, land rights were passed from one generation to the next."[24]

During South Africa's fraught twentieth-century history, some chiefs honored their social and political responsibilities to their people, while others were co-opted by the apartheid regime, becoming a favored class of despots that happily profited from the extended powers conferred on them by the apartheid—now democratic—state.[25] At the same time, according to custom chiefs and kings are charged with weighty responsibilities to ancestors, citizens, and descendants yet to come. Their responsibilities included safeguarding and stewarding their ancestral territories for the benefit of all people in the community in the past, present, and future. While corruption and the abuse of power by traditional leaders are very real features of modern South Africa, these leaders are also part of a complicated history that includes centuries of resistance in which generations of chiefs and kings died defending their lands and people from colonizers. As Zolani Mkiva explains,

> Yes, you have traditional leaders that were used by the apartheid system. . . . Yes, there were those bad apples but you had traditional leaders who were part of the liberation struggle. Even for that matter, my sister, let me hasten to say this to you: that our people only here in the Eastern Cape fought nine frontier wars and the tenth war that put the final nail in the coffin was the psychological warfare which was put to them by Sir George Grey with the Nongqawuse incident.[26] So we fought nine frontier wars, which were physical, which were brutal, where hundreds of thousands of our people over a period of a hundred years died. And ask me a question: who were the commanders and military officers in those wars of dispossession? They were the traditional leaders. Most of them were killed in the front line.[27]

However, David Yali-Manisi contradicts this, stating, "Even in the past, it was not the chiefs who fought for the country: it was the people who were the warriors."[28]

A 2016 exhibit at the Albany Museum in Makhanda offers a nuanced discussion of the historical significance and contemporary role of traditional leaders:

> Traditional leaders of the 1800s guided their people through enormous changes. . . . Now in the 21st century, traditional leaders continue to adapt their roles. Though living within western-style

democracy, they offer leadership which compliments elected officials. Supported by provisions in the South African constitution, they retain a special quality of confidence and respect from their people. Their functions go beyond governance to deal with aspects of human relationships and behavior. Always guided by trusted councillors, they practice African democracy and serve as spiritual and cultural bridges to the African way of living.[29]

Yet despite the respect they receive, the extent to which chiefs practice a democracy cannot go unquestioned, and their role in contemporary South Africa is highly contentious. Chiefs proved instrumental in drumming up ANC support in rural areas, and many gained the support of both Nelson Mandela and Thabo Mbeki in the early years of the new administration. Legislation passed in 2003 and 2005 further strengthened the powers that traditional leaders had enjoyed under apartheid.[30] These undemocratic powers rest "to a significant extent—if variable by region—on their control of rural land and thus of the rural people with a stake in that land."[31] This control over some of South Africa's most vulnerable populations, coupled with the regressive gender politics inherent to traditional leadership, is deeply problematic, particularly in a contemporary society that has largely abandoned the beliefs and customs that may once have provided checks and balances on this power.

On the other hand, many unsavory aspects of traditional leadership—deep conservatism, nepotism, sexism, and abuse of power—appear to be just as much a part of the culture of their democratically elected counterparts. Given the string of ANC scandals over the past decade—ranging from Marikana to Nkandla—and the cozy relationship that has always existed between capital and the South African state, it is painfully clear that liberal democracy leaves much to be desired in terms of instating equality, transparency, and justice.[32] Traditional leadership has had its share of complication and disgrace, yet the ideals it is rooted in could offer valuable models for new relationships between people, communities, and their landscapes. As Mamdani notes, "Although tribes organized under the domination of elders, they contained redistributive mechanisms that thwarted tendencies to reproduce inequalities in a cumulative fashion." He is careful, though, to counter this: "The nature of the relationship between elders on the one hand and juniors and women on the other is still the subject of debate."[33] Meanwhile, Jeff Peires points out that the amaXhosa political system had "no tradition of unconditional obedience to the king," since "the position of the king as lineage head did not permit him to make unreasonable demands at the expense of his subordinates, or to interfere unwarrantedly in their domestic affairs."[34] These comments illustrate that precolonial amaXhosa governance systems involved complex checks and balances developed and refined over millennia of practice to prevent the abuse of power. The cumulative wisdom and culture underpinning traditional leadership could provide insights into alternative understandings of land and land restitution and help find a route toward reconciliation that recognizes the layered meanings held in the land.

The Imbongi's Role in Traditional Leadership

Iimbongi fulfill a fundamental aspect of amaXhosa traditional leadership by helping to maintain linkages between past and future, leaders and commoners, earthly and spiritual realms.[35] In poems delivered at public gatherings before the leaders or dignitaries are about to speak, iimbongi praise and challenge, not only lauding their subjects but also preparing them, through artful provocation or carefully coded messages, for the addresses they deliver. As my interviews show, iimbongi remain a relevant and vital component of contemporary rural culture and are accorded deep respect in their communities. Thus, their function is manifold: even as they pique and critique the leader, they arouse reflection among their lay audiences.

Iimbongi also play a recognized role in holding power to account, acting as mediators between leaders and the citizens they serve.[36] They complicate the alleged "decentralized despotism" of traditional leadership by providing a public avenue for voicing popular concerns, invoking the ancestral responsibilities of leaders, and reminding them of social expectations regarding their conduct. At the same time, iimbongi foreground a variety of cultural imperatives that often countervail those of Western modernity. Through their commentary and critique, iimbongi inject an imaginative constellation of images, emotions, and metaphors into official proceedings. Finally, they act as community historians, which includes the remembrance and recitation of names, genealogies, territories, battles, and notable deeds that are a crucial aspect of their poetry. In Mkiva's words,

> An imbongi as I have said is an historian, according to all the levels that I gave you. Secondly, an imbongi is a go-between. He's an intermediary between the people and leaders. So, he is somebody who has a poetic license to talk truth to power. But at the same time, he is that person who conveys royal messages from leadership to the people. So, he is not just a praise singer, as many Western

people want to believe. He also says some critiques because the license is a proviso for him to say to leaders when they go astray, this that you do is not in sync with what culture, protocol, and heritage expect you to do. Right? So, he has got that license. So, in one way or another the third level is that an imbongi is also a traditional leader in his own right. He assumes that position of being a traditional leader because he also provides leadership to leaders, he also provides guidance to leaders. He also reminds leaders how to do certain things in line with African customs.[37]

The recitation of names and genealogies is fundamentally linked to the culture and politics of land. As Opland explains, "The names of their ancestors held particular significance within the system of ancestor veneration, for not only is an individual descended from individuals, ritually he *is* his ancestors, *and his ancestors are identified with their dwelling places.*"[38] To invoke ancestral lineages is to invoke their homelands, and vice versa. The imbongi, as a spokesperson for both departed ancestors and their living descendants, is responsible for reminding people of their responsibilities to each group. Or, in the words of Thokozani Ntshuntsha, an imbongi from Willowvale: "What are the clan names? They are the people that live upon you. The forefathers. The people that made you to be what you are. Because we believe that although they're dead, they still live upon all things. They still live with you." This dwelling with the ancestors has implications for both the present and the future, as Ntshuntsha went on to explain: "There is a saying that says that if you don't know who you are you cannot determine your future. If you don't know where you come from, you cannot even understand where you are going to."[39] Thus, the ancestral presence that the poet calls forth stirs the audience to reflect on their own dwelling places on these ancestral lands, their obligations to family and clan, and the direction of their own lives within the larger collective.

"Thembu Spatterings"

The recollection of ancestral dwelling places carries different meanings in different locations; such recollections may be deeply painful in instances where ancestral homelands have been seized and dispossessed people have been denied access to their traditional homelands where they could fulfill their ancestral responsibilities. Yet even in these cases, revisiting historical wrongs can help communities make sense of their current situation, as Jeff Opland describes in his discussion of a poem by David

Livingstone Phakamile Yali-Manisi. Born in 1926 in the Khundulu valley in the northwestern region of the former Transkei, Yali-Manisi showed a powerful aptitude for poetry from a young age. Like other iimbongi from rural areas, he grew up tending animals, and he was accustomed to hearing men praise their cattle. He recounts,

> It was really pleasant to listen to those supernatural men delineate their delightful praises with their pitched voices and sweet tongues ... I was encouraged to accomplish my poetic inspiration, because, later on, old men would call and ask me to praise anything for their amusement and pleasure, and in turn, I would be congratulated and encouraged to keep up the spirit.[40]

In 1945, while working as a laborer, Yali-Manisi encountered Rev. Storr Lister, who agreed to sponsor him as a student at the Lovedale Missionary Institution in Alice. Yali-Manisi reached form two of his secondary education before being expelled in 1948 following an incident that reveals both his early political convictions and his dedication to his art. As he explains,

> One Sunday afternoon a certain student of the amaZizi clan from Middledrift stood in front of our dormitory and recited Mpinda's poem which he read from *Imibengo* by Bennie. He had a stick in his right hand. I, then and there, took my knobbed stick and moving towards him I praised the children of Rharhabe. He ran away from me and I continued following him praising all the time. The students came out of the dormitories and followed hailing us, making a hell of a noise. This upset the Institution.[41]

Yali-Manisi was reacting to the inappropriate utterances of his fellow student, yet these subtleties were lost on school administrators. Opland remarks that Yali-Manisi's expulsion from Lovedale must have been painful for him, "yet he was never bitter when he talked of the episode: he simply presented it, as he does here, as something he had to do, yet another action misinterpreted by whites in authority for which an innocent black person suffered." Opland goes on to explain that "the poetry of Xhosa iimbongi is essentially political, and in his poetry Manisi fearlessly expressed his political conviction."[42] This is true of his poem "Thembu Spatterings," which recounts the history of the abaThembu chieftaincy. The poem reveals a complex politics of landscape that developed over hundreds of years of habitation and that transcends the limited economic relationships with land that dominate within the contemporary political economy. In

1970, when the poem was composed, Ntshiza Manzezulu Mthikrakra was chief in Yali-Manisi's Glen Grey district.[43] In violation of custom, Kaiser Mathanzima had been illegitimately installed as paramount chief of the entire Transkei by the Pretoria government, despite political opposition from his distant cousin and rightful paramount chief Sabata Dalindyebo, who was forced into exile in 1980.[44] As the greatest imbongi practicing at the time, Yali-Manisi was the poet laureate de jure of Chief Mathanzima. However, as an active member of the banned ANC who disagreed strongly with both Mathanzima's illegitimate leadership and his politics, Yali-Manisi "voluntarily withdrew from the poetic patronage of his chief," an act of principle which condemned him to lasting obscurity as a poet and intellectual.[45] Yali-Manisi offers his poems "because it's one of the ways to make our people feel what one is telling them. So I write poetry to keep that form of language for generations and generations to come, which we think is a right form of putting right what is wrong, of elaborating to make people understand what is right."[46]

The excerpt discussed below is taken from the translated transcription of a performance by Yali-Manisi recorded by Jeff Opland in 1970 and published in 2015 as "Thembu Spatterings" in *Iimbali Zamanyange: Historical Poems*.[47] The full poem, performed in isiXhosa by Yali-Manisi at Opland's request, recounts the history of the abaThembu people in a five-hundred-line improvised performance that lasted thirty-four minutes, demonstrating the poet's remarkable ability to act as a historian for his people.[48] The depth of his historical knowledge is demonstrated not only by the length and detail of the poem but also by his ability to recall and narrate this history at a moment's notice in improvised poetic form.

Awu! E-e-ewe!	Oh yes! Oh yes!
Yivani lusapho lukaNdaba	Listen, Ndaba's people,[49]
Yivani lusapho lukaNdab'enyamakazi	listen people of News of Game, of Object of Hatred, Leapfrogger,
KaZondwa kaSokhawulela	Strutter, Appearer and they exposed
KaNgqolomsila kaVelabambhentsele!	themselves.
Sasilusapho lukaThembu sivel'eluhlangeni	We were Thembu's people, a nation and we migrated, moving southwards.
Saza sehla sasing' ezantsi	
Sawuwela kamb' uMsimvubu	Then we crossed the Mzimvubu,
Saliwel' iDedesi	we crossed the Dedesi
Saza kuwel' uMthatha	and we crossed the Mthatha,[50]

Safika see zinzi ngxingxilili	we arrived at a place to settle and stay
Kule mixethuka nale mixawuka	on these steep inclines and rocky mountains
Alo mhlaba ingokaNdaba	of this land which belonged to Ndaba.
Sithe sesizinzile sizinile	When we were stable we put down roots,
See zinsi see xangxe	we settled down and expanded.

The poem goes on to describe the subsequent battles with British invaders, concluding with the lines:

Ukuz' ibe nguGungubele noMfanta kubaThembu	So the Thembu Mfanta and Gungubele,
Ukuz' ibe nguGonya noTini kumaNgqika	the Ngqika Gonya and Tini,
Noluny' uwelekehle lweenkosi	as well as another group of chiefs
Bathathwa basiw' eSiqithini	were sent to Robben Island.
Wafel' apho k' uMfanta kaMthikrakra	There Mthikrakra's Mfanta died. We're on his land today,
Nakaloku sisekumhlaba wayo	for when Ngangelizwe moved with Mathanzima,
Kuba wawel' uNgangelizwe noMathanzima	they left Cacadu to Mfanta,
Balishiy' iCacadu ligcinwe nguMfanta	who guarded his father's land with a passion.
Etshel' ebhatyin' egcin' umhlaba kayise	That's why this land is still Mthikrakra's,
Kungoko lo mhlab' usengokaMthikrakra	it's the land of the old Hala kraal, for here Mthikrakra lies buried.
Ngowona mhlab' uligquba lamaHala	There we must stop for the moment:
Kuba kulapho walala khon' uMthikrakra	there will be other occasions.
Xa kulapho masibek' ingca	
Kub' imihl' ayiphelanga	

In this poem Yali-Manisi describes an ancestral lineage and progressive inhabitation of the landscape spanning hundreds of years. The excerpt describes the inheritance of land and attendant responsibility as Ngangelizwe and Mathanzima "crossed over" to the realm of the ancestors, leaving Mfanta to defend the land on behalf of his father. As the poem asserts, this land still belongs to the deceased Mthikrakra, whose ownership has been preserved by his son's fierce defense of the land, by the presence of his descendants, and by the continued dwelling of his buried remains. The poem articulates a complex sense of land ownership that is tightly bound to history, lineage, relatedness, and habitation.

Unlike many izibongo that lack an obvious narrative structure, "Thembu Spatterings" is an epic account crowded with characters and events. Opening with a characteristic sequence of praise names, Yali-Manisi invokes the spirit of Ndaba by name and by the deeds and qualities by which he became known through his life. In narrating the history and genealogy of amaXhosa settlement on the landscape in the Thembu region, the imbongi affirms the amaXhosa right to own and dwell upon their lands. In turn, he documents the struggle for these lands, rebuking the British settlers for their illegitimate tenure and asserting the rightful ancestral claim of the Thembu chieftaincy. At the same time, he invokes emotional registers, articulating the strength and resolve of past chiefs, inducing a sense of communal obligation with respect to their sacrifices, and conjuring images of place and belonging inherent to the inhabited landscape. In sum, the poem presents an outlook and episteme antithetical to the legal and market-based discourse that defines Western systems of land tenure and private property ownership.

Yet the poem has additional layers of meaning not obvious to the average Western reader. What may seem to be minor details for many readers in fact form part of a cascade of linked meanings that recount a political history entangled with amaXhosa spirituality. The "kraal" referred to in the closing stanza is a circular cattle corral made of brush woven between upright posts. Located at the center of the homestead, the kraal is an embodiment of the central aspects of amaXhosa spiritual life: ancestors and cattle. Traditionally, the family patriarch is buried under a central post, and the kraal is thus the dwelling place of the ancestors of a homestead. Cattle serve as an important point of connection with the ancestral realm through ritual sacrifice, as they are the preferred animal for the most important ceremonies held to honor the ancestors. Land is necessary for the maintenance of cattle. There is a circularity in the poem, echoed in the shape of the kraal, as it articulates history's continued presence in everyday life. Yet these cycles have suffered a rupture that remains unresolved. As Opland describes in his discussion of the poem,

> The sacral chief *is* the people: his strength is theirs, and his well-being is ensured by the sympathetic attention of his ancestors to his

Fig. 5. Nguni cattle in their kraal. (Photo by the author)

affairs and to the affairs of the chiefdom. But this ritual relationship is ruptured because Mfanta lies buried on Robben Island, where he was dumped by the whites for resisting white encroachment and fighting for the rights of his people. *And so* Manzezulu's people are destitute, and they will remain destitute and troubled as long as Mfanta's bones lie restless in foreign soil.[51]

Manisi's poem describes the history of the present: Mfanta's remains lie far from his ancestral territories, and his spirit has not been appeased by the ritual sacrifice of a head of cattle and the accompanying ceremony that would connect him to his ancestors. His descendants continue to suffer physically as a result of "the knowledge that they have been unable to perform essential ritual acts."[52] These layered meanings, embedded in amaXhosa spirituality, create an alternative conception of landscape and of human relationships to landscape that is opposed to Western views about the nature of land and environment. Yali-Manisi's poetry draws us out of a narrow concept of land as commodity, and instead conveys the history, genealogy, language, and spirituality of the poet's home place through the affective power of the oral poem.

The King's Speech
NQADU

As described in the previous chapter, on 4 December 2015 I attended an invitational event at King Zwelonke's Great Place at Nqadu, near the town of Idutywa. Born in 1968 to King Xolilizwe C. Sigcawu (1926–2011) and Queen Mother Nozamile Sigcawu, King Zwelonke Mpendulo C. Sigcawu officially took office in 2009, becoming the twenty-second and current monarch of the greater nation of isiXhosa-speaking people.[53] His lineage includes the ancestor Gcaleka, senior son of Phalo and father of Khawuta, who was in turn the father of Hintsa, a king brutally murdered and dismembered by British invaders in 1835 and who subsequently became a martyr of the amaXhosa people. Following a leadership dispute between Gcaleka and his brother Rharhabe, the defeated Rharhabe went into exile across the Kei River where he established his own chieftaincy, now known as the amaRharhabe people. Despite this historical rift among the amaXhosa, Zwelonke, as the amaGcaleka leader, acts as a "symbol of national unity" whose leadership, at least symbolically, extends beyond the amaGcaleka to the amaRharhabe and to isiXhosa-speaking people in general.[54] Yet this symbolic unity is not without complications: Zwelonke's own coronation also involved a leadership dispute over genealogy: "Although he is biologically born from the 3rd House lineage, [Zwelonke] was adopted and raised to the Great House of Queen Nondwe Sigcawu as her own son . . . because of the health problems of Queen Nondwe's only son, Prince Siseko (Nondoda), which rendered him incapable of becoming king. Thus Zwelonke was the only son who could rightfully take over the reins."[55]

As Zwelonke's chosen imbongi at the December event, Thukela Poswayo performed immediately before the king's address.[56] Poswayo grew up in a small village some twenty kilometers from the Transkeian town of Engcobo. Like most of the landscape of the former Transkei, the area around Engcobo is rural, and people who live in the region derive much of their livelihood from the land, whether through crop production and livestock husbandry or by foraging for natural foods, medicines, and building supplies. This reliance on the land brings them into contact with the cycle of the seasons and with the plants and creatures around them, and Poswayo's poetry reflects these tight relationships with homeland and nature.

In December 2015 Poswayo began his isibongo in the traditional manner, drawing his audience in with a rousing greeting:

Imbongi: A Zwelonke!	Imbongi: Hail Zwelonke!
Abantu: A Zwelonke!	Audience: Hail Zwelonke!
Imbongi: A! Zweloooonke!	Imbongi: Hail! Zweloooonke!
Abantu: A! Zweloooonke	Audience: Hail! Zweloooonke!
Iyakhumbulana mntane nkosi.	We miss each other, child of a chief.
Iyakhumbulana thole leduna.	We miss each other, son of a bull.
Ndelula amehlo ndayibona imilambo,	I stretched my eyes and saw the rivers,
Ndanga ndinga qhayisa ndixele uthekwane	I wish I can boast like the uthekwane Saying I'm ugly on this side, beautiful on that.
Ndithi ndimbi ngapha ndimhle ngapha.	

In the second stanza, Poswayo uses a familiar expression, "*ndimbi ngapha ndimhle ngapha*" (literally, I'm ugly here, I'm beautiful here) associated with a common South African waterbird, the *uthekwane*, or hammerkop, a name that refers to the hammer-shaped crest at the back of its head. The uthekwane has a unique way of feeding in which it peers sideways into the water, turning its head from side to side to gaze downward first with one eye and then with the other. The comical behavior gives it the appearance of admiring its own reflection so that it is mocked for its vanity. Among the amaZulu and some isiXhosa-speaking peoples, the uthekwane is also associated with the lightening bird and may be viewed as a harbinger of misfortune or even death. As Poswayo explained when we discussed the translation of his poem,

> Black people, they hate this bird. They hate it because they say it brings bad luck. If you see the bird. They usually say it likes looking at the river water, they say it's a bird that likes itself that much, it's a very ambitious bird. . . . They say the reason it is there at the river, it is not just there to eat frogs and stuff, it's there to look at itself. Looking at the water, seeing itself there. Then it will go back and go again. It likes watching itself. So that's what I was just telling. These two lines are from the folklore that tells about the bird.[57]

This explanation reveals much about the knowledge and orientation of both Poswayo and his audience: the lines incorporate not only folklore but also references to the natural environment that the audience is assumed to understand and appreciate thanks to their proximity and attention to the creatures around them. The uthekwane is familiar to people who are equally knowledgeable about its diet and behaviors and their larger significance. Thus, the poem opens with a well-known image that immediately introduces layers of complex and contradictory meaning. In these lines, the mention of the uthekwane also alludes to the situation of Buyelekhaya Dalindyebo, the abaThembu king who in 2009 "was sentenced to 15 years in prison for culpable homicide, assault with intent to do grievous bodily harm, arson, and kidnapping."[58] Dalindyebo made headlines again at the end of 2015 following an unsuccessful supreme court appeal followed by his incarceration. As the well-known imbongi to the disgraced Dalindyebo, Poswayo is aware that his appearance before the prominent and respected amaGcaleka king may arouse concern or even suspicion among the members of his audience. Here he encourages his listeners to look at the matter from all angles, considering both the ugly and beautiful aspects of a person or situation before drawing conclusions.

From here, Poswayo shifts into a praise of rivers in stanzas three and four. The parallelism in this section is a common stylistic trope of isiXhosa izibongo, particularly in the opening sequences of poems. Here it acts as a sort of prelude, laying out a repetitive series of names or images as both poet and listener to warm to larger subjects.

Ewe kaloku thole leduna	Yes then, son of a bull,[59]
Siyinqamle imilambo.	We crossed rivers.
Sawubona uMbhashe.	We saw the Mbhashe.
Sayinqaml' imilambo	We crossed rivers
Sawusel'uMgwali.	And drank the Mgwali.
Sawubona uMthatha, sawubona uMthamvuna.	We saw the Mthatha, we saw the Mthamvuna.
Salibona iThukela, salibona iCongo,	We saw the Thukela, we saw the Congo.
Salibona iZambezi, salibona iLimpopo,	We saw the Zambezi, we saw the Limpopo.
Siyibonile imilambo	We've seen the rivers,
Ngoba neLubhelu siyibonile.	why, we've even seen the Lubhelu.
Ewe kaloku ndibiza ngabom.	Yes, now I name them deliberately.
Ngoba kaloku ukuze kulunge	So that all may go well
Ndithi Zwelonke	I say Zwelonke;
Funeka ndiyibiz'imilambo ye Afrika.	I must name the rivers of Africa.

If this stanza appears simple, it is deceptively so. In naming rivers, Poswayo names the lifeblood of amaXhosa society. Rivers and their tributaries are perhaps the fundamental points of connection between people and their landscapes, ancestors, and history in that they determined historical patterns of migration, settlement, and transhumance movements. Each river traditionally was associated with a chiefdom and each tributary to sub-chiefdom such that only citizens of that chiefdom and their cattle were entitled to use the water of their local streams. Well-watered areas with many rivers and streams could support more communities and residents than dry areas, and amaXhosa place-names, largely derived from the names of their watercourses, reflect their intimacy with local topography.[60]

Apart from their obvious practical value, rivers and streams are also of vital spiritual importance. Incanting the names of the rivers, Poswayo names amaXhosa communities and their ancestral dwelling places and in the process makes an allegorical reference to the ancestral spirits who inhabit their waters. Importantly, he begins by naming rivers that flow through the heart of King Zwelonke's territories and then moves on to rivers progressively farther away. As he does so, he maps both spatial and temporal distance, symbolically stepping backward along an ancestral lineage as he links the present company to other isiXhosa-speaking peoples, tracing their historical migration from northern regions of the Eastern Cape and beyond. The movement concludes with the mythical land of Lubhelu, perhaps in the Great Lakes region of East Africa, from which the amaXhosa are purported to have originally traveled. "I name them deliberately," says Poswayo, "that all may go well." In naming the rivers, he symbolically invokes the distant ancestors whose presence can help to ensure success at the event and during the king's reign more generally.

In the stanzas that follow, Poswayo asserts the king's place in the royal lineage and in so doing reminds his audience of the king's duty and obligation to his people and to uQamata the creator; Zwelonke accepts the position not as an individual but as the child of a previous king and of an entire nation. He must therefore "act with care."

Ewe kaloku! Le ndawo ukuyo	Yes of course! The position you hold
Kwakukhe kwahlala omnye umntu kuyo	Was held by someone before you,
	As there will be someone after.
Kusezaw'hlal'omnyumntu	That is why you must act with care,
Yiyo lo nto funek'uchul'ukunyathel'uchule	Counting your steps,
Uwabal'amanyathelo	For the river you're crossing,
Ngob'umlambo owela kuwo kwedini	young man,
Uzele amatye agcwel'ucolothi.	Is full of slippery stones,
Ngentla ziziziba, ngezantsi ziziziba	Deep pools to the north, deep pools to the south.[61]

Fig. 6. The landscape near Thukela Poswayo's ancestral home, not far from the town of Engcobo. (Photo by the author)

Far from describing an absolute leader with absolute power, the poem sketches out some of the layered and interlocking relationships and responsibilities that the king, in using his power and authority honorably and for the benefit of his people, is obliged to abide by. Failure to behave honorably with respect to his people and their ancestors could result in a loss of balance on the river's slippery stones and loss of life in its deep pools, the domain of ancestors and of the *abantu bomlambo* (people of the river). As Poswayo explains, "In this position [kingship], it's not going to be smooth. That's what it simply tells. The position you hold now will not make things smooth for you. You must always [be aware] that you will have enemies, and you may also create [them]—yes there are enemies that you will find there, but the others will be created by you." Traditional leadership is not characterized simply by wealth and privilege; it is both arduous and difficult, rife with dangerous rivalries and opportunities for corruption. It is the leader's responsibility to govern nobly despite these obstacles and to inspire his people to act in a similarly principled manner. Shifting from the theme of lineage to that of speech, the remainder of the poem tracks this notion of responsibility. The king must bring honor to his lineage by serving his people not only with the strength of his backbone but also with the strength of his voice; he must right things with his words.

Thetha ke! Nasi isizwe sakokwenu	Speak then! Here is your nation.
Nang'amaGcaleka ka Khawuta.	Here are the Gcalekas of Khawuta.[62]
Nalusapho luka Zanzolo.	Here are the children of Zanzolo.
Nal'usapho luka Sarhili.	Here are the children of Sarhili.[63]
Thetha ke nalo	So speak to them.
Ngoba kaloku okwakh'ukuthetha	For certainly your words
Ngekhe kulambathe	Will not be in vain
. . . .	. . . .
IAfrika yakokwethu inyembezana.	Our Africa is crying.
Ifuna amadoda anomqolo,	It wants men with backbones,
Ifun'amadoda anelizwi elimbombo	It needs men with bold voices
Ukuze ath'akuthetha kulunge	To right things with their words.
Thetha ke,	Speak then,
Ngoba uThixo wakukhomba kuqala.	For God pointed at you first.
Thetha beve abantwana beli lizwe,	Speak so that the children of this nation can hear you,
Thetha senz' isizwe sikayihlomkhulu	Speak, that your forefathers' nation may do as you ask,
Ngob'ungathetha, zonke izinto zakulunga	For when you've spoken, things will fall into place.

Here the poet calls upon the king to speak. It is this speaking, above all, that will act as a guiding light to align a disordered society. Through the leader's speaking, teaching, and instructing his people wisely and judiciously, the people can in turn act confidently and honorably. In Poswayo's words,

> This is what the message is now: because you know that there will be other kings as you come after the one [before you]. Then there's the one after you. So, all what you do now, do it knowing that you're not doing it for yourself, you're doing it for the generations to come. That's what is said there. . . . So now that you know that all what you're doing you're doing it for the next generation, for now stand firm. Stand firm. Because the reason why we were there on that special day, the king had a message to pass to his people. Now I'm encouraging him, that is what is happening. I'm encouraging him that he must stand firm and he must know that what he tells people now, God is listening. God will simply make his words stick to the minds of the people that he's talking to. Because he's not doing it for himself, he's doing it for God. Because he's God-chosen.

Not until the closing stanzas of the poem does Poswayo turn to the occasion at hand: the launch of a campaign to counter the rampant consumption of alcohol during the holiday season that wreaks havoc on communities in the form of violence and automobile accidents. Here he condemns alcohol as one of three devices associated with treacherous white colonizers to ensnare and undermine the strength of the amaXhosa people. In a nod to the great poet S. E. K. Mqhayi, Poswayo cites a well-known passage from one of his poems.

Ngemihl'abelungu besiqhatha	When White people arrived to
Basinika utywala bebhotile	cheat us
De wath'umQhayi,	They delivered alcohol in bottles
Ngubani nalo? NguYeye.	Until Mqhayi said,[64]
Uhamba nabani?	Who is this? It is Yeye.
Noyise. Umphathe ntoni?	Who is walking with him?
Amasi. Ngendeb'enjani?	His father. What has he brought
Ebomvu.	for me?
	Sour milk. What is the color of the container?
	It is red.

Poswayo explains the meaning of the lines as follows:

[Mqhayi] saw a chief with his son next to him. The chief was drunk and had a bottle of brandy in his hand. Then uMqhayi started writing a poem. *Ngubani nalo*—who is that? And he said here it is the younger boy. And whom is he going with? He's going with his father. And what is this that his father is carrying? Then the other boy said he's carrying a sour milk. With what? What is he carrying it with? What is it that container? Then they said it's a red container because what they knew was that whatever that is in a container should be a sour milk. Because that's what they knew. . . . But no, it's not a red container, it's a clear bottle with a red brandy inside. Then he asked the boys and the boys told him innocently that this was the father carrying sour milk for his son. uMqhayi in that poem was condemning liquor. He was condemning the usage of brandy or the usage of liquor within our society.

Poswayo's linking of colonization and alcohol echoes earlier poems, such as Mqhayi's boisterous address to the Prince of Wales on the occasion of his visit to Port Elizabeth during his 1925 tour of the empire.[65]

> She sent us the preacher, she sent us the bottle;
> She sent us the bible, and barrels of brandy;
> She sent us the breechloader, she sent us the cannon;
> O, Roaring Britain! Which must we embrace?[66]

Poswayo, like Mqhayi before him, links alcohol to the larger ills of colonialism and British imperialism and their lasting hangover. On 4 December 2015 people assembled at Nqadu to receive a message from the king—a message denouncing not only the excessive consumption of alcohol but also the ongoing colonization of the spirit that alcohol represents. This message and its delivery, explains Poswayo, held profound symbolic importance:

> Africa needs people like you. Africa has been robbed. Africa needs strong men. Strong men that can say words straight, that can put the straight message, that can tell a direct message. Straight messages that will revive righteousness with the people. Now you have to revive African people. They're coming from a rough background. When the white people came with brandy and wine, they gave us brandy, they gave us wine. They took all the wealth of our people.

The arrival of whites resulted in the theft of land and cattle; alcohol and alcoholism were delivered in exchange. What may have appeared to be a minor public event at Nqadu can also be seen as one more milestone in the ongoing process of denouncing colonialism and its lasting effects on amaXhosa communities. Alcohol, as Mqhayi makes clear and Poswayo reminds us, was as damaging to amaXhosa people as the bible, the cannon, and the breechloader; it was one of the weapons of colonization and is therefore implicated in the loss of land and wealth. With his poetry Poswayo draws connections between land and lineage; alcohol and theft; power, autonomy, and speech. Like Yali-Manisi, he links resonant meanings and histories to the land itself, acknowledging the layers of human dwelling and feeling that reside in each place.

GWADANA

I returned to the Mbashe municipality several months later to see Thukela Poswayo perform again, this time at the village of Gwadana on 11 March 2016. The event, attended by several hundred people, was much larger and more formal than the previous occasion at Nqadu and marked the ceremonial bestowing of a leopard skin on a prominent chief from the

Gwadana area. Relatively few chiefs ever receive this honor, which is linked both to lineage and chiefly conduct. Poswayo performed twice: once immediately before King Zwelonke delivered his official address and again after the king presented Chief Mthetho with the leopard skin, before Mthetho delivered a speech.

The first poem was a spontaneous oration that lasted nearly seven minutes, delivered from the podium set up on a raised platform beside a row of dignitaries (other chiefs, the king, and government officials) seated at a table that faced the audience. From this position, Poswayo could address both dignitaries and the seated crowd from an elevated position that conferred symbolic authority. The second poem, following the emotionally charged presentation ceremony, was briefer, lasting only three and a half minutes. During this second performance, the chief stood at the podium while Poswayo addressed him from the grass below.

In Gwadana as at Nqadu, Poswayo was simply and elegantly dressed in button-down shirt and slacks and lacked the imbongi's common accoutrements. Once again he performed with a focused clarity and confidence and few gestures, yet this time with a voice more typical of iimbongi, roaring throughout. By opening in such strong tones, Poswayo did not have room to build strength of volume as in the previous performance, and there were moments during this performance when his voice faltered under the strain. However, judging from my recordings, this mode of delivery appeared to be more effective in capturing and holding the attention of his audience from the start compared to the quieter beginnings of the previous poem. The opening stanzas are presented below.

Imbongi: A! Zwelonke	Imbongi: Hail! Zwelonke
Abantu: A! Zwelonke	Audience: Hail! Zwelonke
Imgongi: A! Zweloooonke!	Imbongi: Hail! Zweloooonke!
Abantu: A! Zwelonke!	Audience: Hail! Zwelonke!
Mntan'omhle[67]	Honorable one,
Amehl'am ath'akukhangela ndabon'imilambo	Opening my eyes, I saw rivers. When I looked across
Ndathi ndakujonga ngaphesheya	I saw your family's cattle,
Ndazibon'iinkomo zako kwenu	I saw my family's cattle.
Ndazibon'iinkomo zako kwethu	
Ndiyazaz'ezako kwenu	I know those of your family
Ndiyazaz'ezako kwethu	I know those of my family.
Ndiyazehlula ngemibala	I know them by their colors[69]

Kuba zingaphesheya kwemilambo zicacile.	For even across the river they are distinct.
Zicacile zizakuhle	They are beautifully distinct
Zibonakala ngok'tyhobo	They appear now, charging.
Ewe kaloku!	Yes then!
Yithi khe ndicaphule ndenjenje	Let me say something
Ngoba kaloku ukuze kulunge maLawundini[68]	For in order for things to improve, maLawundini,
Vumani kuba sendiliphethibhozo Ndabel'izizwe	Allow me, for I already have the knife.
Vumani kaloku	I distributed among nations.
Ndabel'iQamata	Allow me then,
Ndabel'umhlaba kalok'omagqagala	I gave to Qamata[70]
Ndabela kaloku umhlaba kaloku wakulo Daliwonga	I gave the land with its dry boulders. I gave the land from Daliwonga's family[71]
Kuba kaloku kulapho zaphuma khon'iinkomo	From which the cattle came,
Zaqweqwema zadl'amathafa	Running to the fields.
Zafika kwaChotho zamila	They reached Chotho and stopped,
Zabuya nentombi	Returning with a girl.[72]
Yafika yazal'amadodana	She arrived and gave birth to young boys.

Cattle are central to amaXhosa culture and economy. Not only are they the primary form of wealth and exchange, they are traditionally the only route to marriage through the practice of *lobola*, in which cattle from the groom's family are given to the family of the bride. They therefore represent not only the present wealth of a family but also its future productive and reproductive potential.[73] As described earlier, cattle are also a key point of connection with the ancestral realm through ritual sacrifice during ceremonies held to honor the ancestors.[74]

From this perspective, the tight relationships between water, land, people, and cattle gain additional complexity. Although hospitable in many respects, a large proportion of the landscape inhabited by the amaXhosa is arid or otherwise unsuitable for year-round grazing. While the deep soils of river valleys produce a lush valley bushveld, much of the landscape is vegetated with scrubby Eastern Province thornveld that provides limited forage. Importantly, although the lush sourveld of the valley bushveld provides good summer grazing, after several months its nutritional value declines significantly such that grazing exclusively on these pastures results in sicknesses. Sweetveld, on the other hand, remains nutritious year-round but is fragile and vulnerable to overgrazing, which can cause permanent damage to pastures.[75] In response to these environmental circumstances, amaXhosa pastoralists found various solutions, ranging from burning off grasses to seasonal transhumance to the maintenance of cattle stations away from the permanent homesteads established in areas more suitable for cropping. Social life, settlement patterns, and seasonal movements were all adapted to fit the needs of the pastures—and of the cattle that, much more than mere economic entities, were valued for their own sake and for their individual and collective beauty.

Given the centrality of cattle to amaXhosa people and their livelihoods, they have always figured prominently in izibongo. In the first foreign travel account of isiXhosa poetry, which was written by Gustav Fritsch during his tour of southern Africa between 1864 and 1866, Fritsch noted, "The ideal of the [umXhosa], the object of his daydreams and the favorite subject of his songs (Liedern), is his oxen, which are his most valuable possession. With the praise songs (Lobgesängen) of the cattle those of the chief mix themselves, and in these in turn the chief's cattle figure prominently."[76] Traditionally, the individual cattle in a herd are named; the name of the bull in the herd of a king or chief is often used as one of that leader's praise names in izibongo or everyday speech. AmaXhosa cattle are also prized for the diversity of their colors and markings, and Nguni languages are replete with poetic terms to describe these.[77]

Like many other iimbongi, Poswayo developed his talents praising cattle in his boyhood: "Since the young age I was [an imbongi]. But the platform then was different from the platform I'm using now. I was following cattle and all those things. I would just sing the praises for the cattle." His familiarity with his neighborhood cattle is evidenced by his lines,

> I know those of your family
> I know those of my family.
> I know them by their colors
> For even across the river they are distinct.

In this poem as well, Poswayo's references to animals reveal their importance in the everyday life of amaXhosa people. Later in the poem, he speaks of the *ihahane*, a hadeda ibis: a large brown and iridescent ground-feeding bird with a long, curved bill and an obnoxiously loud voice.

| Ndakufika phezu kwentaba | I arrived at the top of the mountain, |
| Ndivul'amaphiko | Opened my wings, |

Ndime kaloku ndixel'in-tsikiz'im'emaweni	And stood on the cliffs commanding as a hornbill
Iqhayise'amahahane	Boasting to the hadedas,
Isithi mna ndihluthi	Saying I am full,
Ndihluth'amaqonya	I'm full of maqonya.[78]
Kazi wena hahane uyakurhayisa ngantoni	I wonder, what would you boast about, hadeda?[79]

The *intsikizi*, or southern ground hornbill, is another loud-voiced bird whose calls can be heard from as far as three kilometers away. In the stanza in which they appear, the imbongi slows his pace, articulating the alliterative lines. Filled with enormous caterpillars, the larger and louder hornbill is able to outboast the hadeda. Sadly, although the hadeda is common throughout most of the African continent, the southern ground hornbill is listed as critically endangered in South Africa due to loss of habitat. Despite its strength, voice, and cultural status, the ground hornbill's boasting may fall silent soon enough.

Like Poswayo's earlier performance at Nqadu, both Gwadana poems contain literal and symbolic exhortations to speak, and to do so wisely and judiciously. Once again, the imbongi reminds the king of the precariousness of kingship. Although Zwelonke holds a position granted him by divine ordinance (i.e., the will of the amaXhosa god uQamata), he retains his power through the people's respect and goodwill, which he must work to earn and maintain. The poem concludes with a strong admonition to the chief to attend to the wishes of his people who have the power to marginalize and topple him; the king's power is ultimately determined by what people are willing to accept.[80]

In rural communities of the former Transkei, as in other parts of the country, the institution of traditional leadership continues to carry considerable social, emotional, and symbolic weight, though their role and importance in land tenure arrangements is disputed.[81] The politics of chieftainship is complex, and the relationship between leader and commoner is nuanced. To some extent such dynamics are captured in these poems, whose lines remind leaders of their limits and the audience of its collective power. The poems also provide one example of the checks and balances inherent to this leadership, illustrating how citizens, now as in the past, have the power to defy, marginalize, and even depose leaders of whom they do not approve. This sense of mutual responsibility is pervasive in Poswayo's poems. We see it in the following lines:

Le ngub'uyambetheyo	This blanket that covers your body
Asingubo yakho	Is not yours,
Kub'ukh'oyilindeleyo ngasemva	For someone behind you waits for it.
Ewe kaloku	Yes, then,
Isikhundl'okuso kwedini	The position you occupy,
Sasikhe sahlal'omny'umntu ngaphambili	young man, Belonged to someone else before.
Kuba kakade	For it is true,
Le nt'umntu yinto yalo nto, ngumngcelele	People are like that, there is always a queue.
Ngemihla oyihl'omkhulu aba besilw'iimfazwe	The days when your forefathers were at war,
Bevul'umhlaba ukuze balime, wawusewukho	Opening up the ground to plough, you already existed.

Here Poswayo reiterates the reminder to Chief Mthetho that he is part of a lineage that extends before and behind him, and that he owes much to those who preceded him. There is also a sense in this excerpt, echoed in the earlier poems, that the chief's life, like the blanket or animal skin covering his body, is not his own. Rather, the ancestral lineage has dominance over his life and life choices; as the one ordained to follow in a line of chiefs, it falls to him to perform his role and serve his people honorably. The poet also reminds Mthetho that the hereditary designation by no means assures his success, since past chiefs "have been deposed or superseded for being 'cruel,' 'stingy,' or even 'stupid.'"[82] He must therefore be both attentive and responsive to the wishes of his people.

Imbongi, too, are tied to ancestral lineages in specific ways. Among traditional communities they are known to be among the amathwasa, spiritual healers with the ability to receive messages from the ancestral realm that are their responsibility to transmit. Failure to respond to the call to speak would be to defy the ithwasa spirit and, by implication, ancestral wishes, which could have grave consequences for the health of both the poet and his family. Poswayo opens the poem by chiding his audience for their inattention during his previous performance and then turns to the chief: "In order for me to be healthy, honorable one, / allow me to do this." With these lines, he reminds the chief that his personal health and wellbeing are contingent on being able to communicate the message contained in the lines that follow, which requires a respectful audience. In this way, Poswayo excuses himself for the delivery of a message that may be unwelcome or strongly worded; his role as messenger is not one that he has chosen, and he cannot be held entirely responsible for what he is compelled to say.

In the second poem, Poswayo gets at the notion of food, here reminding the chief that "it is not right for a man to eat too much / And forget that his cattle / Are tended by the dogs outside." That is, a chief should not become so caught up in his own wealth that he neglects its source. Dogs, like their owners, are bound by mutual responsibility; starved dogs cannot tend cattle. Yet even as it urges humility and conscientiousness on the part of the chief, this imagery offers a glimpse of another reality: the chief maintains "the right of capture and the distribution of spoils."[83] Despite its sophistication, traditional leadership is ultimately a system of power, and as such it is prone to corruption and failure. An imbongi's words can encourage conscientious behavior, but they are no guarantee of it.

On 16 October 2018, the Pan South African Language Board issued a press release designating "land expropriation without compensation" as its word of the year. The choice, they explained, was due to the phrase being used some 25,000 times across South African print, broadcast, and online media over the course of the year.[84] This prevalence, bordering on obsessive, hints at the degree of public emotion and anxiety stirred up by government announcements during the year as well as by the abundant pressing questions these communiqués have left unresolved.

Whether changes to South Africa's constitution will succeed in curing the ailing land reform system and establishing material and symbolic justice for South Africa's vulnerable dispossessed remains to be seen. Yet given the manifold problems that continue to plague land reform processes, it seems that a constitutional amendment that would enable the state to acquire more land more easily skirts the real issue. Instead, the EFF and ANC could direct their efforts toward improved practices of land registration and distribution that currently fall far short of policy objectives and that often appear arbitrary and unfair.[85] As leaders with inherited responsibilities to land and people, traditional leaders might assist in such efforts, but only if their power can be held in check by democratic governance systems and the members of their own communities, perhaps in part through regulatory systems established in precolonial times.

This chapter suggests that in establishing processes to distribute land justly and with due consideration for past, present, and future inhabitants, there is much wisdom to be found within the social groups who would benefit most from such reforms. The poems discussed here, voiced by ordinary rural people living in difficult situations, present an alternative land ethic and environmental sensibility. The poems foreground the importance of the natural world, of collectivity, and of solidarity with ancestral spirits and generations of unborn descendants. Both poets emphasize continuity, insisting that the positions that traditional leaders occupy, the regalia they wear, even the land they inhabit does not belong to them. Rather, in taking their brief place in a lineage that extends into past and future, king and chief are called upon to act boldly and meaningfully but with humility, generosity, and dignity as their actions will affect future generations and will be remembered for years to come. Poswayo, in delivering a series of images and metaphors, demonstrates the ongoing importance of the rivers, plants, and creatures of the Eastern Cape landscape. He also calls on king and chief to show true leadership, to act for the betterment of their people, and to address the legacies of their nation's difficult past. Crucially, he reminds them that the effects of their leadership extend well beyond their immediate time, place, and community.

These aspects of the poems also show how, as a cultural force and counterpoint to power, iimbongi could play a valuable role in propagating an ethic that sees land not as a commodity to be accumulated by either individuals or the state but as ancestral territories for which many fought and died. These territories will remain the cultural and spiritual homelands of their descendants for the imaginable future. The poets' invocation of the ancestors, their reminder to people of who they are, their insistence on the individual's place within a collective, a lineage, and a territory combine to hold not only power but also people to account. It is not government alone that makes a democracy. In these poems the iimbongi rouse king and citizens alike to answer the call of ancestral responsibility and individual potential on the long walk to justice.

Conclusion

Any human power can be resisted and changed by human beings. Resistance and change often begin in art, and very often in our art: the art of words.
—URSULA LE GUIN

Nelson Mandela observed that after climbing a great hill, one only finds that there are many more hills to climb. In the years since South Africa's transition to democracy in 1994, reconciliation and decolonization have been ongoing. From a despotic regime of racial segregation, the country has emerged as a culturally dynamic nation of politically active citizens striving to overturn the residual inequalities of generations of discrimination. Yet like other African nations that felt a surge of optimism at the time of independence only to be confronted by subsequent challenges, South Africa in the years following the triumphant elections of 1994 has struggled with questions about how to ensure that prosperity and governance are inclusive and how to undertake a profound and equitable decolonization.

These questions are not unique to South Africa. The country's geography mirrors broader relationships of power and inequality that repeat at all scales in our troubled and divided world. In an era in which racist, xenophobic, and misogynist rhetoric increasingly appears on political mainstages worldwide, it is important to remember that although apartheid is particular to South Africa, it grew out of a history similar to that of many nations, my own included. South Africa's story is humbling in what it reveals of human hearts and their capabilities, in all their shades of courage, determination, and hate. Colonialism, racism, gender oppression, and the exploitation of nature and animals are differing but consubstantial aspects of inequitable and destructive relationships. Over the past several centuries such relationships have devastated colonized societies and have brought us to a state of environmental crisis as powerful factions have exerted their dominance over the resources and creative energies of others. Ultimately, this study of South African iimbongi is a study of such relationships and, within them, of the power of speech: who wields it and what kinds of damage can occur when that power is unjustly distributed.

Today's iimbongi are part of a progressive enfranchisement and decolonization that began long before 1994 and continues in the present as marginalized groups assert their rights and call for increased equality regarding the distribution of wealth, the right of wellbeing, and the responsibility of representational authority. The process of decolonization involves dismantling the structures of oppression in all their forms, including the cultural forces that hold colonialist power in place and that persist despite political independence.[1] Iimbongi voice a very particular ecopoetry—one that differs significantly from the geographically and epistemologically limited set of texts that much existing ecopoetics has considered. Their poetry springs from environmental experiences ranging from deep intimacies with landscape, cattle, and ancestral spirits to industrial drudgery in mines and factories to invocations of the nature that is eminently present in the ingenious engineering and unregulated lifeways of informal settlements. In examining the ecopoetry of the iimbongi, we see clearly that there is ample room for ecopoetics to become a more radical project of egalitarianism and inclusivity. We are only just beginning the work of deep listening to the multilingual voices of the world's poets speaking from the margins. The work of seeking these voices out, attending with care, and, in the process, learning anew what poetry is and does is a contribution to an equitable and decolonized global society that respects the perspectives and creative contributions of all peoples.

This work brings us up against the limitations of the narratives of land and environment that have emerged from North American experiences. North American environmentalism and wilderness conservation, and the critique of these processes in the transforming realm of ecocriticism and ecopoetics, represent only a small sampling of the many versions of environmental relatedness and care. Given the perpetual state of social and environmental crises that has come to define the current period of late capitalism, we must consider both local particularities and global universalities, understanding that ideological transformation underpins political change and that the transformation of hegemonic ideologies involves attending to voices that articulate alternative worldviews. These voices speak most plainly from the margins, in their own venues and in their own languages.

In bringing various bodies of scholarship into conversation here, my aim was not only to open new avenues for ecocritical scholarship but also to offer a new perspective on the figure and literature of the imbongi. The poets I spoke with affirmed that iimbongi have license to speak their minds; indeed, the imbongi has functioned as both a counterpoint to power and an integral part of traditional leadership. The eulogistic genre of izibongo requires a subject who in turn needs the courage that izibongo offer and the social legitimization they provide through their ability to air grievances. Since 1994 iimbongi have played a visible role in South African politics, performing at such events as the opening of provincial legislatures and the State of the Nation Address.[2] These findings accord with previous scholarship that emphasized the political function that iimbongi performed during the apartheid period, linking it to the iimbongi's pre-colonial connection with traditional leadership and their role in speaking truth to power through their public performances.

Yet there is a darker side to contemporary transformations, which includes the "intricate relationship between those who control power, *and their continued legitimisation through political oratory* produced by the poet."[3] Iimbongi are not necessarily political progressives and may reinforce aspects of traditional society that are damaging to some groups. They may invoke notions of a precolonial African identity that are no longer relevant or recoverable in a society transformed by centuries of Western influence or are no longer desirable from the standpoint of human rights and equality. They may lend support to traditional leaders who abuse their power in despotic and repugnant ways or to elected leaders whose actions are no less reprehensible. In a deeply patriarchal world troubled by extreme rates of domestic violence, iimbongi too often perform and reiterate male power and male voices when women's voices badly need to be heard. Meanwhile, as we have seen, iimbongi may also be unreliable in delivering their message, either because they are unable to fully articulate it for political reasons or because they are unable to receive and transmit it for reasons relating to the soul and the spirit.

My research suggests that the iimbongi's transition from rural, traditional realms to urban, political ones is not as smooth as has sometimes been described. By presenting iimbongi primarily as political commentators and izibongo as a political genre, scholars not only have neglected the multiple levels on which the poetry works but also may have inadvertently placed unrealistic expectations on practitioners and on the art form itself. In particular, many writings on iimbongi and izibongo omit or gloss over the spiritual aspects that remain central to the tradition. Arguably, it is the spiritual understandings of the genre that endow iimbongi with the "poetic license" to criticize figures of authority with impunity. Operating in the fullest spiritual sense articulated by participants in my research, iimbongi are rare and gifted people with a sacred duty to receive and transmit messages—not only from people to their leaders, as previous commentators have pointed out, but also between the realm of living humans and realms beyond. They may carry out this task at great personal cost, yet may do so because failure to accept the call could cost them even more. Performing spontaneously and in response to the event and people at hand, they are carried along on a flow of words that, after their performance, they are often entirely unable to recall. They perform a healing role in society, similar to that of amagqirha, possessing the power to "revive a spirit of ubuntu" and move people with their words. For these reasons, an imbongi who is seen as a spiritual figure with the responsibility of promoting harmonious relations between God (whether uThixo or uQamata), the ancestral shades, and their earthly kin, is fundamentally different from a poet seen primarily as a secular figure speaking truth to power.

As these aspects of the imbongi's art were explained to me, I became increasingly convinced that a literary figure understood to be connected to and inspired by God and/or ancestral shades cannot perform the same cultural and artistic function in a secular political realm characterized by censorship and corruption. The idea that iimbongi can, should, or do continue to speak an uncensored version of truth to power, unfavorable political circumstances notwithstanding, seems not only misleading but also unfair to those poets compelled to withhold difficult truths. Even in more traditional contexts, the vision of imbongi as healer and medium may well be exaggerated or idealized. The removal of the spiritual checks and balances that might have prevented iimbongi from functioning as propagandists for those in power makes it unlikely that mainstream iimbongi—such as those who perform at the State of the Nation Address, the opening of provincial parliamentary sessions, and other high-profile public events—are able to perform the social functions they would have done historically. While some iimbongi, such as David Yali-Manisi, have refused to perform on stages where patronage by corrupt politicians would compromise their own political convictions and personal integrity, extending such an expectation to all iimbongi would be to overlook the multilayered social significance of their work.

Furthermore, the very term "political" warrants unpacking because it can obscure an important distinction between the party politics of contemporary society and the complex relationships between land and lineage, power and obligation, privilege and responsibility that define traditional forms of leadership. Most of my research participants distinguished between contemporary politics and traditional affairs and did *not* ascribe a political role to the latter because traditional leaders are not partisan figures. Particularly in the rural setting, where people were less familiar with televised performances of iimbongi at high-profile political events, they associated iimbongi primarily with traditional leadership, which they did not consider to be political. The reasons for this are clear: a chief or king, who has inherited his position through divine ordinance, occupies a position of authority very different from that of an elected representative accountable to party members, the party line, and voting constituents. Instead, traditional leaders represent and are responsible for defending the rights and interests of *all* people in their chiefdom or kingdom, not merely supporters and party members, and they are moreover deeply responsible to ancestral spirits, to unborn generations yet to come, to the animals in their care, indeed to the very land itself. Their responsibilities and roles dramatically transcend the political tenure of any given politician, who occupies a leadership position thanks to his or her ability to curry the favor of the majority of the electorate. Traditional leaders are not faced with the same need to establish themselves as popular figures; thus, in the traditional context the danger that the imbongi will function as a propagandist is at least somewhat reduced. Although the tradition has indeed shifted and adapted to reflect changing political circumstances in the country, and although iimbongi have certainly played a political role outside the traditional realm from colonial times to the present, the movement of iimbongi between traditional and political realms seems to me to be neither straightforward nor simple. The foreign systems of land tenure, governance, spiritual worship, and legal procedure imposed alongside the Western capitalist order have produced a complex society with many overlapping obligations and beliefs.

In a certain sense, the genre as traditionally practiced is inherently ecological because of its imbrication with landscape and ancestral dwelling upon that landscape. Yet in all locations it is a form with strong ties to the environment in which it is performed, since the poet draws inspiration from the place, the event, and the people and spirits gathered there. When iimbongi operate as paid performers within the stifled political climate of postapartheid South Africa—particularly when they recite memorized rather than impromptu verses—the environmental relatedness is obscured. Rather than being figures with a message or with a duty to question and provoke, iimbongi in the political realm have their power undermined by the public's understanding that their performances are designed to bolster the image of the political figure in question. Finally, iimbongi operating in urban, political worlds are differently equipped when it comes to the language needed to fulfil their role as provocateur and critic in the difficult circumstances of contemporary South Africa. As my research participants made clear, certain words, idioms, metaphors, and linguistic constructions used by rural iimbongi performing in "deep Xhosa" are unavailable to iimbongi working in urban contexts as they will not be understood. While urban performers and their audiences may have the expectation that iimbongi will be able to "work around" a contentious political topic by delivering a message or criticism obliquely rather than directly through skillful poetic means, I will leave it to future researchers with fluency in the language to comment further.

It seems clear that some contemporary iimbongi *have* been coopted; their work *has* been commodified. Moreover, as predominantly male figures attached to conservative traditions that can be oppressive in themselves, they do not necessarily represent or voice progressive ideologies of acceptance and equality. This does not signal a failure of iimbongi or of the izibongo genre to adapt to changing circumstances, nor is it a sign that the genre on the whole is becoming commercialized and that the beauty and integrity of the art form is being lost. It is clear that oral literature is alive and well in rural and township areas alike, that in many contexts iimbongi are noble and exemplary figures producing literary art of the highest order, and that it needs more opportunities to flourish so that wider range of voices can be heard. Above all, it is clear that ample opportunity for further research exists. I hope that future scholars will take up the many questions that this work leaves unanswered.

As participants in my research acknowledged almost universally, iimbongi certainly remain a vital component of amaXhosa culture and identity. Their importance is manifold: iimbongi play an important healing role and open new possibilities for amaXhosa traditions and spiritualities to flourish. Whether they perform on the compromised terrain of the corporate and commercial mainstream or on the stages of family and community gatherings, iimbongi animate African identities and histories for their audiences. They insist on the beauty of the isiXhosa language and the importance of traditions of mutual encouragement and support. In the townships they perform hybridity, opening new possibilities for learning and culture by creatively mingling very different languages and traditions. In the process, iimbongi present opportunities for challenging and redefining Western notions of "development" by offering a form of active development practice. They open spaces for discussion and decolonization, for appraising and reimagining the political order that has so polarized South Africa. Resisting the reductionist and utilitarian discourse of Western capitalism, they restore depth, meaning, and beauty to the world and the word.

Appendix A
FOSATU by Alfred Themba Qabula

Nguye wavela!	It is he who has appeared!
Basho bonke bathi wavela!	They all said that he had appeared!
Wena hlathi elihambayo laseAfrika.	You moving forest of Africa.
Ngifike amawele elilelana	When I arrived the twins were all crying
Kanti ngabasebenzi	
Abasebenza ezimbonini	These were the workers,
Bexoxelana ngezinkinga	Industrial workers,
Ezibahlupha ezimbonini	Discussing the problems
Abazisebenzela eAfrika.	That affect them in the industries They work for in Africa.
Ngibone omunye edudza abanye,	I saw one of them consoling others,
Ebesula izinyembezi emhleweni.	Wiping their tears from their eyes.
Ngibone umhlola	I saw wonders because even in his
Ngoba nakuye zisuke zagobhoz'iz inyembezi emhleweni.	Eyes the tears did flow.
Basebenzi ngowani na lowo Maye!?	Worker, about what is that cry, Maye!?
Nikhala nje ngubanina onihluphayo?	You are crying, who is troubling you?
Balekani ningene kulelohlathi	Escape into that forest,
Hlath'limnyama elabonwa ngabaqashi balibalekela labonwa	The black forest that the employers saw and ran away from for safety.
Ngabasebenzi	The workers saw it too.

Bathi: 'ngelethu masingeneni sicashe
Ukuze siphephe kubazingeli bethu.
Bangena kulelihlathi baphuma
Sebelashwe uvalo nengebhe
Yokwesaba izitha zabo.

It belongs to us, let us hide they said.
Let us take refuge in it and be safe from our hunters.
Deep in the forest they hid themselves, and then came out,
And when they came out
They were free from fear.

Sikhukhukazi esimaphikw'abanzi
Okufukumel'amatshwele aso,
Sifukamele nathi,
Ngalawamaphiko akho angena ubadlululo.
Sikhukhumeze nathi,
Ukuze sihluzele'ingqondo sihlakaniphe.
Anolak'amadodana akho,
Ingabe uwachela ngaluphi uhlobo lwentelezi
Sichele nathi
Ukuze siwafuze senze njengawe
Uzele phela FOSATU
Amadodana akhe angcwele iAfrika yonkana
Nangaphesheya onyana bakhe bakhona
FOSATU ulibhubesi,
Elingquma ePitoli eseNyakatho
Unesihovisi zenyunyane kulo lonke.

You are the hen with wide wings
That protects its chickens,
Protect us too,
With those sacred wings of yours that know no discrimination.
Protect us too,
So that we gain wisdom.
Militant are your sons and daughters,
One wonders what kind of muti they use.
Sprinkle it so that we take
After them and act likewise.
FOSATU has given birth.
Its sons are spread all over Africa.
Even overseas you find its sons
FOSATU, you are the lion,
That roared at Pretoria North.
With union offices everywhere.

FOSATU sukukhethile,
Ukuba sihole kade sasibakhetha abaholi.
Sikhetha abantu esasibathemba
Abantu esazalwa nabo sakhula nabo
Abantu abalwaziyo lonke usizi lwethu
Nesasigqilazeke kanye nabo
Sabakhetha ngoba sasikholwa

FOSATU, we have chosen you to lead us,
Time and again we have been electing leaders,
Electing people we trusted,
And with whom we were born and with whom we grew up,
People who know all our sufferings,
Together with whom we were enslaved,

Ukuthi balubhaqa olunkhanyisa indlela yethu eya enkululekweni Kanti kuzothi sesibaphakamisele Basiphedukela Basithuthela izimpimpi Zasihlupha	We had elected them because we believed, They found a lamp to brighten the way to freedom, But to our dismay They turned against us, They brought impimpis into our midst to inflict Sufferings upon us.
Amathambo ami nabalozi bangi-shela ukuthi Yebo, uzele amadodana akho mahle Futhi ahlakaniphile ekanti aphilile kodwa Kukhona isifo esingukufa Enye indodana akho iyagula impela Lesisifo esingukufa Singawathelela namanye amadodana akho Nawo agcine onke esegula Ngempela eguliswa yisifo esibi kakhulu Isifo somdlavuza, ewe umdlavusa.	My bones and my abalozi are telling me this, Yebo, handsome are your sons, Intelligent and healthy, But a deadly disease threatens them, One of your children is ailing, And this disease called Death May infect your other sons, Leaving them all sick, With this horrible disease, Cancer, yes Cancer.
Ngikubhekile konke Okwenzayo! Ulibinda FOSATU! Bayethe! Amandla kubasebenzi!	I am watching all that you are Doing! You are great, FOSATU! Hail! Power to the workers!

Reprinted with permission from Russell Kaschula's "The Transitional Role of the Xhosa Oral Poet in Contemporary South African Society."

Appendix B
Isibongo Performed at the State of the Nation Address, 2016

Gamuza le nyang'ephum'emafini	Gamuza, this moon that emerges from the sky,
Inyang'exhoph'ubumnyama	The moon that disturbs the darkness
Yaxhoph'iikhonkwane zobanjululo	
Kwaze kwas'amabhul'ezulazul'ephi-thizela	And disturbed apartheid nails Until the Boers were confused.
Ukuba niyiyekiiiiile boDemethi	If you leave it you, Demetis.
Ngob'enkhulul'amaAfrik'onke	Because he liberated you, all Africans,
Umdon'omile phezu kweNkandla	A wild tree standing on Nkandla.
Haye bawulabalabela	My goodness they play around!
Unomfundi woqobo abethi akafundile	The learned they said he's not:
Ngiyo baphikisa ngiyoze ngife	I'll disagree with them till I die.
Ufundil'okaMsholoz'ufundisiwe	The son of Msholozi is educated,
Kungafakaz'unina khulu	His grandmother can bear witness.
UMayengwaye Mpindamshaye	Mayengwaye Mpindamshaye,
Kuye kufakaze ngisho ogazi lakhe kwabaka Bhengu	His relative from Bhengus will also witness it.
Inkosana kaKhongolose	The prince of Congress,
Abayibeka beyibangis'abakhulu	Placed there despite competition with great ones,
Inkosana abayibeka ngobuqhawe nangobuhlakani bayo	The prince placed for his heroism and courage,
Abanye babekwa ngokuzabalaza kooyise	

Sihlahl'esikhulu, esihlula ngisho sebethi bayasisephula	Unlike others whose fathers struggled, paving the way for their sons. The great branch which is difficult to cut.
Chief of intelligence Indla beyiphikisa ngish'ezikhundlen'eziphezulu Mthetho kaZuma kaSophinokhombangosophakathi Babemfel'umona Ubuholi k'abufundelwa maAfrika Ubuholi busegazini kuwe Msholozi Obahol'ekudingiswen'eLusaka Phaya bakukhothamela	Chief of intelligence! They stood against him even in higher positions, The law of Zuma of Sophinokhombangosophakathi.[1] They were jealous of him You don't need schooling to be a leader, Africans. Leadership style is in your blood, Msholozi. You lead them in exile in Lusaka, There they bowed to you.
Nanamhlanjena amaAfrik'ayakukhothamela Uqhajan'akaviki ngasihlangu Akanje ngasotha mlilo Iindab'engizwe ngimncane Ngaze ngamdala ngaybona ngamehlo Ngiyibone nyakana ka 2005 Bethiwa okaZum'unecala Icalokutyholwa ngosopolitik'epalamente Amany'amacala etyholwa ziimanty'enkantolo UGedlehlekisa, abanye bemkhamfula Umazul'az'ayithole Nanamhlanjena ziyathakaza izizwe zonke Uvula bevalile Umgoq'abawuvale phakath'epalamente Bethi ke asoyiphind'ibus'eka Msholozi	Even today, Africans bow to you. The small one who does not hide behind the shoe, He's not like one next to the fire. News I heard when I was still young, When I grew I saw with my own eyes, I saw it in year 2005: They said Zuma is guilty. Charges which were brought by politicians in parliament, Other charges were brought by judges in court. Gedlehlekisa, others disrespected him, He who walks around until he finds it. Even today nations are excited, He opens where it is closed. They conspired against him in parliament, Saying Msholozi will never lead again

Nanamhlanj'iyangena	And today he is entering.
Kwaye kwajampa ngisho nozwe ngephepha	They even jumped those who read from the newspapers.
Isithol'esimagqapagqapa	The plant with different colors.
Hebo kwezakithi kooZuma	Yes, to ours, to the Zumas.
Esibhekwe zizizwe zonke, zasmoyizelela	All nations are watching with a smile,
AmaKomanisi asimoyizelela	Communists are smiling, too.
Eze Cosatu zisbhekile zonke zisbhekile zasmoyzelela	All the Cosatu members looked at it and smile.
Msholozi ngekhe ngikqede Nxamalala	Msholozi, I'll never finish, Nxamalala.

Appendix C
Izibongo Performed by Thukela Poswayo

Address to King Zwelonke, 4 December 2015

Imbongi: A Zwelonke!	Imbongi: Hail Zwelonke!
Abantu: A Zwelonke!	Audience: Hail Zwelonke!
Imbongi: A! Zweloooonke!	Imbongi: Hail! Zweloooonke!
Abantu: A! Zweloooonke	Audience: Hail!Zweloooonke!
Iyakhumbulana mntane nkosi.	We miss each other, child of a chief.
Iyakhumbulana thole leduna.	We miss each other, son of a bull.[1]
Ndelula amehlo ndayibona imi-lambo,	I stretched my eyes and saw the rivers,
Ndanga ndinga qhayisa ndixele uthekwane	I wish I can boast like the thekwane, Saying I'm ugly on this side, beauti-ful on that.
Ndithi ndimbi ngapha ndimhle ngapha.	
Ewe kaloku thole leduna	Yes then, son of a bull,
Siyinqamle imilambo.	We crossed rivers.
Sawubona uMbhashe.	We saw the Mbhashe.
Sayinqaml' imilambo	We crossed rivers
Sawusel'uMgwali.	And drank the Mgwali.
Sawubona uMthatha, sawubona uMthamvuna.	We saw the Mthatha, we saw the Mthamvuna.
Salibona iThukela, salibona iCongo,	We saw the Thukela, we saw the Congo.

Salibona iZambezi, salibona iLimpopo,	We saw the Zambezi, we saw the Limpopo.
Siyibonile imilambo	We've seen the rivers,
Ngoba neLubhelu siyibonile.	Why, we've even seen the Lubhelu.
Ewe kaloku ndibiza ngabom.	Yes, now I name them deliberately.
Ngoba kaloku ukuze kulunge	So that all may go well
Ndithi Zwelonke	I say Zwelonke;
Funeka ndiyibiz'imilambo ye Afrika.	I must name the rivers of Africa.
Ewe kaloku kwakudala,	Yes, you see, even long ago
Le mini yayi saziwa iyakuz'ifike	It was known this day would come.
Ungeka qashulwa, engekakuzali unyoko	Before you were conceived, before You were born to your mother, you
Wawusele uzelwe.	existed.
Ke kambe okwethu kukungqina	Now we need only witness,
Sithi nal'ithole lika Xolilizwe.	Saying that this is Xolilizwe's calf.²
Nants' inkonyane yohlanga	This is the calf of the nation,
Eyabizwa ingekaveli.	Named before he was born.
Ewe kaloku! Le ndawo ukuyo	Yes of course! The position you hold
Kwakukhe kwahlala omnye umntu kuyo	Was held by someone before you, As there will be someone after.
Kusezaw'hlal'omnyumntu	That is why you must act with care,
Yiyo lo nto funek'uchul'ukunyathel'uchule	Counting your steps, For the river you're crossing,
Uwabal'amanyathelo	young man,
Ngob'umlambo owela kuwo kwedini	Is full of slippery stones,
Uzele amatye agcwel'ucolothi.	Deep pools to the north, deep pools
Ngentla ziziziba, ngezantsi ziziziba	to the south.³
Chula ke ukhangele ngaphesheya	Be steady then and look across,⁴
Ngoba kaloku ukwenza kwakho namhla	Because what you do in this time Will follow you when you depart.
Kuyakulandela ngemihla sewungasekho	
Ngoba kaloku okwenzayo namhla	Because what you do today
Kwakukhe kwenziwa ngaphambili	Was done before.
Yima ke thole lomThembukazi	Stand still then, lamb of the Thembukazi,⁵
Yim'uthi gomololo.	Stand firm as ever.⁶

Amandl'uwanikiwe	You've been given the power,
Ngob'igunya walinikwa kuqala	For you've been given authority from the start.
Thetha ke! Nasi isizwe sakokwenu	Speak then! Here is your nation.
Nang'amaGcaleka ka Khawuta.	Here are the Gcalekas of Khawuta.[7]
Nalusapho luka Zanzolo.	Here are the children of Zanzolo.
Nal'usapho luka Sarhili.	Here are the children of Sarhili.[8]
Thetha ke nalo	So speak to them.
Ngoba kaloku okwakh'ukuthetha	For certainly your words
Ngekhe kulambathe	Will not be in vain
Ngoba kaloku uThix'uMdali, uQamata	Just as God the creator, Qamata[9] of our forefathers,
Woobawo mkhulu,	Pointed with his finger,
Wakhomba ngomnwe wakhe	Choosing a man to lead others,
Wakhomb'indoda'emayi khokel'amanye amadoda,	So to your voice he turns his ear.
Ke ngelakh 'ilizwi uyakubeka indlebe.	Listen well! And make things right for us.
Aphulaphule enze kulunge kokwethu.	
IAfrika yakokwethu inyembezana.	Our Africa is crying.
Ifuna amadoda anomqolo,	It wants men with backbones,
Ifun'amadoda anelizwi elimbombo	It needs men with bold voices
Ukuze ath'akuthetha kulunge	To right things with their words.
Thetha ke,	Speak then,
Ngoba uThixo wakukhomba kuqala.	For God pointed at you first.
Thetha beve abantwana beli lizwe,	Speak so that the children of this nation can hear you,
Thetha senz' isizwe sikayihlomkhulu	Speak so that your forefathers' nation may do as you ask,
Ngob'ungathetha, zonke izinto zakulunga	For when you've spoken, things will fall into place.
Ngemihla besithatha abantwana	In the days when we filed into the mountains
Sibaqukuqela sibasa entabeni	With our children, kindling fires,
Besisenza amadoda okumela eli lizwe.	We made strong men for this world.
Hayi imbunye nembudede yentw'esiyibona kulemihla.	There was not the confusion we see now.

Elankhw'ilizwi ke, hleze lingathetha Kobakh'umtha welanga. Thetha ke ngoba thina Sizakv'ukuthetha kwakho.	Raise your voice then, that your speaking May bring a ray of sun. Speak to us, That we may hear your words.
Siyiwelile ke imilambo, Sizibonil'izinto. Sasikho thina kwakuqala Ngemihl'abelungu besiqhatha Basinika utywala bebhotile De wath'uMqhayi, *Ngubani nalo? Ngu Yeye.* *Uhamba nabani?* *Noyise. Umphathe ntoni?* *Amasi. Ngendeb'enjani?* *Ebomvu.*	We've crossed the rivers, We've seen many things. We were here even in the beginning When white people arrived to cheat us They delivered alcohol in bottles Until Mqhayi said,[10] *Who is this? It is Yeye.* *Who is walking with him?* *His father. What has he brought for me?* *Sour milk. What is the color of the container?* *It is red.*
Kaloku ngalo mihla Umlungu ufike esiteketisa ngebhotile. Sathi sokuy'jonga Safika ifanekile ngathi ngumfundisi Engen'ecaweni Sathi kuzakulunga kanti kumhla konakala	In those days A white man came to charm us with a bottle. As we gazed It became as beautiful as a church minister Entering the church. We said things will improve, but things got worse.
Khalime ke ukuze siy'bhebhethe, Hayi ngobubi kodwa ngok'qiqa kwengqondo. Chulak'ukunyathela Ngoba abakowenu bath'inkos'itheth'apha Suke batolike phaya.	Lament then and banish it, Not with misery but diplomacy. And tread with care, For though the chief says this, The people chase that.
Nathi sikho ke. Okuthethileyo, Whina sohamba nako siye ezizweni.	Here we are. What you say We'll take to the people.

Address to King Zwelonke, 11 March 2016

Imbongi: A! Zwelonke
Abantu: A! Zwelonke
Imgongi: A! Zweloooonke!
Abantu: A! Zwelonke!

Mntan'omhle
Amehl'am ath'akukhangela ndabon'imilambo
Ndathi ndakujonga ngaphesheya
Ndazibon'iinkomo zako kwenu
Ndazibon'iinkomo zako kwethu

Ndiyazaz'ezako kwenu
Ndiyazaz'ezako kwethu
Ndiyazehlula ngemibala
Kuba zingaphesheya kwemilambo zicacile.
Zicacile zizakuhle
Zibonakala ngok'tyhobo

Ewe kaloku!
Yithi khe ndicaphule ndenjenje
Ngoba kaloku ukuze kulunge maLawundini
Vumani kuba sendiliphethibhozo
Ndabel'izizwe
Vumani kaloku
Ndabel'iQamata
Ndabel'umhlaba kalok'omagqagala
Ndabela kaloku umhlaba kaloku wakulo Daliwonga
Kuba kaloku kulapho zaphuma khon'iinkomo
Zaqweqwema zadl'amathafa
Zafika kwaChotho zamila
Zabuya nentombi
Yafika yazal'amadodana

Imbongi: Hail! Zwelonke
Audience: Hail! Zwelonke
Imbongi: Hail! Zweloooonke!
Audience: Hail! Zweloonke!

Honorable one,[11]
Opening my eyes, I saw rivers.
When I looked across
I saw your family's cattle,
I saw my family's cattle.

I know those of your family.
I know those of my family.
I know them by their colors,[12]
For even across the river they are distinct.
They are beautifully distinct.
They appear now, charging.

Yes then!
Let me say something,
For in order for things to improve, maLawundini,[13]
Allow me, for I already have the knife.
I distributed among nations.
Allow me then,
I gave to Qamata.[14]
I gave the land with its dry boulders.
I gave the land from Daliwonga's family[15]
From which the cattle came,
Running to the fields.
They reached Chotho and stopped, returning with a girl.[16]
She arrived and gave birth to young boys.

Namhla ke kuthi mandithi	Today I want to say only
Ukuze kulunge kum	That things are well with me.
Zikho kalok'iinkomo zakulo Mvuzo	There are the cattle from Mvuzo's family,
Zikho kalok'iinkomo zakulo Thambekile	There are the cattle from Thambekile's family.
Nawe nkonyana yakulo Thambekile	And you, calf of Thambekile's family,
Yithi ndithi rhuthu	Let me take out
Nang'umwangalala ndikwabele	These scattered coins to share with you.[17]
Ewe kaloku!	Yes then!
Ukuze kulunge maLawundini	So that things will be well, maLawundini,
Vumani kaloku ndiwele kalok'imilambo,	Allow me to cross these rivers.
Ndiwel'uMbashe, ndiwel'iXuka	I crossed the Mbashe, I crossed the Xuka
Ndinyuke kaloku ngoMkhonkotho.	And ascended Mkhonkotho.[18]
Ndakufika phezu kwentaba	I arrived at the top of the mountain,
Ndivul'amaphiko	Opened my wings,
Ndime kaloku ndixel'intsikiz'im'emaweni	And stood on the cliffs commanding as a hornbill
Iqhayise'amahahane	Boasting to the hadedas,
Isithi mna ndihluthi	Saying I am full,
Ndihluth'amaqonya	I'm full of maqonya.[19]
Kazi wena hahane uyakurhayisa ngantoni na	I wonder, what would you boast about, hadeda?[20]
Kuhluth'intsundwan'enje.	Since the other is so full.
Kulapho kaloku	So that is where
Zikhoy'iinkomo zakulo Biya	The cattle of Biya's family are.
Kulapho kaloku	So that is where
Zikhoy'iinkomo zakulo Mgangatho	The cattle of Mgangatho's family are.
Ukuze kulunge kaloku	So that things will be well then
Nawe nkonyana kaDaluxolo	Even you, lamb of Daluxolo,
Vuma ndithi kuwe sendikho.	Let me say it fell, but I am still here.
Yima kaloku! Ungayiyizeli	Wait now! Don't celebrate
Kuba hlez'ubhideke.	For you may be confused.
Akufane kuyiyizelwe ngemihl'enje	Times like these aren't for celebrating,
Ngoba kaloku imihl'enje	Times like these

Yeyokuba kukhutshw'iinyaniso	Are for revealing truths,
Zibekw'elubala badl'abantu	Putting them on the surface for
Ngoba kaloku	people to eat,
Abantu badla mhla ngatheko	For, you see,
Kuba kalok'amazw'angawo	People eat when there is an event.[21]
Ngaw'afanel'abantwana beenkosi	Thus, encouraging words
Ukuze bave ngeendlebe zabo	Are most suitable for chief's children,
Benze kulung'esizweni	For they attend well with their ears
	And act, returning the nation to normal.
Kube mnandi kokwethu kube chosi kubehele	So that we'll enjoy and be happy.
Sigide siguye sidindithe	We'll dance, sing and clap.
Kube mnandi kokwethu si thetsul'oMayeka	We'll enjoy and Mayekas will take heed,
Kube mnandi kokwethu	And be happy at home.
Sidle kube mnandi	We'll eat and enjoy,
Sityibilik'ebhotolweni.	Falling as the ground grows slick with butter.[22]
Yima kaloku nkonyana kaXolilizwe	Wait, bull calf of Xolilizwe,[23]
Nas'isizwe sakokwenu	Here is your nation.
Kuba kaloku!	For then!
Sewumanangananga nje, zizadwendwe	If you are adorned with colorful guests
Kukwaphuka kwemikhonto yamaphakathi	It is because of the spears of your councillors,
Esilwel'ooyihlo	Broken in the fight for your fathers.[24]
Kukwaphuka kwemikhonto yamadoda	It is because of men's spears, broken
Esilwel'eli lizwe	In the fight for this country
Ukuze kaloku kubekhon'indoda	So that there can be a man,
Ikhonjw'ibenye yenz'izinto	A willow spear thrown down to do things
Phakathi kwamany'amadoda	Among other men,
Kuthiwe lo ndod'ukubizwa kwayo yikumkani.	And that man is called their king.
Ukuze kukholiseke kophezulu	To please the one above
Yithobeleni ke kuba kakad'ayizibeke	Obey him, for he did not appoint himself.
Yakhonjwangomnwe woQamat'o-wayekho kwakudaladala	He was appointed by Qamata who has always existed.

Thetha ke!	Speak then!
Nas'isizwe sakokwenu	Here is your nation.
Nas'isizwe sezizwe	Here is the nation of nations.
Nas'isizwe sakulo Mcothama	Here is the nation of Mcothama,
Nas'isizwe sakulo Dwayi	Here is the nation of the Dwayi family,
Nas'isizwe kaloku sakulo Ndlambe	Here is the nation, then, from the Ndlambe family,
Kuba kaloku wena kwedin'uyingqalo	For you, young man, are the beginning.
Kwamhla mnene kwazalwa tanc'indoda	Even before the man was born
Yathi gqolo ukuzal'amany'amadoda	And it carried on raising other men
Ukuze kalok'amany'azalwa kuzikunene namaqad'ayiphahle	In order those from other polygamous[25]
Namhla k'akuphahlil'amaqad'akokwenu	And from young polygamous protect him.
	Today your brothers from your father's other wives surround you.[26]
Namhlak'isizwe sakokwenu siyakuvumela ngazwi nye	Today your nation agrees in one voice.
Yolul'isandla njengemihla yoyihlo	Extend your hand as in the days of your fathers,
Njengemihl'oyihlo bawel'imilambo	As in the days when your fathers crossed the rivers,
Bolul'iizandla banquml'iiphonoshono	Extending their hands they stopped on the near side
Nephesheya kweNciba	Then crossed over the Kei.
Belul'iizandla yadabuk'umdangala	Extending their hands, laziness was gone.
Namhla ke kwedini yima	Today then, young man, stand,
Ngoba kaloku	For, you see,
Ngendalo kwavunywa k'qala	In nature it was agreed before:
Akungakuzalwa tanci	It is not by being a first born,
Koko kungokuzalwa ngokwesiko	It is only by traditional right's birth.
Yingoko ke kwedini ndisitsho	That's why I'm saying, young man,
Ngegunya loyihlo yima	By the authority of your fathers[27]
Nank'uyihlo mncinci	Here is your uncle.[28]
Namhla melulel'izandla	Today extend him your hands,
Namhla mambathise	Today cover him

Ukuz'isizwe sivume	So that as a nation we can agree
Sithi ngomnwe wakho kwenzeka	And say that by your finger it happened,
Ukuz'abakh'apha namhlanje	For the ones present today
Baqalis'ukubek'imbali	Begin this history.
Nathi ke siyavuma	We also agree,
Sithi beka ngob'izinto zale mihla ziyabhida	We say respect, for things of these times are perplexing.
Hlez'usakuvilapha	If you become lazy here,
Bakungene ngasemva kwedini bakugawule.	They'll stab you from behind, young man, and chop you down.
Kuba banjal'abantu	For people are like that,
Namhla bakubeka phezulu	Today they place you on high,
Kanti ngomso baya kugawula bakudl'izithende	But tomorrow they will chop and eat your heels.²⁹
Kodwa k'asizok'thetha lo nt'apha	But we won't speak of that here.
Sith'ekho nj'uQamata	We say that while Qamata lives
Likhw'izwi lakho nje	And your voice is present
Wakukhomba ngomnwe wakho nje	You will point with your finger
Uyakuthetha kwedini kulunge	And speak, young man, and all will be well.
Thetha ke, nathi sikho	Speak then, we are also present.
Ngezeth'iingqondo neendlebe simamele	With our minds and our ears we listen.
Sakuva ke sixelel'abanye	We'll hear you tell others
Sithi namhl'ithethil'inkonyana yesizwe	We'll say today the calf of the nation has spoken.
Yath'uk'thetha yegqabagqaba yegqabagqaba	He said these few words, few words.³⁰
Kazi lelaphin'elirhanuga?	I wonder, who is this one with such nonsense?
Kweewu!	My goodness!³¹

Address to Chief Mthetho, 11 March 2016

Kukub'izinto zisuka zigqwetheke	Things just become a mess.
Zithi bezifane'ukuba beziphethwe sisandla sokunene	They were to be carried by the right hand,
Zisuke ziphamb'isandla	But they confuse the hand and escape,
Singene kwesokunxele	Moving on to the left.

Vuma mntan'enkosi
Mabini mathathu ndigoduke
Kuba ndinganga ndingafuman'amaz-
  w'okubik'ekhaya
Ndikhe ndanxunguphala
Kuba suke ndabonga phakathi
  kwamarhanuga
Ndathi ndithetha nje
Ab'eman'ukuphikel'ethi gram
Zen'khe nithule marhanuga
Kuba kuthi le nto yimpilo
Nakufak'amazwi athint'iindlebe
  zethu
Embilinini kuthi kuyonakala
Ukuze ndiphile ke mntan'omhle
Vuma nawe ndenjenje
Le ngub'uyambetheyo
Asingubo yakho
Kub'ukh'oyilindeleyo ngasemva
Ewe kaloku
Isikhundl'okuso kwedini
Sasikhe sahlal'omny'umntu
  ngaphambili
Kuba kakade
Le nt'umntu yinto yalo nto,
  ngumngcelele
Ngemihla oyihl'omkhulu aba
  besilw'iimfazwe
Bevul'umhlaba ukuze balime,
  wawusewukho
Kuba kakade
Ngemihla kwedini
URhili eleqwa ngamadlagusha
Wawukho use sinqeni kuye
Yima ke uthi gomololo
Kub'imits'oyakuyenza namhla
Hlez'ixolis'ilizwe kwimihl'elandelayo
Kuba kwakunjalo kwakuqala
Le nt'iyindoda yint'okuphilel'enye

Allow me, honorable one,
These few words and then I'll go
  home.
For I hope for a few encouraging
  words to say
To those at home.
I was troubled,
For, rising to bonga among the igno-
  rant people,
I saw as I was speaking
That they disputed while I spoke.
Could you please keep quiet, igno-
  rant people,
For to us this is life.
When we hear you
It becomes a mess in our spirits.
In order for me to be healthy, honor-
  able one,
Allow me to do this.
This blanket that covers your body
Is not yours,
For someone behind you waits for it.
Yes, then,
The position you occupy,
  young man,
Belonged to someone else before.
For it is true,
People are like that, there is always
  a queue.
The days when your forefathers were
  at war,
Opening up the ground to plough,
  you already existed.
For it is true
In those days, young man,
Rhili was chased by sheep eaters[32]
And you existed already in his loins.
Stand firm, then,
For what you will do today

Ukuze kulunge kaloku
Phila namhla, uphilel'abazayo
Kub'akunto ukutya kwendod'ibhu-
  kuxe
Ilibal'intokokuba iinkomo zayo
Zikhangelwe zizinja ngaphandle
Yity'ushiye zity'izinja zikhonkothe
Yima ke uthi gomololo
Le nt'umnt'umzi kwedin'ayince-
  kelelwa
Khe ndamv'umzukulwana ka-
  Mvuz'esitsho ngeny'imini
Uz'ungasingcekeleli k'isizwe
Uz'usibambe ngezandla zozibini
Kuba kaloku, amava nembali ngawe
Iyakwakhiwa ngamadod'owakho-
  keleyo
Yima ke, uxhas'ikokwenu
Kuba kwedini angathi abhatyaz'um-
  ntan'omhle
Ziyakukhonjwa kuwe
Ngamadod'alandela ngasemva
Kuba namhla solul'iizandla nje
Uzakhel'iintsika zokuwel'imilambo
Imilamb'eniyiwelay'izel'amatye
  alucolothi
Uz'ume ke
Umxhas'uxhathise
Ukuz'igama lakokwenu lingacimi
Imb'indod'ethi iphunga nje
Ib'ijonge ngaphesheya kuba ziyo-
  nakal'izinto
Uz'ume ke, uzinz'ukhange'ucok-
  is'ukunyathela
Kub'umzil'okhonjwayo
Ngumzila wezilwanyan'ezicok-
  is'ukunyathela
Yima ke uthethe ungenzi mazwi
  maninzi
Kub'asikubekelanga kuthetha

Could please the nation in days to
  come,
For it has been so before.
Men are meant to live for others.
For things to be well then,
Live these days for the ones who
  have yet to come,
For it is not right for a man to eat
  too much
And forget that his cattle
Are tended by the dogs outside.
Don't finish the food, but let the
  dogs eat and bark.
Stand tall then,
You cannot put a house on your
  head.
I heard Mvuzo's grandchild saying
  that one day.
Don't put the nation on your head,
But hold it with both hands,
Because experience and your history
Will be built by the men you lead.
Stand, then, and look after your
  home,
For if you, honorable one, trip up,
You will be blamed
By men behind you.
For today as we stretch our hands,
You build the foundation to cross
  rivers.
The rivers you cross are full of slip-
  pery stones.
Stand then
And support him, stand strong
So that your family name will
  continue.
It is not good for a man to sit drink-
  ing tea
While he looks across, for things are
  messy.

Sikubekel'ukwenza.
Yenza ke, sibone sibuke.
Thina mbongi sibonge
Kub'ukuthetha kokwethu kakade.

Be strong then and careful,
For the direction pointed
Is the route of cautious animals.
Stand then and speak, but not too much,
For we've not appointed you to speak,
But appointed you to act.
Act then, for all to see.
We the iimbongi will bonga,
For speech is certainly ours.

Poems in this series translated by Dumisa Mpupha and Emily McGiffin.

GLOSSARY

Certain words used in this book will be unfamiliar to some readers; others are contested and weighted with ongoing debate. I present this glossary to help orient the reader and to expand on some of the contentious or potentially ambiguous terms. In this text I have opted to use the new orthography issued by the Pan South African Language Board that incorporates the prefixes *isi-* (pertaining to language) and *ama-* (pertaining to people). However, when quoting other scholars or research participants I have not modified their words to suit the orthography.

amaXhosa Used in this book to indicate the nations and peoples unified by their use of various dialects of the isiXhosa language.
-*bonga* The root word for praise poetry that takes the form of a verb (*ukubonga*, "to praise, extol loudly and impromptu by songs or orations") or of a noun (imbongi, "the poet who praises, an impovisator"; isibongo: praise poem). See Kropf, *Xhosa-English Dictionary*, 42.
amagqirha Spiritual healers (commonly referred to as *sangomas*)
black A racial category for people of African origin that does not distinguish between linguistic, cultural, or religious affiliation or country of origin. I have generally tried to use "black" (which is more common in North America) in this text in lieu of "African," the more common South African equivalent, to avoid confusion with peoples from elsewhere on the African continent and to avoid appearing to make sweeping generalizations about the continent as a whole. I have avoided using the term "indigenous" as synonymous with "black" or "African" out of

respect for the important cultural and political distinctions between African peoples whose presence in present-day South Africa dates back tens of thousands of years and those who have migrated to these lands at more recent points in the past.

Ciskei   A pre-1994 geographical designation; a former Bantustan area on the southwest side of the Kei River.

colored   Under the 1950 Population Registration Act, a colored person was defined as "a person who is not a white person or a native." Instead, this racial class consists of people of mixed heritage, including any combination of South Africa's African, European, South Asian, and East Asian cultural groups.

igqhirha   A spiritual healer

iimbongi   amaXhosa poets

imbongi   umXhosa poet

isibongo   A single poem performed by an imbongi

isiXhosa   The language of the amaXhosa people; formerly known as Xhosa.

izibongo   The genre of poetry performed by iimbongi; plural of isibongo (yet often treated as a collective noun taking the singular verb form).

North, Northern, global North   As scholars increasingly acknowledge processes of internal colonization and the unequal distribution of economic wealth within nations, terms such as global North/global South (like older terms such as center/periphery and First World/Third World) are becoming increasingly complex and harder to define. I have used "global North" here to refer to nations whose geopolitical power enables them to shape global affairs. I have avoided terms such as "developed," "developing," and "underdeveloped" that impose a colonial teleology, although they do appear here in the discussion about development in chapter 5.

traditional   A problematic term that I have used in this text to refer to beliefs, practices, and relationships that predate the arrival of Europeans in South Africa. The presence of traditional lifeways is uneven across South Africa, where some areas and cultures have changed much more radically in response to the social and environmental transformations of the past two centuries. Yet even in those areas where precolonial practices and beliefs strongly persist, the traditional is dynamic; nowhere is it static or fixed.

Transkei   A pre-1994 geographical designation; a former Bantustan area on the black side of the Kei River that became the first and only Bantustan to be granted nominal independence by the apartheid government.

township   The residential areas formerly reserved for colored and black people that remain more or less exclusively inhabited by these groups. Townships are invariably located on the peripheries of settlements, at varying remove from centers historically reserved for whites. There is considerable variability within and between townships, which range from relatively prosperous areas to informal shack settlements without running water, sewers, or electricity.

umoya   A spirit or ghost; wind, air, breath. See Kropf, *Xhosa-English Dictionary*, 237.

West/Western   Another tricky term used here to denote primarily Anglo-American imperialist centers and the cultural and economic ideologies that have emanated from them, particularly in the postwar years.

white   Often an unstated or normative class, the term "white" is used here as a racial category for people of European heritage. This classification does not distinguish between linguistic, cultural, or religious affiliation, and in South Africa the term lumps together people of two significantly different linguistic and cultural groups, English and Afrikaans, as well as immigrants from a hodgepodge of European and other settler-colonial nations.

NOTES

Introduction

1. This account of the initial meeting between Opland and Yali-Manisi is adapted from Opland's own version, described at length in *Dassie and the Hunter,* 79–103; and "First Meeting." The lines of the poem are taken from *Dassie and the Hunter,* 87, and are also available in "First Meeting." Although the circumstances under which the performance occurred were unusual (Kaschula notes that the relationship between poet and scholar has been considered controversial ["Intellectualisation," 20]), there is no doubt that this encounter set in motion a scholarly career that has had a profound on South African literature.

2. However, previous South African ecocriticism on African-language texts does exist; this work includes Biyela, "Securing Women"; Wylie, "//Kabbo's Challenge."

3. Iheka, *Naturalizing Africa,* 25.

4. Glotfelty and Fromm characterize ecocriticism as "predominantly a white movement" (*Ecocriticism Reader,* xxv); Gersdorf and Mayer offer a definition of ecocriticism in *Nature in Literary Studies,* 9.

5. Discussed at length in both Clark, *Introduction to Literature;* and Ray, *Ecological Other.*

6. A vast and increasing range of critical writing exists, for example, in the collections of Catriona Mortimer-Sandilands and Bruce Erickson, eds., *Queer Ecologies: Sex, Nature, Politics, Desire* (Bloomington: Indiana University Press, 2010); Greta Gaard, Simon C. Estok, and Serpil Oppermann, eds., *International Perspectives in Feminist Ecocriticism* (New York: Routledge, 2013); Joni Adamson, Mei Mei Evans, and Rachel Stein, eds., *The Environmental Justice Reader: Politics, Poetics, and Pedagogy* (Tucson: University of Arizona Press, 2002).

7. Glotfelty and Fromm, *Ecocriticism Reader,* xxv.

8. Recent ecocritical titles reveal the truly global nature of this literary movement: Oppermann, *New International Voices in Ecocriticism;* Oppermann, Özdag, Özkan, and

Slovic, *Future of Ecocriticism*; Goodbody, *Ecocritical Theory*; Slovic, *Ecocriticism in Taiwan*; Slovic, Rangarajan, and Sarveswaran, *Ecocriticism of the Global South*; Iovino, *Ecologia letteraria*; and Wake, Suga, and Yuki, *Ecocriticism in Japan*.

9. See Roos and Hunt, *Postcolonial Green*; and DeLoughrey and Handley, *Postcolonial Ecologies*.

10. Huggan and Tiffin, *Postcolonial Ecocriticism*.

11. Roos and Hunt, *Postcolonial Green*, 3.

12. Caminero-Santangelo, *Different Shades of Green*, 1.

13. Caminero-Santangelo, *Different Shades of Green*, 2.

14. Nixon, *Slow Violence and Environmentalism*, 22–23; Stanley and Phillips, "South African Ecocriticism," 000.

15. Rigby, "Ecopoetics," 79.

16. Elder, *Imagining the Earth*; Rutella, *Reading and Writing*; Gifford, *Green Voices*; Scigaj, *Sustainable Poetry*; Bate, *Song of the Earth*; Quetchenbach, *Back from the Far Field*; Gilcrest, *Greening the Lyre*; Bryson, *West Side of Any Mountain*.

17. Bryson, *Ecopoetry*.

18. See, for example, Knickerbocker, *Ecopoetics*; Lidström, *Nature, Environment, Poetry*; Nolan, *Unnatural Ecopoetics*.

19. Ramazani, introduction to *Cambridge Companion to Postcolonial Poetry*, 1.

20. Bery opens his monograph with the observation that "the bulk of literary criticism in the field of Anglophone postcolonialism is devoted to fiction" (*Cultural Translation*, 1). Patke notes in his preface that "many books with 'postcolonial' in their titles ignore or marginalize the genre of poetry" (preface to *Postcolonial Poetry in English*, vii). Ramazani similarly states that "with some exceptions, poetry has been largely ignored in postcolonial studies" (introduction to *Cambridge Companion*, 5).

21. Ramazani, introduction to *Cambridge Companion*, 5.

22. Hume and Osborne, *Ecopoetics*.

23. Postmentier, *Cultivation and Catastrophe*.

24. Ergin, *Ecopoetics of Entanglement*.

25. Cooke, *Speaking the Earth*.

26. For other examples of postcolonial ecopoetics, see also Bristow's discussion of John Kinsella's *Jam Tree Gully* in *Anthropocene Lyric*, 19–46, and Lidström's discussion of Seamus Heaney's work in *Nature, Environment, Poetry*.

27. Guha and Martínez Alier, "Radical American Environmentalism," 96.

28. Martínez Alier, "Environmentalism of the Poor." This article develops the themes presented in his 2002 article of the same title.

29. Caminero-Santangelo, *Different Shades of Green*, 13

30. I have elected to treat *izibongo* as a collective noun taking the singular verb form (equivalent to "poetry").

31. Abram, *Spell of the Sensuous*; Ong, *Orality and Literacy*; Furniss and Gunner, *Power, Marginality*.

32. Ong, *Orality and Literacy*.

33. Opland, *Xhosa Poets*; Gérard, "Xhosa Literature."

34. Mgqwetho, *Nation's Bounty*.

35. Dickinson, "Lyric Ethics," 4.

36. Zwicky, "What Is Lyric Philosophy?"

37. The first quote is from Eagleton *How to Read a Poem*, 90; the latter are from DeLoughrey and Handley, *Postcolonial Ecologies*, 5.
38. Eagleton, *How to Read a Poem*, 51.
39. Opland, *Dassie and the Hunter*.
40. See Bringhurst, *Everywhere Being Is Dancing*.
41. Okunoye, "Postcolonial African Poetry," 31.
42. In taking this approach, I hope to minimize the situation that Gayatri Spivak criticizes: "The ventriloquism of the speaking subaltern is the left intellectual's stock-in-trade." *Critique of Postcolonial Reason*, 255.
43. Bate, *Song of the Earth*, 75–76.
44. Huggan and Tiffin, *Postcolonial Ecocriticism*, 29.

1 / A Brief History of IsiXhosa Literature

1. The terms "bushman" and "San" are derogatory. A resurgence in the use of "bushman" is part of a move by these groups to reclaim the term; however, "'San' is currently the most commonly used referent in academic, advocacy, and political circles" (Ellis, "Ons Is Boesmans," 123); see also Raper, "Ethnonyms"; "San, Bushmen or Basarwa." On early human habitation, see Mallick et al., "Simons Genome Diversity."
2. A. B. Smith, "Origins and Demise of the Khoikhoi."
3. Beleza, Gusmão, Amorim, Carracedo, and Salas, "Genetic Legacy."
4. Ross explains that their alienation from their territories and the mass slaughter of local fauna provoked vigorous Khoisan resistance, creating a vicious cycle of human and animal relationships. "Khoesan and Immigrants," 200.
5. Polanyi, *Great Transformation*; Lawrence, "Exporting Culture"; Cain and Hopkins "Gentlemanly Capitalism."
6. Niemandt and Greve, "Fragmentation Metric Proxies"; Corrigan, Kneen, Geldenhuys, and van Wyk, "Spatial Changes."
7. Opland, *Xhosa Oral Poetry*; Fry, "Siyamfenguza"; Lester, "Margins of Order." South Africa's various amaMfengu groups have a complex identity that derives from their historical roots as isiZulu-speaking refugees fleeing King Shaka's Mfecane.
8. Peires, *House of Phalo*; Dold and Cocks, *Voices from the Forest*.
9. Reader, *Africa*; Peires, *House of Phalo*.
10. Peires, *House of Phalo*, 2.
11. Opland, *Xhosa Oral Poetry*.
12. This approach to naming more accurately reflects how amaXhosa self-identify than do outdated terms such as Southern Nguni, while it also respects the fact that many unique lineages, dialects, and identities coexist within the amaXhosa nation.
13. Peires, *House of Phalo*.
14. Peires, *House of Phalo*; Opland, *Xhosa Oral Poetry*.
15. Opland, *Xhosa Oral Poetry*.
16. Maho, "Bantu Noun Classes." Note that the anthropological term "Bantu," here denoting a linguistic category and historical event, carries strong echoes of its derogatory use throughout the apartheid period. Both "Nguni" and "Bantu" are dated terms that are used in this technical context for want of an alternative. Although "Bantu" simply means "people" in isiXhosa, in other contexts the word carries highly charged political and emotional baggage. Given the misappropriation and derogatory usage of anthropo-

logical and linguistic referents by the apartheid regime, updated terms are long overdue. For details on Bantu languages and the Bantu expansion, see Rexová et al., "Cladistic Analysis"; Berniell-Lee et al., "Genetic and Demographic"; Beleza, Gusmão, Amorim, Carracedo, and Salas, "Genetic Legacy"; and Gunnink, Sands, Pakendorf, and Bostoen, "Prehistoric Language Contact."

17. Marten, "Bantu Languages"; Maho, "Bantu Noun Classes"; Nurse and Philippson, *Bantu Languages*.

18. Gunnink, Sands, Pakendorf, and Bostoen, "Prehistoric Language Contact."

19. Maho, "Bantu Noun Classes."

20. Bryant, *Xhosa for Second-Language Learners*.

21. Dold and Cocks, *Voices from the Forest*.

22. Kaschula, "Transitional Role" and *African Oral Literature*; O'Brien, *Against Normalization*; Opland, *Xhosa Poets*; Seddon, "Written Out, Writing In"; Sitas, "Peoples' Poetry in Natal"; Neser, *Stranger at Home*.

23. Finnegan, *Oral Literature in Africa*, 121.

24. Opland and McAllister, "Xhosa Imbongi as Trickster," 157–67.

25. Neser, *Stranger at Home*; Finnegan, *Oral Literature in Africa*.

26. Opland, *Xhosa Poets*, 89.

27. Yali-Manisi, *Imbongi Entsha*.

28. Kaschula, "Transitional Role."

29. Opland, *Xhosa Poets* and *Xhosa Oral Poetry*.

30. See, for example, Kaschula and Diop, "Political Processes"; Neser, *Stranger at Home*.

31. Mpupha, personal communication, Makhanda, South Africa, 2016.

32. Nxasana, "Mgqwetho's *The Nation's Bounty*."

33. For a more complete description of this history, see the excellent accounts in Peires, *House of Phalo*; Gérard, *Four African Literatures*; Opland, *Xhosa Poets* and *Xhosa Oral Poetry*.

34. Gérard, *Four African Literatures*, 33.

35. Mamdani, *Citizen and Subject*.

36. Beinart, Delius, and Trapido, *Putting the Plough to the Ground*; Yudelman, *Emergence of Modern South Africa*; Trapido, "Imperialism, Settler Identities"; Nattrass and Seekings, "Economy and Poverty."

37. Nattrass and Seekings, "Economy and Poverty."

38. Fanon, *Black Skin, White Masks*.

39. Rhodes, *Last Will and Testament*, 58.

40. Rhodes, *Last Will and Testament*, 58.

41. Rhodes, *Last Will and Testament*, 149.

42. Castle, "Oxford Will Keep Statue."

43. Luxemburg, *Accumulation of Capital*.

44. Posel presents a critique of this debate in her introduction to *Making of Apartheid*, 1–22.

45. Friedman, *Race, Class and Power*; Wolpe, "Capitalism and Cheap Labour"; Legassick, "South Africa."

46. Friedman, *Race, Class and Power*; Mamdani, *Citizen and Subject*.

47. Fraser, "Land Reform"; Ramutsindela, "Resilient Geographies."

48. Furniss and Gunner, *Power, Marginality*; Ngugi, *Decolonising the Mind*; Harlow, *Resistance Literature*.
49. Mlama, "Oral Art."
50. Kaschula, "Transitional Role," "Role of the Xhosa," and *African Oral Literature*; O'Brien, *Against Normalization*; Opland, *Xhosa Poets*; Seddon, "Written Out, Writing In"; Sitas, "Labour Poets" and "Moving Black Forest."
51. Kaschula, "Myth and Reality"; Opland, *Dassie and the Hunter*.
52. Gibson, "Promised Land," 53.
53. Gibson, "Promised Land," 53.
54. The first quote is from Ferguson, "Uses of Neoliberalism," 170; the second is from Harvey, *Brief History of Neoliberalism*, 2.
55. Mbembe, *Critique of Black Reason*, 3; Harvey, "Neoliberalism as Creative Destruction" and "Brief History of Neoliberalism."
56. Giroux, "Neoliberalism and the Death," 588.
57. Bond, *Elite Transition*, 1.
58. Peet, "Ideology, Discourse."
59. Marais, *South Africa Pushed*, 7.
60. Harvey, "Neoliberalism as Creative Destruction," 22, 23.
61. Monbiot, "Neoliberalism—The Ideology."
62. Giroux, "Neoliberalism and the Death."
63. McCarthy and Prudham, "Neoliberal Nature," 275.
64. Gibson, "What Happened to the 'Promised Land'?"
65. Hart, "Provocations of Neoliberalism."
66. See, for example, Bond, *Elite Transition*; Marais, *Limits to Change*.
67. Rodney, *How Europe Underdeveloped Africa*; Duffield and Hewitt, *Empire, Development*; Rist, *History of Development*. See the glossary for a discussion of the term "global North."
68. Soske, "Dissimulation of Race"; Ndikumana, "Integrated yet Marginalized."
69. Bond, *Looting Africa*; Schmidt, Mittelman, Cheru, and Trip, "Development in Africa."
70. Evans and Glenn, "TIA—This is Africa"; Baker, "Media Portrayals." Notable exceptions: Ryan Coogler's *Black Panther* is only the third US film to top $700 million in domestic box office sales. McNary, "Black Panther."
71. Yrjölä, "Invisible Violence."

2 / Verse, Violence, and the Migrant Labor System

1. The c. 1885 photograph by H. R. Gros appears online in Rod Kruger, "Northcliff Hill Then and Now," 9 March 2015, Heritage Portal website, accessed 6 December 2018, http://www.theheritageportal.co.za/article/northcliff-hill-then-and-now.
2. Churchill, *Men, Mines and Animals*, 58.
3. Worsfold, *South Africa*, 57.
4. Beinart, *Twentieth-Century South Africa*.
5. Remmington, "Solomon Plaatje's Decade"; Jordan, *Towards an African Literature*.
6. Opland, *Xhosa Oral Poetry* and *Xhosa Poets*, 223.
7. See, for example, Mqhayi, *Abantu Besizwe*; Gqoba, *Isizwe Esinembali*; Mgqwetho, *Nation's Bounty*; Solilo, *Umoya Wembongi*.

8. Opland, introduction to *Nation's Bounty*, xiv.
9. Opland, introduction to *Nation's Bounty*.
10. Mgqwetho, *Nation's Bounty*.
11. Opland, introduction to *Nation's Bounty*.
12. Opland, introduction to *Nation's Bounty*, xxvi.
13. Caminero-Santangelo, *Different Shades of Green*, 7–8.
14. See Hume's discussion of Claudia Rankine, "Toward an Antiracist Ecopoetics," 169–86.
15. Trapido, "Imperialism, Settler Identities," 89.
16. Rösner and van Schalkwyk, "Environmental Impact"; Weissenstein and Sinkala, "Soil Pollution with Heavy Metals."
17. Friedman, *Race, Class* and "Struggle within the Struggle."
18. Amin *Capitalism*; Biel, *New Imperialism*; N. Smith, *Uneven Development*.
19. Nxasana, "Mgqwetho's *The Nation's Bounty*."
20. Apartheid Museum, Johannesburg, 2015, https://www.apartheidmuseum.org.
21. Crush, Jeeves, and Yudelman, *South Africa's Labor Empire*, xiv.
22. Bourne, *Forced Labor*, 7.
23. Bourne, *Forced Labor*, 8.
24. Beinart, Delius, and Trapido, *Putting the Plough to the Ground*.
25. Fairweather, *Common Hunger*; Mbeki, *Peasants' Revolt*; Allen, *History of Black Mineworkers*; Crush, Jeeves, and Yudelman, *South Africa's Labor Empire*.
26. Fairweather, *Common Hunger*.
27. For a detailed account of this history see Mostert, *Frontiers*.
28. Peires *Dead Will Arise*, 12.
29. Mqhayi, *Abantu Besizwe*.
30. Peires, *Dead Will Arise*, 79.
31. Sources disagree on the number of animals killed. Peires cites Rev. John Brownlee's estimate of 400,000 slaughtered cattle, commenting that the number "is probably a conservative estimate of total cattle loss if we count in deaths from lungsickness as well" (*Dead Will Arise*, 319); in *Four African Literatures*, Gérard puts the number at 150,000 to 200,000.
32. Peires, *Dead Will Arise*; Davies, "Raising the Dead."
33. Peires, *Dead Will Arise*.
34. Apartheid Museum exhibit, Johannesburg, 2015.
35. Marais *Limits to Change*, 9.
36. Marais *Limits to Change*; Fairweather, *Common Hunger*.
37. Fairweather, *Common Hunger*.
38. Fairweather, *Common Hunger*; Mbeki, *Peasants' Revolt*.
39. Mbeki, *Peasants' Revolt*.
40. Amin, *Capitalism*, 58.
41. Fairweather, *A Common Hunger*.
42. Mbeki, *Peasants' Revolt*; Biko, *I Write What I Like*; Qabula, *Working Life*.
43. Krikler, "Women, Violence."
44. Lauretta Ngcobo describes how mothers in traditional amaXhosa society held a central cosmological role in which they enabled the passage of children from the spiritual to the human realm; see "African Motherhood."
45. Wilson, *Labour in Gold Mines*.

46. Allen, *History of Black Mineworkers*, 304.
47. Allen, *History of Black Mineworkers*.
48. Trapido, "Imperialism, Settler Identities," 89.
49. Allen, *History of Black Mineworkers*.
50. Thompson, *History of South Africa*, 174.
51. Thompson, *History of South Africa*; "African National Congress (ANC)," South African History Online, accessed 6 December 2018, http://www.sahistory.org.za/organisations/african-national-congress-anc.
52. See Allen, *History of Black Mineworkers*; and "Rand Rebellion," South African History Online, accessed 6 December 2018, https://www.sahistory.org.za/article/rand-rebellion-1922.
53. Crush, Jeeves, and Yudelman, *South Africa's Labor Empire*.
54. Thompson, *History of South Africa*; Jeeves *Migrant Labor*, 3.
55. See Opland, *"Abantu-Batho,"* for a detailed description of Mgqwetho's early career.
56. Iheka, *Naturalizing Africa*, 27.
57. Mgqwetho, *Nation's Bounty*, 122.
58. Mgqwetho, *Nation's Bounty*, 221.
59. See Caminero-Santangelo's commentary on indigenous pastoralism in *Different Shades of Green*.
60. Mgqwetho, *Nation's Bounty*, 52.
61. Mgqwetho, *Nation's Bounty*, 176.
62. Mgqwetho, *Nation's Bounty*, 213.
63. Fanon notes, "The country people are suspicious of the townsman. The latter dresses like a European; he speaks the European's language, works with him, sometimes even lives in the same district; so he is considered by the peasants as a turncoat who has betrayed everything that goes to make up the national heritage. . . . Here, we are not dealing with the old antagonism between town and country, it is the antagonism which exists between the native who is excluded from the advantages of colonialism and his counterpart who manages to turn colonial exploitation to his own account." *Wretched of the Earth*, 89.
64. Mgqwetho, *Nation's Bounty*, 2.
65. Mgqwetho, *Nation's Bounty*, 80.
66. Nxasana, "Mgqwetho's *The Nation's Bounty*."
67. Beinart, *Twentieth-Century South Africa*, 107.
68. Nxasana, "Mgqwetho's *The Nation's Bounty*," 15.
69. Ong, *Orality and Literacy*, 32.
70. Neser, *Stranger at Home*, 67.
71. "Shades," i.e., ancestral shades.
72. Nxasana, "Ambivalent Engagement," 76.
73. The quotes are from Nxasana, "Ambivalent Engagement," 76.
74. Hofmeyr, foreword to *Nation's Bounty*.
75. Nxasana, "Ambivalent Engagement," 76.
76. Mgqwetho, *Nation's Bounty*, 50.
77. Mgqwetho, *Nation's Bounty*, 208.
78. Mudimbe, *Invention of Africa*.
79. Mudimbe, *Invention of Africa*, 47.
80. Mudimbe, *Invention of Africa*, 52.

81. Opland, *Xhosa Poets*, 195.
82. Opland, *Xhosa Poets*.
83. "History of Abantu-Batho Newspaper, 1912–1931," South Africa History Online, accessed 6 December 2018, http://www.sahistory.org.za/topic/history-abantu-batho-newspaper-1912-1931.
84. "History of Abantu-Batho Newspaper."
85. Limb, "They Must Go."
86. "History of Abantu-Batho Newspaper."
87. Couzens 1985, quoted in Opland, *Xhosa Poets*, 252.
88. Opland, *Xhosa Poets*, 252–53.
89. Opland, "*Abantu-Batho.*"
90. Opland, "*Abantu-Batho.*"
91. Mgqwetho, *Nation's Bounty*.
92. Mkhonza, "Queen Labotsibeni," 143.
93. Mgqwtho, *Nation's Bounty*, 158.
94. Mgqwetho, *Nation's Bounty*, 170.
95. A more literal translation of *ukutshutshiswa* is "persecute" ("oppress" is *ukucinezela*).
96. Mgqwetho, *Nation's Bounty*, 230.
97. Mgqwetho, *Nation's Bounty*, 230.
98. Mies, *Patriarchy and Accumulation*.

3 / *Black Mamba* and the Durban/Rural Nexus

1. Sitas, "Alfred Temba Qabula"; Qabula, "FOSATU."
2. Malange, interview with the author, 14 January 2016.
3. Mamdani, *Citizen and Subject*; Friedman, *Race, Class*.
4. Mashige, "Mi Hlatshwayo and Temba Qabula."
5. Mamdani, *Citizen and Subject*, 219.
6. Fairweather, *Common Hunger*.
7. International Defense and Aid Fund, "South Africa: 'Resettlement.'"
8. Hill, *Bantustans*, 13.
9. International Defense and Aid Fund, "South Africa: 'Resettlement.'"
10. Biko, *I Write What I Like*, 91.
11. Biko, *I Write What I Like*, 91; Hill, *Bantustans*, 2.
12. Mamdani, *Citizen and Subject*, 102; Platzky and Walker, *Surplus People*.
13. Mamdani, *Citizen and Subject*, 102.
14. Fairweather, *Common Hunger*.
15. Fairweather, *Common Hunger*; Mbeki, *Peasants' Revolt*.
16. Beinart, Delius, and Trapido, *Putting the Plough to the Ground*; Mbeki, *Peasants' Revolt*.
17. Mbeki, *Peasants' Revolt*, 67.
18. Biel, *New Imperialism*; N. Smith, *Uneven Development*.
19. Nixon, *Slow Violence and Environmentalism*, 165.
20. Dubow, *Apartheid*; Mager and Mulaudzi, "Popular Responses to Apartheid," 369–408.
21. Mamdani, *Citizen and Subject*, 29.

22. Mamdani, *Citizen and Subject*; Marais, *Limits to Change*.
23. Marais, *Limits to Change*.
24. Bond, *Elite Transition*.
25. Mamdani, *Citizen and Subject*, 231, 275.
26. Sitas, "Moving Black Forest," 166.
27. Sitas, "Moving Black Forest," 166.
28. Marais, *Limits to Change*, 43.
29. Mamdani, *Citizen and Subject*, 234.
30. Beinart, *Twentieth-Century South Africa*; Lodge, "Resistance and Reform."
31. O'Brien, *Against Normalization*, 177.
32. O'Brien, *Against Normalization*, 177.
33. D. Brown, *Oral Literature and Performance*; Gunner, "Remaking the Warrior?"
34. Furniss and Gunner, *Power, Marginality*, 227.
35. Malange, interview with the author, 14 January 2016.
36. Mahaye, "Life Cruel Beyond Belief."
37. Kaschula, *Bones of the Ancestors*.
38. Lodge, "Resistance and Reform"; Malange, interview with the author, 14 January 2016.
39. Malange, interview with the author, 14 January 2016.
40. See, for example, Mashige, "Mi Hlatshwayo and Temba Qabula" and "Oral Performance"; D. Brown, *Oral Literature and Performance*; Kaschula, *Bones of the Ancestors*; Sitas, "Alfred Temba Qabula."
41. Sitas, "Moving Black Forest."
42. Kaschula, "Transitional Role," 145.
43. O'Brien, *Against Normalization*, 190.
44. Qabula, *Working Life*.
45. Qabula, *Working Life*, 13–18.
46. Qabula, *Working Life*, 25.
47. Qabula, *Working Life*.
48. Sitas, "Moving Black Forest."
49. Dold and Cocks, *Voices from the Forest*, 11.
50. Quoted in Dold and Cocks, *Voices from the Forest*, 12.
51. Dold and Cocks, *Voices from the Forest*, 12.
52. Qabula discusses this in his autobiography, *Working Life*.
53. Dold and Cocks, *Voices from the Forest*.
54. Dold and Cocks, *Voices from the Forest*, 15.
55. Qabula, Hlatshwayo, and Malange, *Black Mamba Rising*, 21.
56. Qabula, Hlatshwayo, and Malange, *Black Mamba Rising*, 15.
57. Sitas, "Moving Black Forest," 171.
58. Mashige, "Oral Performance," 23.
59. Malange, interview with the author, 14 January 2016.
60. Qabula, *Working Life*, 83.
61. Harvey, "Body as an Accumulation Strategy," 401, 404.
62. Harvey, "Body as an Accumulation Strategy."
63. Qabula, *Working Life*, 67.
64. Qabula, *Working Life*, 78.

65. Qabula, *Working Life*, 109.
66. Nixon, *Slow Violence and Environmentalism*, 104. Derek Attridge explains, "Literature does make something happen in the material sense, not just the passive expression/reflection of modes of production and material conditions." He specifies, "I'm a different person from what I would have been had I never picked up a book or attended a play. A society in which art has flourished is not the same as one in which it has been stifled. But since these literary effects arise from a multiplicity of singular experiences and the changes they produce may not be registered consciously, it's impossible to predict or accurately chart them. And it's important to register that they may be changes for the bad as well as for the good, since the openness to alterity that I'm suggesting lies at the heart of both artistic production and artistic reception means that there is no possibility of knowing in advance what one is opening oneself to." *Work of Literature*, 7.
67. Mahaye, "Life Cruel Beyond Belief," 4.
68. Evill and Kromberg, *Izinsingizi*, 6.
69. Van Dyk and Brown, "Ari Sitas."
70. Van Dyk and Brown, "Ari Sitas."
71. Van Dyk and Brown, "Ari Sitas."
72. Cooper, *To Lay These Secrets Open*, 146, 153.
73. Abrahams and Asvat, "Poetry Is Difficult," 16; see also Cronin, "Poetry: Élitist Pastime."
74. Gordimer, "Who Writes?," 36.
75. Abrahams and Asvat, "Poetry Is Difficult," 16.
76. Abrahams and Asvat, "Poetry Is Difficult."
77. Sitas, "Qabula: Working Class Poet," 25.
78. The "Thesis Tape," recorded in Makhanda, South Africa, n.d., courtesy of Russell Kaschula.
79. Kaschula presents this juxtaposition in "Transitional Role."
80. Kaschula, "Transitional Role."
81. Eagleton, *How to Read Literature*, 3 (emphasis in original).
82. "Nise Bulelwa Malange," KZN Literary Tourism website, accessed 6 December 2018, http://literarytourism.co.za/index.php?option=com_content&view=article&id=502:nise-bulelwa-malange&catid=13:authors&Itemid=28.
83. Malange, "Breaking the Silence."
84. Marismulu, "Labour and South African Literature," 264.
85. Evill and Kromberg, *Izinsingizi*, 18–19.
86. Marismulu, "Labor and South African Literature," 265.
87. Quoted in O'Brien, *Against Normalization*, 183.
88. Quoted in Marismulu "Labor and South African Literature," 264.
89. Issue 1, no. 2 of *Writers' Notebook* includes the "Focus on Women" and Mahaye, "Life Cruel Beyond Belief." O'Brien also discusses the imbalance in *Against Normalization*.
90. O'Brien, *Against Normalization*.
91. Qabula, Hlatshwayo, and Malange, *Black Mamba*, 59–60.
92. "Bundu" is the bush.
93. CTA is the acronym for Cape Town Area.
94. Cowdung is used for polishing the floors of rondavel houses.
95. "Samp" is corn grits.

96. Soweto is the syllabic abbreviation of South Western Townships, the site of a mass uprising in 1976 that was met with the murderous violence Malange describes here. "Panga" is a type of machete. Evill and Kromberg, *Izinsingizi*, 14–17.
97. Malange, "Breaking the Silence," 12.
98. Malange, "Let Women Be Heard," 20.
99. Malange, "Let Women be Heard."
100. Malange, "Let Women be Heard," 20.
101. Malange, interview with the author, 14 January 2016.
102. Sitas, "Alfred Temba Qabula," 172.
103. Qabula, *Working Life*, 7.
104. Sitas, "Alfred Temba Qabula," 172–73, translated from the isiXhosa by Harold Nxasana.

4 / Versions of Silence

1. Elbra, "Forgotten Resource Curse."
2. "Impimpis" are black police informants.
3. Qabula, Hlatshwayo, and Malange, *Black Mamba*, 12.
4. Bruchhausen, "Understanding Marikana."
5. Alexander, "Marikana, Turning Point."
6. Alexander, "Marikana, Turning Point"; Bruchhausen, "Understanding Marikana"; Desai, "Miners Shot Down."
7. Fanon, *Wretched of the Earth*.
8. A. Desai, *We Are the Poors*, 9.
9. Gibson, "What Happened to the 'Promised Land'?"; Hart, "Provocations of Neoliberalism"; J. Brown, *South Africa's Insurgent Citizens*.
10. A. Desai, *We Are the Poors*.
11. Gibson, *Fanonian Practices*.
12. Gibson, *Fanonian Practices*.
13. See Qabula, *Working Life*, as an example.
14. Neser, *Stranger at Home*.
15. Kaschula, "Role of the Oral Poet"; Kaschula and Diop, "Political Processes and the Imbongi"; Van Dyk and Brown, "Ari Sitas"; Gunner, *Remaking the Warrior?*; Cronin, "Rine of Terror"; Mashige, "Oral Performance."
16. Mandela, *Long Walk*, 36.
17. Mandela, *Long Walk*, 36.
18. On Biko, see Biel, *New Imperialism*; on the rise of black print culture, see Lodge, "Resistance and Reform"; on the influence of iimbongi, see Opland, *Dassie and the Hunter* and *Xhosa Poets*.
19. Mandela, "Address to Rally in Durban."
20. Lodge, "Resistance and Reform."
21. Mangosuthu Buthelezi founded the IFP in 1975 and was chief minister of the KwaZulu Bantustan until 1994. P. W. Botha was a prime minister (1978–84) and state president (1984–89) of South Africa. He was instrumental in the development of apartheid and a staunch opponent of black majority rule. Malange, personal communication with the author, 2016.
22. Marais, *Limits to Change*, 74.
23. Gumede and Dikeni, *Poverty of Ideas*, 2.

24. Gumede, "Building a Democratic Political Culture," in *The Poverty of Ideas: South African Democracy and the Retreat of Intellectuals*, ed. William Gumede and Leslie Dikeni (Auckland Park, SA: Jacana, 2009), 14–17.

25. Malange, interview with the author, 14 January 2016.

26. Peet, "Ideology, Discourse."

27. Kaschula and Diop, "Political Processes and the Imbongi."

28. Malange, interview with the author, 14 January 2016.

29. Dyakala, interview with the author, 23 February 2016. In this and subsequent chapters, I have quoted extensively from my interviews with both iimbongi and their audiences, since the opinions and ideas of these research participants, as voiced in their own words, are such a valuable resource for understanding iimbongi and their work. In most cases the lengthy quotations included here could not have been paraphrased or shortened without compromising the context, voice, and thread of thought that are central to the participants' ideas.

30. Sixham, interview with the author, 5 January 2016 (emphasis added); translated from isiXhosa by Dumisa Mpupha.

31. Finnegan, *Oral Literature in Africa*, 84.

32. Ntshuntsha, interview with the author, 20 December 2015.

33. Mkiva, "Poet of Africa."

34. D'Abdon, "Commercialization of Celebratory Poetry."

35. D'Abdon, "Commercialization of Celebratory Poetry," 315.

36. D'Abdon, "Commercialization of Celebratory Poetry," 318.

37. Mkiva, "Poet of Africa."

38. Mkiva, interview with the author, 28 December 2015.

39. For example, see Hill, "Decline of Academic Bilingualism."

40. Brown and Kiguli, "People Feel No Event Is Complete," 132–47, quote on 144.

41. Mkiva, "Poet of Africa."

42. Rawlings, "Rawlings Receives Another Award."

43. Rawlings, "Rawlings Receives Another Award."

44. "Jerry J. Rawlings: Head of State, Ghana." *Encyclopedia Britannica*, accessed 8 December 2018, https://www.britannica.com/biography/Jerry-J-Rawlings.

45. Kaschula, "Remembering Mandela."

46. Kaschula, "Remembering Mandela."

47. Matthews, "Democracy, Dissidence," 57.

48. For an index of these speeches, see "State of the Nation Address," South African Government website, accessed 8 December 2018, http://www.gov.za/state-nation-address.

49. "President Jacob Zuma: State of the Nation Address, 2016," South African Government website, accessed 11 December 2018, https://www.gov.za/speeches/president-jacob-zuma-state-nation-address-2016-11-feb-2016-0000.

50. An assegai is a traditional spear.

51. Martin Legassick, "Jacob Zuma," *Britannica Academic*, https://academic.eb.com.

52. Kavanagh and Riches, "Zuma, Jacob Gedleyihlekisa."

53. De Wet, "Timeline: Spy Tapes Saga."

54. Legassick, "Jacob Zuma."

55. Gqirana, "DA's Bid Fails"; Powell, "Charges Misuse of SA Law"; Haden, "Cape Town Turns Out."

56. Finnegan, *Oral Literature in Africa*, 85.
57. Msholozi is Zuma's clan name.
58. Tabane, "Zuma No Fool"; Suttner, "Zuma Rape Trial"; Vetten, "Losing the Plot"; Ferreira, "Judgement in Spy Tapes"; Southall, "Briefing: Family and Favour"; Pather, de Wet, Clifford-Holmes, and Evans, "Zuma's Nkandla"; Elgot, "Zuma Breached Constitution."
59. Kaschula and Diop, "Political Processes and the Imbongi," 13.
60. Anonymous interview with author, Makhanda, 5 March 2016.
61. Ngcobo, "African Motherhood."
62. Jewkes and Abrahams, "Epidemiology of Rape."
63. Davis, *Women, Culture, and Politics*, 37.
64. D. Smith, "Zuma the Chameleon"; Palitza, "Culture (Ab)Used."
65. Buiten and Naidoo, "Framing the Problem of Rape."
66. Vetten, "Losing the Plot."
67. Buiten and Naidoo, "Framing the Problem of Rape."
68. Machisa, Jewkes, Morna, and Rama, "War at Home."
69. "Factsheet: South Africa's 2015/16 Crime Statistics," Africa Check website, accessed 8 December 2018, https://africacheck.org/factsheets/factsheet-south-africas-201516-crime-statistics.
70. Jewkes and Abrahams, "Epidemiology of Rape."
71. Malange, interview with the author, 14 January 2016.
72. Nicholson, "Anti-Rape Protestors."
73. Nicholson, "Anti-Rape Protestors."
74. Mkiva, interview with the author, 28 December 2015.

5 / Literature, Iimbongi, and Ideologies of Development

1. See, for example, Demombynes and Özler, "Crime and Local Inequality"; Gibson, "What Happened to the 'Promised Land'?"; Gibson, *Fanonian Practices*; Hart, "Provocations of Neoliberalism"; Bond, *Elite Transition*; Desai, *We Are the Poors*; Bond and Ruiters, "Uneven Development and Scale Politics."
2. Kruger, "Crime and the Physical Environment."
3. Richardson et al., "Forced Removals Embodied as Tuberculosis."
4. Short and Hammett, "Informal Settlement."
5. Evans, "Resettlement"; Fairweather, *Common Hunger*; Friedman, *Race, Class and Power*.
6. Richardson et al., "Forced Removals"; Short and Hammett, "Housing and Health"; Jewkes and Abrahams, "Epidemiology of Rape"; and Buiten and Naidoo, "Framing the Problem of Rape."
7. Biko, *I Write What I Like*; Mashige, "Mi Hlatshwayo and Temba Qabula"; Sitas, "Moving Black Forest."
8. "Human Development Reports," United Nations Development Programme website, accessed 8 December 2018, http://hdr.undp.org/en.
9. "Human Development Reports"; Posel, "Adult Literacy Rates."
10. Mallinson, "Thando Mgqolozana."
11. Memmi, *Colonizer and the Colonized*; Ngugi, *Decolonising the Mind*.
12. Seddon, "Written Out, Writing In"; D. Brown, *Voicing the Text*.
13. For example, McGiffin, "Iimbongi of the Resistance" and "Yim'uthi Gomololo."

14. Eagleton, *How to Read a Poem*, 90; Attridge, *Work of Literature*; Carper and Attridge, *Meter and Meaning*.

15. For example, see Barford, "Emotional Responses"; Jasper, "Emotions and Social Movements"; and Hercus, "Identity, Emotion."

16. Barford, "Emotional Responses," 25.

17. Neser, *Stranger at Home*, 14.

18. Ong, *Orality and Literacy*; Furniss and Gunner, *Power, Marginality*; Abram, *Spell of the Sensuous*.

19. See, for example, Kaschula, *Bones of the Ancestors*; Opland, *Dassie and the Hunter*.

20. Furniss and Gunner, *Power, Marginality*.

21. Neser, *Stranger at Home*, 14.

22. Tsheola, "Basic Needs"; Marais, *South Africa Pushed to the Limit*.

23. "Sustainable Development Agenda," United Nations website, accessed 8 December 2018, https://www.un.org/sustainabledevelopment/development-agenda/.

24. "Sustainable Development Agenda."

25. Rist, *History of Development*, viii.

26. Kapoor, *Postcolonial Politics of Development*, 19.

27. Harvey, "Neoliberalism as Creative Destruction"; Selwyn, *Global Development Crisis*; N. Smith, *Uneven Development*; Biel, *New Imperialism*.

28. Rist, *History of Development*, 258.

29. Kapoor, "Queer Third World"; see also Escobar, *Encountering Development*.

30. Huggan and Tiffin, *Postcolonial Ecocriticism*, 35.

31. See, for example, Kepe and Ntsebeza, *Rural Resistance*; Mbeki, *Peasants' Revolt*; Beinart, "Beyond Homelands."

32. Opland, "Structural Patterns," *Xhosa Oral Poetry*, and *Xhosa Poets*; Kaschula "Role of the Xhosa Oral Poet"; d'Abdon, "Commercialization of Celebratory Poetry"; and Sitas "Moving Black Forest."

33. For example, Hirst, "Dreams and Medicines"; Booi and Edwards, "Becoming a Xhosa Healer"; Mabona, *Diviners and Prophets*.

34. Opland, *Xhosa Oral Poetry*, 270

35. The name Fundiswa is a pseudonym. The letter Q represents a palatal click—a strong, alliterative consonant. *Usiba* means pen (literally, "feather"); *yosiba* translates to "of the pen."

36. See, for example, Kaschula and Mostert, "Analyzing, Digitizing, and Technologizing"; Opland, *Dassie and the Hunter*.

37. Mpupha, personal communication, Makhanda, South Africa, 2016.

38. Opland *Xhosa Oral Poetry*, 126, 130.

39. For example, Kaschula and Mostert, "Analyzing, Digitizing, and Technologizing"; Opland, *Dassie and the Hunter*.

40. Ntshuntsha, interview with the author, 20 December 2015.

41. Mpupha, personal communication, Makhanda, South Africa, 2016.

42. Ntshuntsha, interview with the author, 20 December 2015.

43. Mabona, *Diviners and Prophets*, 327.

44. Booi and Edwards, "Becoming a Xhosa Healer"; Hirst, "Dreams and Medicines."

45. Discussed in detail in Mabona, *Diviners and Prophets*, 322–28.

46. Mabona, *Diviners and Prophets*, 379.

47. Mabona explains the importance of guidance for an apprentice healer: "Both the master diviner and the people attending the novice have an insightful understanding of the ukuthwasa phenomenon and of how the novice must be shepherded along her/his difficult path." *Diviners and Prophets*, 335.
48. Booi and Edwards, "Becoming a Xhosa Healer."
49. Mabona, *Diviners and Prophets*, 314–15.
50. Ntshuntsha, interview with the author, 20 December 2015.
51. Opland, *Xhosa Oral Poetry*, 127; Ainslie and Kepe, "Understanding the Resurgence."
52. Khawuta was the father of the ancestor Gcaleka, for whom an amaXhosa kingdom is named.
53. Sarhili was the son of Hintsa and a major figure in amaXhosa history.
54. uQamata is the amaXhosa god (whereas the Christian god is uThixo).
55. Opland, *Xhosa Oral Poetry*, 264.
56. For example, Fraser, "Land Reform"; Ainslie and Kepe, "Understanding and Resurgence."
57. Dyakala, interview with the author, 23 February 2016.
58. Ntshuntsha, interview with the author, 20 December 2015.
59. A. Desai, *We Are the Poors*; Wood and Jewkes, "'Dangerous' Love."
60. For a discussion on censorship in contemporary South Africa, see Gumede and Dikeni, *Poverty of Ideas*.
61. Ndileka is a pseudonym.
62. Opland, *Xhosa Poets*; Kaschula, "Oppression of IsiXhosa Literature."
63. Ngugi, *Decolonising the Mind*, 4.
64. Kaschula, "Oppression of isiXhosa Literature," 117–18.
65. Sosibo, "Thando Mgqolozana."
66. Memmi, *Colonizer and Colonized*, 107.
67. Ntshuntsha, interview with the author, 20 December 2015.
68. "Uthini's this?" translates as "What's this?"
69. Dyakala, interview with the author, 23 February 2016.
70. Sixham, interview with the author, 5 January 2015.
71. Lewis, Rodgers, and Woolcock, "Fiction of Development."
72. Nyamnjoh, "Fiction and Reality"; Sylvester, "Development Poetics"; Lewis, Rodgers, and Woolcock, "Fiction of Development."

6 / Land Expropriation without Compensation and the Vocal Dispossessed

1. Walker, "Redistributive Land Reform."
2. Bourdreaux, "Land Reform as Social Justice."
3. Walker and Cousins, introduction to *Land Divided, Land Restored*.
4. Bourdreaux, "Land Reform as Social Justice." Bourdreaux notes that although the process took longer than originally hoped (with several thousand outstanding claims as of 2009) it was largely successful.
5. Thurner, "Land Reform and Hunger"; Cousins, "Small-Scale Farmers" and "Reforming Communal Land Tenure."
6. Jager, "Land Reform"; Kepe, "Unjustified Optimism"; Kepe, Lewison, Ramasra, and Butt, "Elusive 'Fair Deal'"; Hall and Kepe, "Elite Capture and State Neglect," 122.

7. Kepe, Lewison, Ramasra, and Butt, "Elusive 'Fair Deal'"; Hall and Kepe, "Elite Capture"; Bourdreaux, "Land Reform as Social Justice."
8. See, for example, Kepe, Lewison, Ramasra, and Butt, "Elusive 'Fair Deal'"; Fay, "Keeping Land"; Giroux, "Neoliberalism and the Death."
9. See, for example, Kepe, Lewison, Ramasra, and Butt, "Elusive 'Fair Deal.'"
10. Aliber, "Unravelling 'Willing Buyer.'"
11. Aliber, "Unravelling 'Willing Buyer.'"
12. Kepe, Lewison, Ramasra, and Butt, "Elusive 'Fair Deal,'" 372.
13. Hall and Kepe, "Elite Capture," 123.
14. Hall and Kepe, "Elite Capture," 126.
15. Boudreaux, "Land Reform as Social Justice."
16. Lowman, "Cyril Ramaphosa"; "President Cyril Ramaphosa: 2018 State of the Nation Address," South African government website, https://www.gov.za/speeches/president-cyril-ramaphosa-2018-state-nation-address-16-feb-2018-0000.
17. EFF South Africa (@EFFSouthAfrca_), "On Tuesday, the CIC @Julius_S_Malema will lead a Motion on Expropriation of Land without Compensation for Equal Redistribution at 14h00. Here is the Proposed Resolution," Twitter, 25 February 2018, 2:14 a.m.
18. Parliament of the Republic of South Africa, "NCOP Approves Recommendation to Amend Section 25 of Constitution," 5 December 2018, accessed 4 January 2019, https://www.parliament.gov.za/press-releases/ncop-approves-recommendation-amend-section-25-constitution.
19. "About Us," EFF website, accessed 4 January 2019, https://www.effonline.org/about-us.
20. Hall and Kepe, "Elite Capture," 129.
21. Fraser, "Land Reform"; Mathis, "Politics of Land Reform."
22. Constitution of the Republic of South Africa, Government of South Africa website, accessed 8 December 2018, http://www.gov.za/documents/constitution/constitution-republic-south-africa-1996-1.
23. Ntsebeza, *Democracy Compromised*; Fraser, "Land Reform"; Mnwana, "Why Giving."
24. Mnwana, "Why Giving."
25. Mamdami, *Citizen and Subject*.
26. Nongqawuse was the prophetess who called for the slaughter of all the cattle of the amaXhosa people. The prophecy deeply divided the nation and brought widespread famine and the capitulation of the amaXhosa to British colonialists. Note that here Mkiva espouses the theory that the British, under Sir George Grey, were ultimately responsible for the incident, by way of their influence over the prophetess or others in her immediate circles. Mkiva, interview with the author, 28 December 2015.
27. Mkiva, interview with the author, 28 December 2015.
28. Opland, *Dassie and the Hunter*, 23–24.
29. *AmaXhosa Kingdom*, exhibit at the Albany Museum, Makhanda, 2016.
30. Ainslie and Kepe, "Understanding the Resurgence."
31. Ainslie and Kepe, "Understanding the Resurgence," 23.
32. Alexander, "Marikana, Turning Point"; Elgot, "Zuma Breached Constitution"; Pather, de Wet, Clifford-Holmes, and Evans, "Zuma's Nkandla."
33. Mamdani, *Citizen and Subject*, 41.
34. Peires, *House of Phalo*, 28.
35. Brown and Kiguli, "No Event Is Complete," 138; Opland, *Xhosa Oral Poetry*

36. Brown and Kiguli, "No Event Is Complete."
37. Mkiva, interview with the author, 28 December 2015.
38. Opland, *Dassie and the Hunter*, 50 (emphasis added).
39. Ntshuntsha, interview with the author, 20 December 2015.
40. Yali-Manisi, *Imbongi Entsha*, 275.
41. Opland, *Dassie and the Hunter*, 19.
42. Opland, *Dassie and the Hunter*, 20, 22.
43. Opland, "Bones of Mfanta."
44. Opland, "Bones of Mfanta."
45. Opland, introduction to *Imbongi Entsha*, 2.
46. Opland, *Dassie and the Hunter*, 25.
47. Yali-Manisi, *Imbongi Entsha*, 234–56.
48. Opland, *Dassie and the Hunter*.
49. An ancestor whose name translates as "News" and whose praise name, Ndab'enyamakazi, means "News of Game."
50. The abaThembu are an isiXhosa-speaking nation descended from an ancestor named Thembu. The Mzimvubu and Mthatha Rivers are among the most important of the Eastern Cape province; the Dedesi River is a tributary of the Mzimvubu.
51. Opland, "Bones of Mfanta," 48 (emphasis in original).
52. Opland, "Bones of Mfanta."
53. *AmaXhosa Kingdom*, exhibit at the Albany Museum, Makhanda, 2016.
54. Peires, *House of Phalo*.
55. *AmaXhosa Kingdom*, exhibit at the Albany Museum, Makhanda, 2016.
56. The entire address is included in appendix C in this volume.
57. Poswayo, interview with the author, 4 December 2016. The quotes in the ensuing discussion of Poswayo's work are from the same interview.
58. Shange, "King Dalindyebo Hands Himself Over."
59. In other words, the son of a warrior, a brave person.
60. Peires *House of Phalo*, 2.
61. "Deep pools" are mentioned by the imbongi because it is known that there are people dwelling at the bottom of the river pits (a site of initiation for spiritual people).
62. The father of the ancestor Gcaleka.
63. Sarhili was the son of Hintsa and a major figure in amaXhosa history.
64. S. E. K. Mqhayi was an imbongi, historian, and major literary figure of the early twentieth-century South Africa.
65. Opland, *Dassie and the Hunter*.
66. Jordan, *Towards an African Literature*.
67. "Mntan'omhle" means, literally, "beautiful child."
68. "MaLawundini" is someone without a tradition or custom who wants to fit in somewhere. The term is sometimes offensive but is not meant to be so in this case. It could mean that the king may feel like amalawundini because the imbongi is going to say things that he may not understand.
69. Cattle colors are often particular to clan.
70. In this case, the town of Qamata (iQamata) rather than the god (uQamata).
71. The family includes Kaiser Daliwonga Mathanzima, who was installed as chief of the Transkei by the apartheid government.
72. These cattle were the lobola (bridewealth) for the girl from Chotho.

73. Peires, *House of Phalo*.
74. Opland, *Xhosa Oral Poetry*.
75. Peires, *House of Phalo*, 9.
76. Quoted in Opland, *Xhosa Oral Poetry*, 6.
77. Opland, *Xhosa Oral Poetry*; Poland, Hammond-Tooke, and Voigt, *Abundant Herds*.
78. "Amaqonya" are large, green-and-silver caterpillars of the emperor moth that feed on the mimosa thorn-bushes. The caterpillars, which can grow to ten centimeters, were traditionally an important food source for people and birds alike. As Kropf describes, "The boys kill it by inverting the head and thus pressing out the intestines; they then roast and eat the remainder" (Kropf, *Xhosa-English Dictionary*, 359). Although a different species, amaqonya are analogous to the more familiar mopane worms, a major protein source throughout southeast Africa.
79. The mispronunciation in the isiXhosa (the correct word is *uyakuqhaisa*) is for alliterative effect, echoing the smoother aspirated *H*s of *hahane* and *kuhluthi* rather than interrupting these mellifluous sounds with a hard, palatal click.
80. Peires, *House of Phalo*, 30.
81. See Fay, "Keeping Land."
82. Peires, *House of Phalo*, 54.
83. Peires, *House of Phalo*.
84. Pan SLB, "Land Expropriation without Compensation Is SA Word of the Year 2018," PanSLB website, accessed 4 January 2019, http://www.pansalb.org/SA%20word%20of%20the%20year%202018.html.
85. Hall and Kepe, "Elite Capture."

Conclusion

1. Ashcroft, Griffiths, and Tiffin, *Postcolonial Studies*, 73.
2. Kaschula, "Imbongi in Profile."
3. Kaschula and Diop, "Political Processes," 13 (emphasis added).

Appendix B

1. Meaning "he points with his long finger."

Appendix C

1. "Son of a bull," i.e., the son of a warrior, a brave person.
2. Xolilizwe was Zwelonke's father.
3. Pools are mentioned by the imbongi because it is known that there are people dwelling at the bottom of the river pits (a site of initiation for spiritual people).
4. "Look across" to the ancestral realm.
5. The root -*kazi* is a feminine suffix; thus "lamb of the Thembu woman."
6. The phrase "*Yim'uthi gomololo*" urges that one should not be shaken by any possible opposition and instead must be brave at all costs, even to the extent of giving up one's life. The various translations could include "stand firm," "be strong," or "be courageous."
7. The father of the ancestor Gcaleka.
8. Sarhili was the son of Hintsa and a major figure in amaXhosa history.
9. uQamata is the amaXhosa god (whereas the Christian god is uThixo).
10. Mqhayi was an imbongi, a historian, and a major literary figure of the early twentieth-century South Africa.

11. "Mntan'omhle" means, literally, "beautiful child."
12. Cattle colors are often particular to clans.
13. "Malawundini" indicates someone without a tradition or custom who wants to fit in somewhere. The term is sometimes offensive but is not meant to be so in this case. It could mean that the king may feel like a malawundini because the imbongi is going to say things that he may not understand.
14. In this case, the town of Qamata (iQamata) rather than the god (uQamata).
15. The family includes Kaiser Daliwonga Mathanzima, who was installed as chief of the Transkei by the apartheid government.
16. The cattle were the lobola (bride price) for the girl from Chotho.
17. "Umwangalala" refers to dispersed objects generally. It is interesting to note the correspondence between money and cattle in Kropf's definition: "Grain thrashed out and lying spread on the floor; small money scattered about, cattle dispersed" (*Xhosa-English Dictionary*, 461). The word also captures the fact that the coins are abundant, befitting to the recipient's status.
18. Mkhonkotho is a mountain near Centane.
19. "Amaqonya" are large, green-and-silver caterpillars of the emperor moth that feed on the mimosa thorn-bushes. The caterpillars, which can grow to ten centimeters, were traditionally an important food source for people and birds alike. As Kropf describes, "The boys kill it by inverting the head and thus pressing out the intestines; they then roast and eat the remainder" (Kropf, *Xhosa-English Dictionary*, 359). Although a different species, amaqonya are analogous to the more familiar mopane worms, a major protein source throughout southeast Africa.
20. The mispronunciation in the isiXhosa (the correct word is *uyakuqhaisa*) is for alliterative effect, echoing the smoother aspirated *H*s of "hahane" and "kuhluthi" rather than interrupting these mellifluous sounds with a hard, palatal click.
21. This stanza contains a veiled warning that the king should remain vigilant, as many people are jealous of his position and may seek to undermine, dethrone, or even kill him.
22. In other words, there is abundant, rich food, reflecting the kingdom's wealth.
23. Xolilizwe was Zwelonke's father.
24. This points out that many people fought and died so that the king could be comfortable in his position.
25. This refers to the "Right Hand" wife, whose son is the heir apparent.
26. This line illustrates the value of polygamy when these siblings are loyal and the potential danger when they are not. These brothers may plot against the king or his mother.
27. That is, his father and his father's brothers, who are also his fathers in amaXhosa tradition.
28. "Mncinci" means an uncle, specifically from the father's side.
29. An expression meaning that people will gossip negatively, preventing one from moving forward.
30. Note the flourish of crowd-pleasing alliteration as the poem reaches its conclusion.
31. "Kweewu" is a word with many possible meanings: We'll see what happens; Hope for the best; Who knows?
32. "Sheep eaters" indicates white people.

BIBLIOGRAPHY

Abrahams, Lionel, and Farouk Asvat. "Poetry Is Difficult: That Is the Price We Pay for Depth." (Johannesburg) *Weekly Mail*, 3 April 1987, 16.
Abram, David. *The Spell of the Sensuous: Perception and Language in a More-Than-Human World*. New York: Vintage Books, 1997.
Ainslie, Andrew. "Harnessing the Ancestors: Mutuality, Uncertainty, and Ritual Practice in the Eastern Cape Province, South Africa." *Africa* 84, no. 4 (2014): 530–52.
Ainslie, Andrew, and Thembela Kepe. "Understanding the Resurgence of Traditional Authorities in Post-Apartheid South Africa." *Journal of Southern African Studies* 42, no. 1 (2016): 19–33.
Alexander, Peter. "Marikana, Turning Point in South African History." *Review of African Political Economy* 40, no. 138 (2013): 605–19.
Aliber, Michael. "Unravelling the 'Willing Buyer, Willing Seller' Question." In *Land Divided, Land Restored: Land Reform in South Africa for the Twenty-First Century*, edited by Ben Cousins and Cherryl Walker, 145–60. Auckland Park, SA: Jacana, 2015.
Allen, V. L. *The History of Black Mineworkers in South Africa*. Vol. 1, *The Techniques of Resistance, 1871–1948*. Keighley, UK: Moor Press, 1992.
Amin, Samir. *Capitalism in the Age of Globalization: The Management of Contemporary Society*. London: Zed Books, 1997.
Ashcroft, Bill, G. Griffiths, and Helen Tiffin. *Postcolonial Studies: The Key Concepts*. 3rd ed. Abingdon, UK: Routledge, 2013.
Attridge, Derek. *The Work of Literature*. Oxford: Oxford University Press, 2015.
Baker, Andy. "Media Portrayals of Africa Promote Paternalism." *Washington Post*, 5 March 2015.

Barford, Anna. "Emotional Responses to World Inequality." *Emotion, Space, and Society* 22 (2017): 25–35.
Bate, Jonathan. *The Song of the Earth*. Cambridge, MA: Harvard University Press, 2000.
Beinart, William. "Beyond 'Homelands': Some Ideas about the History of African Rural Areas in South Africa." *South African Historical Journal* 64, no.1 (2012): 5–21.
Beinart, William. *Twentieth-Century South Africa*. Oxford: Oxford University Press, 2001.
Beinart, William, Peter Delius, and Stanley Trapido. *Putting the Plough to the Ground: Accumulation and Dispossession in Rural South Africa, 1850–1930*. Johannesburg: Ravan Press, 1986.
Beleza, Sandra, Leonor Gusmão, António Amorim, Angel Carracedo, and Antonio Salas. "The Genetic Legacy of Western Bantu Migrations." *Human Genetics* 117 (2005): 366–75.
Berniell-Lee, Gemma, et al. "Genetic and Demographic Implications of the Bantu Expansion: Insights from Human Paternal Lineages." *Molecular Biology and Evolution* 26, no. 7 (2009): 1581–89.
Bery, Ashok. *Cultural Translation and Postcolonial Poetry*. New York: Palgrave Macmillan, 2007.
Biel, Robert. *The New Imperialism: Crisis and Contradictions in North-South Relations*. London: Zed Books, 2000.
Biko, Steve. *I Write What I Like: Selected Writings*. Johannesburg: Picador Africa, 2004.
Biyela, Sr. N. Gloria Irenata. "Securing Women and Children at King Shaka's Well-Resourced and Formidable Refuge, Nkandla Forest." *Alternation* 14, no. 2 (2007): 158–87.
Bond, Patrick. *Elite Transition: From Apartheid to Neoliberalism in South Africa*. London: Pluto Press, 2000.
Bond, Patrick. *Looting Africa: The Economics of Exploitation*. London: Zed Books, 2006.
Bond, Patrick, and Greg Ruiters. "Uneven Development and Scale Politics in Southern Africa: What We Learn from Neil Smith." *Antipode* 49, no. 1 (2017): 171–89.
Booi, Beauty N., and David J. A. Edwards. "Becoming a Xhosa Healer: Nomzi's Story." *Indo-Pacific Journal of Phenomenology* 14, no. 2 (2015): 1–12.
Bourdreaux, Karol. "Land Reform as Social Justice: The Case of South Africa." *Economic Affairs* 30, no. 1 (2010): 13–20.
Bourne, H. R. Fox. *Forced Labour in British South Africa: Notes on the Condition and Prospects of South African Natives under British Control*. London: P. S. King & Son, 1903.
Bringhurst, Robert. *Everywhere Being Is Dancing: Twenty Pieces of Thinking*. Kentville, NS: Gaspereau Press, 2007.

Bringhurst, Robert. *A Story as Sharp as a Knife: The Classical Haida Mythtellers and Their World* [in English and Haida]. Vancouver, BC: Douglas & McIntyre, 2011.
Bristow, Tom. *The Anthropocene Lyric: An Affective Geography of Poetry, Person, Place.* Houndmills, UK: Palgrave, 2018.
Brown, Duncan. *Oral Literature and Performance in Southern Africa.* Athens: Ohio University Press, 1999.
Brown, Duncan. *Voicing the Text: South African Oral Poetry and Performance.* Cape Town: Oxford University Press, 1998.
Brown, Duncan, and Susan Kiguli. "People Feel No Event Is Complete without a Poet." In *Selves in Question: Interviews on Southern African Auto/Biography*, edited by Judith Lütge Coullie, Stephan Meyer, Thengani Ngwenya, and Thomas Olver, 132–47. Honolulu: University of Hawai'i Press, 2006.
Brown, Julian. *South Africa's Insurgent Citizens: On Dissent and the Possibility of Politics.* London: Zed Books, 2015.
Bruchhausen, Sarah. "Understanding Marikana through the Mpondo Revolts." *Journal of Asian and African Studies* 50, no. 4 (2015): 412–26.
Bryant, Alexandra. *Xhosa for Second-Language Learners: Senior School and Beyond.* Self-published, 2007.
Bryson, J. Scott. *Ecopoetry: A Critical Introduction.* Salt Lake City: University of Utah Press, 2002.
Bryson, J. Scott. *The West Side of Any Mountain.* Iowa City: University of Iowa Press, 2005.
Buiten, D., and K. Naidoo. "Framing the Problem of Rape in South Africa: Gender, Race, Class and State Histories." *Current Sociology* 64, no. 4 (2016): 535–50.
Cain, P. J., and A. G. Hopkins. "Gentlemanly Capitalism and British Expansion Overseas: I. The Old Colonial System, 1688–1850." *Economic History Review* 39, no. 4 (1996): 501–25.
Caminero-Santangelo, Byron. *Different Shades of Green: African Literature, Environmental Justice, and Political Ecology.* Charlottesville: University of Virginia Press, 2014.
Carper, Thomas, and Derek Attridge. *Meter and Meaning: An Introduction to Rhythm in Poetry.* New York: Routledge, 2003.
Castle, Stephen. "Oxford University Will Keep Statue of Cecil Rhodes." *New York Times*, 29 January, 2016.
Churchill, Randolph S. *Men, Mines and Animals in South Africa.* London: S. Low, Marston & Co., 1895.
Clark, T. *The Cambridge Introduction to Literature and the Environment.* Cambridge: Cambridge University Press, 2011.
Cooke, Stuart. *Speaking the Earth's Languages: A Theory for Australian-Chilean Postcolonial Poetics.* Amsterdam: Rodopi, 2013.
Cooper, Brenda. *To Lay These Secrets Open: Evaluating African Literature.* Cape Town, SA: David Philip, 1992.

Corrigan, B. M., M. Kneen, C. J. Geldenhuys, and B. E. van Wyk. "Spatial Changes in Forest Cover on the Kwanibela Peninsula, St Lucia, South Africa, during the Period 1937 to 2008." *Southern Forests: A Journal of Forest Science* 72, no. 1 (2010): 47–55.

Cousins, Ben. "Reforming Communal Land Tenure in South Africa." *ESR Review: Economic and Social Rights in South Africa* 3, no. 3 (2002): 7–9.

Cousins, Ben. "Small-Scale Farmers Should Be at the Centre of Land Reform in South Africa." *The Conversation*, 16 April 2018, https://theconversation.com/small-scale-farmers-should-be-at-the-centre-of-land-reform-in-south-africa-94546.

Cousins, Ben, and Cherryl Walker, eds. *Land Divided, Land Restored: Land Reform in South Africa for the Twenty-First Century.* Auckland Park, SA: Jacana Media, 2015.

Cronin, Jeremy. "'Even under the Rine of Terror . . .': Insurgent South African Poetry." *Research in African Literatures* 19, no. 1 (1988): 12–23.

Cronin, Jeremy. "Poetry: An Élitist Pastime Finds Mass Roots." (Johannesburg) *Weekly Mail*, 13 March 1987.

Crush, Jonathan, Alan Jeeves, and David Yudelman. *South Africa's Labor Empire: A History of Black Migrancy to the Gold Mines.* Claremont, SA: Westview Press, 1991.

d'Abdon, Raphael. "The Commercialization of Celebratory Poetry: A Critical Examination of Zolani Mkiva's Post-Apartheid Praise Poetry (Izibongo)." *African Identities* 12, nos. 3–4 (2015): 314–25.

Davies, Sheila Boniface. "Raising the Dead: The Xhosa Cattle-Killing and the Mhlakaza-Goliat Delusion." *Journal of Southern African Studies* 33, no. 1 (2007): 19–41.

Davis, Angela. *Women, Culture, and Politics.* New York: Vintage Books, 1990.

de Wet, P. "Timeline: How the Spy Tapes Saga Contintues to Haunt Zuma since 2001." (Johannesburg) *Mail and Guardian*, 23 May 2016.

DeLoughrey, Elizabeth, and George B. Handley. *Postcolonial Ecologies: Literatures of the Environment.* Oxford: Oxford University Press, 2011.

Demombynes, Gabriel, and Berk Özler. "Crime and Local Inequality in South Africa." *Journal of Development Economics* 76, no. 2 (2005): 265–92.

Desai, Ashwin. *We Are the Poors: Community Struggles in Post-Apartheid South Africa.* New York: Monthly Review Press, 2002.

Desai, Rehad, dir. "Miners Shot Down." 1h 26m. Johannesburg: Icarus Films, 2014.

Dickinson, Adam William. "Lyric Ethics: The Matter and Time of Ecopoetry." PhD diss., University of Alberta, 2005.

Dold, Tony, and Michelle Cocks. *Voices from the Forest: Celebrating Nature and Culture in Xhosaland.* Auckland Park, SA: Jacana Media, 2012.

Dubow, Saul. *Apartheid, 1948–1994.* Oxford: Oxford University Press, 2014.

Duffield, Mark R., and Vernon Marston Hewitt. *Empire, Development, and Colonialism: The Past in the Present.* Woodbridge, Suffolk, UK: James Currey, 2009.

Dyakala, Mandlenkosi. Interview with the author. Makhanda, SA, 23 February 2016.
Eagleton, Terry. *How to Read a Poem*. Malden, MA: Blackwell, 2007.
Eagleton, Terry. *How to Read Literature*. New Haven, CT: Yale University Press, 2013.
Elbra, Ainsley D. "The Forgotten Resource Curse: South Africa's Poor Experience with Mineral Extraction." *Resources Policy* 38, no. 4 (2013): 549–57.
Elder, John. *Imagining the Earth: Poetry and the Vision of Nature*. 2nd ed. Ubana: University of Illinois Press, 1985.
Elgot, Jessica. "Jacob Zuma Breached Constitution over Home Upgrades, South African Court Rules." *Guardian* (UK), 31 March 2016.
Ellis, William F. "*Ons Is Boesmans:* Commentary on the Naming of Bushmen in the Southern Kalahari." *Anthropology Southern Africa* 38, nos. 1–2 (2015): 120–33.
Ergin, Meliz. *The Ecopoetics of Entanglement in Contemporary Turkish and American Literatures*. Cham, Switzerland: Palgrave Macmillan, 2017.
Escobar, Arturo. *Encountering Development: The Making and Unmaking of the Third World*. Princeton, NJ: Princeton University Press, 1995. http://www.library.yorku.ca/e/resolver/id/2496619.
Evans, Laura. "Resettlement and the Making of the Ciskei Bantustan, South Africa, c. 1960–1976." *Journal of Southern African Studies* 40, no. 1 (2014): 21–40.
Evans, Martha, and Ian Glenn. "'TIA—This Is Africa': Afropessimism in Twenty-First-Century Narrative Film." *Black Camera* 2, no. 1 (2010): 14–35.
Evill, Gill, and Steve Kromberg. *Izinsingizi: Loud Hailer Lives: South African Poetry from Natal*. Durban, SA: Culture and Working Life Publications, 1988.
Fairweather, Joan G. *A Common Hunger: Land Rights in Canada and South Africa*. Calgary: University of Calgary Press, 2006.
Fanon, Frantz. *Black Skin, White Masks*. Translated by R. Philcox. Berkeley: Grove Press, 2008.
Fanon, Frantz. *The Wretched of the Earth*. Translated by C. Farrington. 1961; reprint, London: Penguin Classics, 2001.
Fay, Derick A. "'Keeping Land for Their Children': Generation, Migration, and Land in South Africa's Transkei." *Journal of Southern African Studies* 41, no. 5 (2015): 1083–97.
Ferguson, James. "The Uses of Neoliberalism." *Antipode* 41 (2010): 166–84.
Ferreira, Emsie. "Judgement in Spy Tapes Case against Zuma Due on Friday." (Johannesburg) *Mail and Guardian*, 28 April 2016.
Finnegan, Ruth H. *Oral Literature in Africa*. Cambridge, UK: Open Book Publishers, 2012. Originally published as *Oral Literature in Africa*, Nairobi: Oxford University Press, 1976.
Fraser, Alistair. "Land Reform in South Africa and the Colonial Present." *Social and Cultural Geography* 8, no. 6 (2007): 835–51.

Friedman, Steven. *Race, Class and Power: Harold Wolpe and the Radical Critique of Apartheid*. Pietermaritzburg, SA: University of KwaZulu-Natal Press, 2015.

Friedman, Steven. "The Struggle within the Struggle: South African Resistance Strategies." *Transformation: Critical Perspectives on Southern Africa* 3 (1987): 58–70.

Fry, Poppy. "Siyamfenguza: The Creation of Fingo-Ness in South Africa's Eastern Cape, 1800–1835." *Journal of Southern African Studies* 36, no. 1 (2010): 25–40.

Furniss, G., and E. Gunner. *Power, Marginality, and African Oral Literature*. Cambridge: Cambridge University Press, 1995.

Gérard, Albert S. "Xhosa Literature." In *Four African Literatures: Xhosa, Sotho, Zulu, Amharic*, 21–49. Berkeley: University of California Press, 1971.

Gersdorf, Catrin, and Sylvia Mayer. *Nature in Literary and Cultural Studies: Transatlantic Conversations on Ecocriticism*. Amsterdam: Rodopi, 2006.

Gibson, Nigel C. *Fanonian Practices in South Africa: From Steve Biko to Abahlali Basemjondolo*. New York: Palgrave Macmillan; Scottsville, SA: University of KwaZulu-Natal Press, 2014.

Gibson, Nigel C. "What Happened to the 'Promised Land'? A Fanonian Perspective on Post-Apartheid South Africa." *Antipode* 44, no. 1 (2012): 51–73.

Gifford, Terry. *Green Voices: Understanding Contemporary Nature Poetry*. Manchester, UK: Manchester University Press, 1995.

Gilcrest, David W. *Greening the Lyre: Environmental Poetics and Ethics*. Reno: University of Nevada Press, 2002.

Giroux, Henry A. "Neoliberalism and the Death of the Social State: Remembering Walter Benjamin's Angel of History." *Social Identities* 17, no. 4 (2011): 587–601.

Glotfelty, Cheryll, and Harold Fromm, eds. *The Ecocriticism Reader: Landmarks in Literary Ecology*. Athens: University of Georgia Press, 1996.

Goodbody, A. *Ecocritical Theory: New European Perspectives*. Charlottesville: University of Virginia Press, 2011.

Gordimer, Nadine. "Who Writes? Who Reads? The Concept of a People's Literature." *Staffrider* 9, no. 1 (1990): 36–41.

Gqirana, Thulani. "DA's Bid to Impeach Zuma Fails." (Johannesburg) *Mail and Guardian*, 2 September 2015.

Gqoba, William Wellington. *Isizwe Esinembali: Xhosa Histories and Poetry (1873–1888)*. Translated by Jeff Opland, Wandile Kuse, and Pamela Maseko. Pietermaritzburg, SA: University of KwaZulu-Natal Press, 2015.

Guha, R., and J. Martínez Alier. "Radical American Environmentalism and Wilderness Preservation: A Third-World Critique." In *Varieties of Environmentalism: Essays North and South*. London: Earthscan Publications, 1997.

Gumede, William. "Building a Democratic Political Culture." In *The Poverty of Ideas: South African Democracy and the Retreat of Intellectuals*, edited by William Gumede and Leslie Dikeni, 11–34. Auckland Park, SA: Jacana, 2009.

Gumede, William, and Leslie Dikeni, eds. *The Poverty of Ideas: South African Democracy and the Retreat of Intellectuals*. Aukland Park, SA: Jacana, 2009.

Gunner, Liz. "*Remaking the Warrior?* The Role of Orality in the Liberation Struggle and in Post-Apartheid South Africa." In *Oral Literature and Performance in Southern Africa*, edited by Duncan Brown, 50–60. Oxford, UK: James Currey, 1999.

Gunnink, Hilde, Bonny Sands, Brigitte Pakendorf, and Koen Bostoen. "Prehistoric Language Contact in the Kavango-Zambezi Transfrontier Area: Khoisan Influence on Southwestern Bantu Languages." *Journal of African Languages and Linguistics* 36, no. 2 (2015): 193–232.

Haden, Alexis. "Cape Town Turns out for 'Biggest March since the Dawn of Democracy.'" *South African*, 7 April 2017.

Hall, Ruth, and Thembela Kepe. "Elite Capture and State Neglect: New Evidence on South Africa's Land Reform." *Review of African Political Economy* 44, no. 151 (2017): 122–30.

Harlow, Barbara. *Resistance Literature*. New York: University Paperbacks, 1987.

Hart, Gillian. "The Provocations of Neoliberalism: Contesting the Nation and Liberation after Apartheid." *Antipode* 40, no. 4 (2008): 678–705.

Harvey, David. "The Body as an Accumulation Strategy." *Environment and Planning D: Society and Space* 16 (1998): 401–21.

Harvey, David. *A Brief History of Neoliberalism*. Oxford: Oxford University Press, 2005.

Harvey, David. "Neoliberalism as Creative Destruction." *Annals of the American Academy of Political and Social Science* 610, no. 1 (2007): 21–44.

Hercus, Cheryl. "Identity, Emotion, and Feminist Collective Action." *Gender and Society* 13, no. 1 (1999): 34–55.

Hill, Christopher. *Bantustans: The Fragmentation of South Africa*. Edited by London Institute of Race Relations. London: Oxford University Press, 1964.

Hill, Lloyd B. "The Decline of Academic Bilingualism in South Africa: A Case Study." *Language Policy* 8, no. 4 (2009): 327–49.

Hirst, Manton. "Dreams and Medicines: The Perspective of Xhosa Diviners and Novices in the Eastern Cape, South Africa." *Indo-Pacific Journal of Phenomenology* 5, no. 2 (2005): 1–22.

Hofmeyr, Isabel. Foreword to *The Nation's Bounty: The Xhosa Poetry of Nontsizi Mgqwetho*, edited by Jeff Opland. Johannesburg: Wits University Press, 2007.

Huggan, Graham, and Helen Tiffin. *Postcolonial Ecocriticism: Literature, Animals, Environment*. 2nd ed. London: Routledge, 2015.

Hume, Angela. "Toward an Antiracist Ecopoetics: Waste and Wasting in the Poetry of Claudia Rankine." In *Ecopoetics: Essays in the Field*, edited by Angela Hume and Gillian Osborne, 169–86. Iowa City: University of Iowa Press, 2018.

Hume, Angela, and Gillian Osborne. *Ecopoetics: Essays in the Field*. Iowa City: University of Iowa Press, 2018.

Iheka, Cajetan Nwabueze. *Naturalizing Africa: Ecological Violence, Agency, and Postcolonial Resistance in African Literature*. Cambridge: Cambridge University Press, 2018.

International Defense and Aid Fund. "South Africa: 'Resettlement'—The New Violence to Africans." London: Christian Action Publications, 1969.

Iovino, Serenella. *Ecologia letteraria: Una strategia di sopravvivenza*. Milan: Ambiente, 2006.

Jager, Theo de. "Land Reform: The View from Commercial Agriculture." In *Land Divided, Land Restored: Land Reform in South Africa for the Twenty-First Century*, edited by Ben Cousins and Cherryl Walker, 120–26. Auckland Park, SA: Jacana Media, 2015.

Jasper, James M. "Emotions and Social Movements: Twenty Years of Theory and Research." *Annual Review of Sociology* 37 (2011): 285–303.

Jeeves, Alan. *Migrant Labour in South Africa's Mining Economy: The Struggle for the Gold Mines' Labour Supply, 1890–1920*. Kingston, ON: McGill-Queen's University Press, 1985.

Jewkes, Rachel, and Naeema Abrahams. "The Epidemiology of Rape and Sexual Coercion in South Africa: An Overview." *Social Science and Medicine* 55 (2002): 1231–44.

Jordan, A. C. *Towards an African Literature: The Emergence of Literary Form in Xhosa*. Berkeley: University of California Press, 1973.

Kapoor, Ilan. *The Postcolonial Politics of Development*. London: Routledge, 2008.

Kapoor, Ilan. "The Queer Third World." *Third World Quarterly* 36, no. 9 (2015): 1611–28.

Kaschula, Russell H. *African Oral Literature: Functions in Contemporary Contexts*. Claremont, SA: New Africa Books, 2001.

Kaschula, Russell H. *The Bones of the Ancestors Are Shaking: Xhosa Oral Poetry in Context*. Lansdowne, SA: Juta, 2002.

Kaschula, Russell H. "Imbongi in Profile." *English in Africa* 20, no. 1 (1993): 65–76.

Kaschula, Russell H. "Intellectualisation of isiXhosa Literature: The Case of Jeff Opland." *Tydskrif vir Letterkunde* 54, no. 2 (2017): 5–25.

Kaschula, Russell H. "Myth and Reality in the New South Africa: Contemporary Oral Literature." *Alizes* 24 (2004). Accessed 7 September 2006. http://www2.univ-reunion.fr/~ageof/text/74c21e88-611.htm.

Kaschula, Russell H. "The Oppression of IsiXhosa Literature and the Irony of Transformation." *English in Africa* 35, no. 1 (2008): 117–32.

Kaschula, Russell H. "Remembering the Late Nelson Rholihlahla Mandela through the Eyes of the Poet." *Current Writing: Text and Reception in Southern Africa* 30, no. 1 (2018): 12–24.

Kaschula, Russell H. "The Role of the Xhosa Oral Poet in Contemporary South African Society." *South African Journal of African Languages* 11, no. 2 (1991): 47–54.

Kaschula, Russell H. "The Transitional Role of the Xhosa Oral Poet in Contemporary South African Society." PhD diss., Rhodes University, Makhanda, SA, 1991.

Kaschula, Russell H., and Samba Diop. "Political Processes and the Role of the

Imbongi and Griot in Africa." *South African Journal of African Languages* 20, no. 1 (2000): 13.
Kaschula, Russell H., and Andre Mostert. "Analyzing, Digitizing, and Technologizing the Oral Word: The Case of Bongani Sitole." *Journal of African Cultural Studies* 21, no. 2 (2009): 159–75.
Kavanagh, Dennis, and C. Riches, eds. "Zuma, Jacob Gedleyihlekisa." Oxford Quick Reference, http://www.oxfordreference.com/view/10.1093/oi/authority.20110803133556460.
Kepe, Thembela. "Unjustified Optimism: Why the World Bank's 2008 'Agriculture for Development' Report Misses the Point for South Africa." *Journal of Peasant Studies* 36, no. 3 (2009): 637–43.
Kepe, Thembela, Elsie Lewison, Renata Ramasra, and Sadia Butt. "The Elusive 'Fair Deal' in South Africa's Land Reform." *Forum for Development Studies* 38, no. 3 (2011): 371–78.
Kepe, Thembela, and Lungisile Ntsebeza. *Rural Resistance in South Africa: The Mpondo Revolts after Fifty Years*. Cape Town: University of Cape Town Press, 2012.
Knickerbocker, Scott. *Ecopoetics: The Language of Nature, the Nature of Language*. Amherst: University of Massachusetts Press, 2012.
Krikler, Jeremy. "Women, Violence, and the Rand Revolt of 1922." *Journal of Southern African Studies* 22, no. 3 (1996): 349–72.
Krog, Antje. "Baas van die plaas / Izwe Lethu: Essay in Fragments and Two Villanelles Exploring Different Relationships to Land in Some Indigenous Poetic Texts." In *Land Divided, Land Restored: Land Reform in South Africa for the Twenty-First Century*, edited by Ben Cousins and Cherryl Walker, 206–31. Auckland Park, SA: Jacana Media, 2015.
Kropf, Albert. *A Xhosa-English Dictionary*. 2nd ed. Lovedale (SA) Mission Society, 1915.
Kruger, Tinus, and Karina Landman. "Crime and the Physical Environment in South Africa: Contextualizing International Crime Prevention Experiences." *Built Environment* 24, no. 1 (2008): 75–87.
Lawrence, Susan. "Exporting Culture: Archaeology and the Nineteenth-Century British Empire." *Historical Archaeology* 37, no. 1 (2003): 20–33.
Legassick, Martin. "South Africa: Capital Accumulation and Violence." *Economy and Society* 3, no. 3 (1974): 253–91.
Lester, Alan. "The Margins of Order: Strategies of Segregation on the Eastern Cape Frontier, 1806–c. 1850." *Journal of Southern African Studies* 23, no. 4 (1997): 635–53.
Lewis, David, Dennis Rodgers, and Michael Woolcock, eds. *Popular Representations of Development*. London: Routledge, 2014.
Lewis, David, Dennis Rodgers, and Michael Woolcock. "The Fiction of Development: Literary Representation as a Source of Authoritative Knowledge." *Journal of Development Studies* 44, no. 2 (2008): 198–216.

Lidström, Susanna. *Nature, Environment, and Poetry: Ecocriticism and the Poetics of Seamus Heaney and Ted Hughes*. London: Routledge, 2015.
Limb, Peter. "'They Must Go to the Bantu Batho': Economics and Education, Religion and Gender, Love and Leisure in the People's Paper." In *The People's Paper* edited by Peter Limb, 81–115. Johannesburg: Wits University Press, 2012.
Lloyd, Trevor Owen. *Empire: The History of the British Empire*. London: Hambledon and London, 2001.
Lodge, Tom. "Resistance and Reform, 1973–1994." In *The Cambridge History of South Africa*, vol. 2, edited by Robert Ross, Anne Kelk Mager, and Bill Nasson, 409–91. Cambridge: Cambridge University Press, 2011.
Lowman, Stuart. "Cyril Ramaphosa's Maiden State of the Nation Address." *Biz News*, 16 February 2018. https://www.biznews.com/sa-investing/2018/02/16/cyril-ramaphosa-debut-state-nation.
Luxemburg, Rosa. *The Accumulation of Capital*. Translated by Agnes Schwarzschild. Edited by Joan Robinson. 1951; reprint, New Haven: Yale University Press, 2012.
Mabona, Mongameli. *Diviners and Prophets among the Xhosa (1593–1856)*. Münster, Germany: Lit Verlag Münster, 2004.
Machisa, Mercilene, Rachel Jewkes, Colleen Lowe Morna, and Kubi Rama. "The War at Home: Gender Based Violence Indicators Project." Johannesburg: Gender Links & South African Medical Research Council, 2011.
Mager, Anne Kelk, and Maanda Mulaudzi. "Popular Responses to Apartheid: 1948–c. 1975." In *The Cambridge History of South Africa*, vol. 2, edited by Robert Ross, Anne Kelk Mager, and Bill Nasson, 369–408. Cambridge: University of Cambridge Press, 2011.
Mahaye, Zithulele. "A Life Cruel Beyond Belief." *Writers' Notebook* 1, no. 2 (1990): 1–12.
Maho, Jouni. "A Comparative Study of Bantu Noun Classes." PhD diss., Göteborg University, Sweden, 1999.
Malange, Nise. "Breaking the Silence." Paper presented at the Buang basadi: Khulumani makhosikazi (Women Speak: Conference on Women and Writing), Transvaal, SA, 1988.
Malange, Nise. "Let Women Be Heard." *Writers' Notebook* 1, no. 2 (1990): 20–21.
Malange, Nise. Interview with the author. Durban, SA, 14 January 2016.
Mallick, S., H. Li, M. Lipson, et al. "The Simons Genome Diversity Project: 300 Genomes from 142 Diverse Populations." *Nature* 538, no. 7624 (21 September 2016): 201–6.
Mallinson, Theresa. "Thando Mgqolozana: 'The Audience Does Not Treat Me as a Literary Talent, but as an Anthropological Subject.'" (Johannesburg) *Daily Vox*, 15 May 2015.
Mamdani, Mahmood. *Citizen and Subject: Contemporary Africa and the Legacy of Late Colonialism*. Princeton, NJ: Princeton University Press, 1996.
Mandela, Nelson. "Address by Nelson Mandela to Rally in Durban after Release

from Prison." 1990. Accessed 9 January 2019. http://www.mandela.gov.za/mandela_speeches/1990/900225_dbn.htm.
Mandela, Nelson. *Long Walk to Freedom*. Boston: Little, Brown, 1994.
Marais, Hein. *South Africa Pushed to the Limit: The Political Economy of Change*. London: Zed Books, 2011.
Marais, Hein. *South Africa: Limits to Change: The Political Economy of Transition*. London: Zed Books, 2001.
Marismulu, Priya. "Labour and South African Literature in the 1980s." *Alternation* 5, no. 2 (1998): 263–300.
Marten, Lutz. "The Bantu Languages by Derek Nurse and Gérard Philippson." *Bulletin of the School of Oriental and African Studies, University of London* 68, no. 3 (2005): 500–502.
Martínez Alier, Joan. "The Environmentalism of the Poor." *Geoforum* 54 (2014): 239–41.
Mashige, Mashudu. "Mi Hlatshwayo and Temba Qabula: Worker Poets in the Struggle against Apartheid." In *School of Human Sciences Monograph Series*, 2, (2001): 24.
Mashige, Mashudu. "Oral Performance and the Constructs of Identity in Temba Qabula's Poetry." *Southern African Journal for Folklore Studies* 15, no. 2 (2005): 20–33.
Mathis, Sarah M. "The Politics of Land Reform: Tenure and Political Authority in Rural Kwazulu-Natal." *Journal of Agrarian Change* 7, no. 1 (2007): 99–120.
Matthews, James. "Democracy, Dissidence, and the Poet." In *The Poverty of Ideas: South African Democracy and the Retreat of Intellectuals*, edited by William Gumede and Leslie Dikeni, 52–56. Aukland Park, SA: Jacana Media, 2009.
Mbeki, Govan. *South Africa: The Peasants' Revolt*. Hammodsworth, UK: Penguin Books, 1964.
Mbembe, Achille. *Critique of Black Reason*. Translated by Laurent Dubois. Durham: Duke University Press, 2017.
McCarthy, James, and Scott Prudham. "Neoliberal Nature and the Nature of Neoliberalism." *Geoforum* 35, no. 3 (2004): 275–83.
McGiffin, Emily. "Iimbongi of the Resistance: Praise Poets, Trade Unions, and Extractive Capitalism in Apartheid South Africa." *Green Letters* 20, no. 2 (2016): 156–69.
McNary, Dave. "'Black Panther' Is Third Movie Ever to Top $700 Million at Domestic Box Offices." *Chicago Tribune*, 5 August 2018.
Memmi, Albert. *The Colonizer and the Colonized*. Translated by H. Greenfeld. 1957; reprint, Boston: Beacon Press, 1967.
Mgqwetho, Nontsizi. *The Nation's Bounty: The Xhosa Poetry of Nontsizi Mgqwetho*. Translated by Jeff Opland. Johannesburg: Wits University Press, 2007.
Mies, Maria. *Patriarchy and Accumulation on a World Scale: Women in the International Division of Labour*. London: Zed Books, 1998.
Mkiva, Zolani. Interview with the author. Bholotwa, SA, 28 December 2015.

Mkiva, Zolani. "Poet of Africa: His Royal Heritage, Zolani Mkiva." Accessed 24 January 2019. http://www.poetofafrica.com/new1/.

Mkiva, Zolani. "Son of the Soil." World Poetry Movement. Accessed 24 January 2019. http://www.wpm2011.org/node/107.

Mkhonza, Sarah. "Queen Labotsibeni and *Abantu-Batho*." In *The People's Paper: A Centenary History and Anthology of* Abantu-Batho, edited by Peter Limb, 128–50. Johannesburg: Wits University Press, 2012.

Mlama, Penina. "Oral Art and Contemporary Cultural Nationalism." In *Power, Marginality, and African Oral Literature*, edited by G. Furniss and E. Gunner, 22–34. Cambridge: Cambridge University Press, 1995.

Mnwana, Sonwabile. "Why Giving South Africa's Chiefs More Power Adds to Land Dispossession." *The Conversation*, 4 April 2018. https://theconversation.com/why-giving-south-africas-chiefs-more-power-adds-to-land-dispossession-93958.

Monbiot, George. "Neoliberalism—The Ideology at the Root of All Our Problems." *Guardian* (UK), 15 April 2016.

Mostert, Noël. *Frontiers: The Epic of South Africa's Creation and the Tragedy of the Xhosa People*. London: Cape, 1992.

Mpupha, Dumisa Julius. Personal communication. Makhanda, SA, 2016.

Mqhayi, S. E. K. *Abantu Besizwe: Historical and Biographical Writings, 1902–1944*. Translated by Jeff Opland. Johannesburg: Wits University Press, 2009.

Mudimbe, V. Y. *The Invention of Africa: Gnosis, Philosophy, and the Order of Knowledge*. Bloomington: Indiana University Press, 1988.

Mugo, Kagure. "When Comrades Rape Comrades." (Johannesburg) *Mail and Guardian*, 27 November 2015.

Nattrass, Nicoli, and Jeremy Seekings. "The Economy and Poverty in the Twentieth Century." In *The Cambridge History of South Africa*, vol. 2, edited by Robert Ross, Anne Kelk Mager, and Bill Nasson, 518–72. Cambridge: Cambridge University Press, 2011.

Ndikumana, Léonce. "Integrated yet Marginalized: Implications of Globalization for African Development." *African Studies Review* 58, no. 2 (2015): 7–28.

Neser, Ashlee. *Stranger at Home: The Praise Poet in Apartheid South Africa*. Johannesburg: Wits University Press, 2011.

Ngcobo, Lauretta. "African Motherhood—Myth and Reality." In *African Literature: An Anthology of Criticism and Theory*, edited by Tejumola Olaniyan and Ato Quayson, 533–541. Malden, MA: Blackwell, 2007.

Ngugi wa Thiong'o. *Decolonising the Mind: The Politics of Language in African Literature*. London: J. Currey, 1986.

Nicholson, Greg. "How South African Anti-Rape Protesters Disrupted Zuma's Speech." *Guardian* (UK), 9 August 2016.

Niemandt, Corné, and Michelle Greve. "Fragmentation Metric Proxies Provide Insights into Historical Biodiversity Loss in Critically Endangered Grassland." *Agriculture, Ecosystems, and Environment* 235 (2016): 172–81.

Nixon, Rob. *Slow Violence and the Environmentalism of the Poor.* Cambridge, MA: Harvard University Press, 2011.
Nolan, Sarah. *Unnatural Ecopoetics: Unlikely Spaces in Contemporary Poetry.* Reno: University of Nevada Press, 2017.
Ntsebeza, Lungisile. *Democracy Compromised: Chiefs and the Politics of Land in South Africa.* Leiden, Netherlands: Brill, 2005.
Ntshuntsha, Thokozani. Interview with the author. Willowvale, SA, 20 December 2015.
Nurse, Derek, and Gérard Philippson, eds. *The Bantu Languages.* London: Routledge, 2003.
Nxasana, Thulani. "The Ambivalent Engagement with Christianity in the Writing of Ninteenth- and Early Twentieth-Century Africans in the Eastern Cape." Master's thesis, Rhodes University, Makhanda, SA, 2009.
Nxasana, Thulani. "Nontsizi Mgqwetho's *The Nation's Bounty*: A Prophetic Voice towards an African Literary Theory." PhD diss., Rhodes University, Makhanda, SA, 2016.
Nyamnjoh, Francis B. "Fiction and Reality of Mobility in Africa." *Citizenship Studies* 17, nos. 6–7 (2013): 653–80.
O'Brien, Anthony. *Against Normalization: Writing Radical Democracy in South Africa.* Durham, NC: Duke University Press, 2001.
Okunoye, Oyeniyi. "Postcolonial African Poetry." In *The Cambridge Companion to Postcolonial Poetry*, edited by Jahan Ramazani, 45–57. Cambridge: Cambridge University Press, 2017.
Ong, Walter J. *Orality and Literacy.* London: Routledge, 2002.
Opland, Jeff. "*Abantu-Batho* and the Xhosa Poets." In *The People's Paper: A Centenary History and Anthology of* Abantu-Batho, edited by Peter Limb, 201–23. Johannesburg: Wits University Press, 2012.
Opland, Jeff. "The Bones of Mfanta: A Xhosa Oral Poet's Response to Context in South Africa." *Research in African Literatures* 18, no. 1 (1987): 36–50.
Opland, Jeff. *The Dassie and the Hunter: A South African Meeting.* Scottsville, SA: University of KwaZulu-Natal Press, 2005.
Opland, Jeff. "First Meeting with Manisi." *Research in African Literatures* 36, no. 3 (2004): 26–45.
Opland, Jeff. Interview with the author, Hogsback, SA, 17 November 2015.
Opland, Jeff. Introduction to *Iimbali Zamanyange: Historical Poems*, by D. L. P. Yali-Manisi, 1–33. Pietermaritzburg, SA: University of KwaZulu-Natal Press, 2015.
Opland, Jeff. Introduction to *The Nation's Bounty: The Xhosa Poetry of Nontsizi Mgqwetho*, translated and edited by Jeff Opland, xiv–xxx. Johannesburg: Wits University Press, 2007.
Opland, Jeff. "Structural Patterns in the Performance of a Xhosa izibongo." *Comparative Literature* 48, no. 2 (1996): 94–127.
Opland, Jeff. *Xhosa Oral Poetry: Aspects of a Black South African Tradition.* Cambridge: Cambridge University Press, 1983.

Opland, Jeff. *Xhosa Poets and Poetry*. Cape Town: David Philip Publishers, 1998.
Opland, Jeff, and Patrick McAllister. "The Xhosa Imbongi as Trickster." *Journal of African Cultural Studies* 22, no. 2 (2010): 157–67.
Oppermann, Serpil, ed. *New International Voices in Ecocriticism*. Lanham, MD: Lexington Books, 2015.
Oppermann, Serpil, Ufuk Özdag, Nevin Özkan, and Scott Slovic, eds. *The Future of Ecocriticism: New Horizons*. Newcastle Upon Tyne: Cambridge Scholars 2011.
Palitza, Kristin. "Culture (Ab)Used to Dodge Women's Rights." *Agenda* 68 (2006): 108–11.
Pather, Ra'eesa, Phillip de Wet, Lauren Clifford-Holmes, and Sarah Evans. "Zuma's Nkandla: A Timeline." (Johannesburg) *Mail and Guardian*, 18 March 2014.
Patke, Rajeeve S. *Postcolonial Poetry in English*. Oxford: Oxford University Press, 2006.
Peet, Richard. "Ideology, Discourse, and the Geography of Hegemony: From Socialist to Neoliberal Development in Postapartheid South Africa." *Antipode* 34, no. 1 (2002): 54–84.
Peires, J. B. "The Central Beliefs of the Xhosa Cattle-Killing." *Journal of African History* 28 (1987): 43–63.
Peires, J. B. *The Dead Will Arise: Nongqawuse and the Great Xhosa Cattle-Killing Movement of 1856–7*. Johannesburg: Ravan Press, 1989.
Peires, J. B. *The House of Phalo: A History of the Xhosa People in the Days of Their Independence*. Berkeley: University of California Press, 1982.
Platzky, Laurine, and Cherryl Walker. *The Surplus People: Forced Removals in South Africa*. Johannesburg: Ravan Press, 1985.
Poland, Marguerite, W. D. Hammond-Tooke, and Leigh Voigt. *The Abundant Herds: A Celebration of the Cattle of the Zulu People*. Vlaeberg, SA: Fernwood, 2003.
Polanyi, Karl. *The Great Transformation: The Political and Economic Origins of Our Time*. Boston, MA: Beacon Press, 2001.
Posel, Deborah. *The Making of Apartheid, 1948–1961*. Oxford: Oxford University Press, 1997.
Posel, Dorrit. "Adult Literacy Rates in South Africa: A Comparison of Different Measures." *Language Matters* 42, no. 1 (2011): 39–49.
Postmentier, Sonya. *Cultivation and Catastrophe: The Lyric Ecology of Modern Black Literature*. Baltimore: John Hopkins University Press, 2018.
Powell, Cathleen. "How the Charges against Pravin Gordhan Demonstrate a Misuse of SA Law." (Johannesburg) *Mail and Guardian*, 19 October 2016.
Qabula, Alfred. "FOSATU." In *Words That Circle Words: A Choice of South African Oral Poetry*, edited by Jeff Opland, 258–63. Parklands, SA: A. D. Donker, 1992.
Qabula, Alfred Temba. *A Working Life, Cruel Beyond Belief*. Fort Hare: National Union of Metalworkers of South Africa, 1989.

Qabula, Alfred Temba, Mi S'dumo Hlatshwayo, and Nise Malange. *Black Mamba Rising: South African Worker Poets in Struggle*. Durban, SA: Worker Resistance and Culture Publications, University of Natal, 1986.
Qabula, Alfred, and Zithulele Mahaye. "A Life Cruel Beyond Belief." *Writers' Notebook* 1, no. 2 (1990): 1–12.
Quetchenbach, Bernard W. *Back from the Far Field: American Nature Poetry in the Late Twentieth Century*. Charlottesville: University of Virginia Press, 2000.
Ramazani, Jahan. Introduction to *The Cambridge Companion to Postcolonial Poetry*, edited by Jahan Ramazani, 1–15. Cambridge: Cambridge University Press, 2017.
Ramutsindela, Maano. "Resilient Geographies: Land, Boundaries, and the Consolidation of the Former Bantustans in Post-1994 South Africa." *Geographical Journal* 173, no. 1 (2007): 43–55.
Raper, Peter. "The Ethnonyms 'Bushman' and 'San.'" *Acta Academica* 42, no.1 (2012): 168–86.
Rawlings, John Jerry. "Rawlings Receives Another Award in South Africa and Says the World Is Engulfed in Hypocrisy." J. J. Rawlings: Ghana's Former President J. J. Rawlings in the Spotlight, 2013. https://jjrawlings.wordpress.com/2013/10/27/rawlings-receives-another-award-in-south-africa-and-says-the-world-in-engulfed-in-hypocrisy/.
Ray, Sarah Jaquette. *The Ecological Other: Environmental Exclusion in American Culture*. Tuscon: University of Arizona Press, 2013.
Reader, John. *Africa: A Biography of the Continent*. New York: Vintage Books, 1997.
Remmington, Janet. "Solomon Plaatje's Decade of Creative Mobility, 1912–1922: The Politics of Travel and Writing in and beyond South Africa." *Journal of Southern African Studies* 39, no. 2 (2013): 425–46.
Rexová, Katerina, Yvonne Bastin, and Daniel Frynta. "Cladistic Analysis of Bantu Languages: A New Tree Based on Combined Lexical and Grammatical Data." *Naturwissenschaften* 93 (2006): 189–94.
Rhodes, Cecil. *The Last Will and Testament of Cecil John Rhodes: With Elucidatory Notes to Which Are Added Some Chapters Describing the Political and Religious Ideas of the Testator*. London: Review of Reviews Office, 1902.
Richardson, Eugene T., Carl D. Morrow, Theodore Ho, Nicole Fürst, Rebekkah Cohelia, Khai Hoan Tram, Paul E. Farmer, and Robin Wood. "Forced Removals Embodied as Tuberculosis." *Social Science and Medicine* 161 (2016): 13–18.
Rigby, Kate. "Ecopoetics." In *Keywords for Environmental Studies*, edited by Joni Adamson, William A. Gleason, and David N. Pellow, 79–81. New York: New York University Press, 2016.
Rist, Gilbert. *The History of Development: From Western Origins to Global Faith*. 4th ed. Translated by Patrick Camiller. London: Zed Books, 2014.
Rodney, Walter. *How Europe Underdeveloped Africa*. Rev. ed. Washington, DC: Howard University Press, 1981.

Roos, Bonnie, and Alex Hunt. *Postcolonial Green: Environmental Politics and World Narratives*. Charlottesville: University of Virginia Press, 2010.

Rösner, T., and A. van Schalkwyk. "The Environmental Impact of Gold Mine Tailings Footprints in the Johannesburg Region, South Africa." *Bulletin of Engineering Geology and the Environment* 59 (2000): 137–48.

Ross, Robert. "Khoisan and Immigrants: The Emergence of Colonial Society in the Cape, 1500–1800." In *The Cambridge History of South Africa*, vol. 1, edited by Carolyn Hamilton, Bernard K. Mbenga and Robert Ross, 168–210. Cambridge: Cambridge University Press, 2009.

Rutella, Guy. *Reading and Writing Nature: The Poetry of Robert Frost, Wallace Stevens, Marianne Moore, and Elizabeth Bishop*. Lebanon, NH: Northeastern University Press, 1990.

Schmidt, Elizabeth, James H. Mittelman, Fantu Cheru, and Aili Mari Tripp. "Development in Africa: What Is the Cutting Edge in Thinking and Policy?" *Review of African Political Economy* 36, no. 120 (2009): 273–82.

Scigaj, Leonard M. *Sustainable Poetry: Four American Ecopoets*. Lexington: University Press of Kentucky, 1999.

Seddon, Deborah. "Written Out, Writing In: Orature in the South African Literary Canon." *English in Africa* 35, no. 1 (2008): 133–50.

Selwyn, Benjamin. *The Global Development Crisis*. Malden, MA: Polity, 2014.

Shange, Naledi. "King Dalindyebo Hands Himself Over to Correctional Centre." (Johannesburg) *Mail and Guardian*, 31 December 2015.

Shortt, Niamh K., and Daniel Hammett. "Housing and Health in an Informal Settlement Upgrade in Cape Town, South Africa." *Journal of Housing and the Built Environment* 28, no. 4 (2013): 615–27.

Sitas, Ari. "Alfred Temba Qabula, 1942–2002: A Tribute." *Current Writing* 15, no. 1 (2003): 169–73.

Sitas, Ari. "A. T. Qabula: Working Class Poet." *South African Labour Bulletin* 9, no. 8 (1984): 21–26.

Sitas, Ari. "The Labour Poets." *Writers' Notebook* 1, no. 1 (1989): 37–59.

Sitas, Ari. "The Moving Black Forest of Africa: The Mpondo Rebellion, Migrancy, and Black Worker Consciousness in Kwazulu-Natal." In *Rural Resistance in South Africa: The Mpondo Revolts after Fifty Years*, edited by Thembela Kepe and Lungisile Ntsebeza, 165–87. Leiden, Netherlands: Brill, 2011.

Sitas, Ari. "Peoples' Poetry in Natal." *Writers' Notebook* 1, no. 1 (1989): 37–59.

Sixham, Yakobi. Interview with the author. King William's Town, SA, 5 January 2016.

Slovic, Scott. *Ecocriticism in Taiwan: Identity, Environment, and the Arts*. Lanham, MD: Lexington Books, 2016.

Slovic, Scott, Swarnalatha Rangarajan, and Vidya Sarveswaran. *Ecocriticism of the Global South*. Lanham, MD: Lexington Books, 2015.

Smith, Andrew B. "The Origins and Demise of the Khoikhoi: The Debate." *South African Historical Journal* 23, no. 1 (1990): 3–14.

Smith, David. "Jacob Zuma the Chameleon Brings South Africans Joy and Fear." *Guardian* (UK), 20 April 2009.
Smith, Neil. *Uneven Development: Nature, Capital, and the Production of Space*. Athens: University of Georgia Press, 2008.
Solilo, John. *Umoya Wembongi: Collected Poems (1922–1935)*. Translated by Jeff Opland and Peter T. Mtuze. Pietermaritzburg, SA: University of KwaZulu-Natal Press, 2016.
Sosibo, Kwanele. "Thando Mgqolozana on How Can We Decolonize SA Literature." (Johannesburg) *Mail and Guardian*, 14 March 2016.
Soske, Jon. "The Dissimulation of Race: 'Afro-Pessimism' and the Problem of Development." *Qui Parle* 14, no. 2 (2004): 15–56.
Southall, Roger. "Briefing: Family and Favour at the Court of Jacob Zuma." *Review of African Political Economy* 38, no. 130 (2011): 617–26.
Spivak, Gayatri Chakravorty. *A Critique of Postcolonial Reason: Toward a History of the Vanishing Present*. Cambridge, MA: Harvard University Press, 1999.
Stanley, Brooke, and Walter Dana Phillips. "South African Ecocriticism: Landscapes, Animals, and Environmental Justice." In *The Oxford Handbook of Ecocriticism (Supplement)*, edited by Greg Garrard. Oxford: Oxford University Press, 2017.
Suttner, Raymond. "The Jacob Zuma Rape Trial: Power and African National Congress (ANC) Masculinities." *NORA—Nordic Journal of Feminist and Gender Research* 17, no. 3 (2009): 222–36.
Sylvester, Christine. "Development Poetics." *Alternatives: Global, Local, Political* 25, no. 3 (2000): 335–51.
Tabane, Rapule. "Zuma May Not Be Schooled, but He's No Fool." (Johannesburg) *Mail and Guardian*, 4 October 2013.
Thurner, Wolfgang. "Land Reform and Hunger in South Africa: Why the Two go Hand in Hand." *The Conversation*, 29 May 2018. https://theconversation.com/land-reform-and-hunger-in-south-africa-why-the-two-go-hand-in-hand-96684.
Thompson, Leonard. *A History of South Africa*. New Haven, CT: Yale University Press, 2000.
Trapido, Stanley. "Imperialism, Settler Identities, and Colonial Capitalism: The Hundred-Year Origins of the 1899 South African War." In *The Cambridge History of South Africa*, vol. 2, edited by Robert Ross, Anne Kelk Mager, and Bill Nasson, 66–101. Cambridge: Cambridge University Press, 2011.
Tsheola, Johannes. "Basic Needs in the Northern Province and South Africa's Globalization Agenda." *African Development Review* 14, no. 1 (2002): 48–74.
Van Dyk, Bruno, and Duncan Brown. "Ari Sitas: The Publication and Reception of Worker's Literature." *Staffrider* 8, nos. 3–4 (1989): 61–68.
Vetten, Lisa. "Losing the Plot in Zuma Rape Trial's Stories." (Johannesburg) *Mail and Guardian*, 14 August 2014.

Wake, Hisaaki, Keijiro Suga, and Masami Yuki. *Ecocriticism in Japan*. Lanham, MD: Lexington Books, 2017.
Walker, C. "Redistributive Land Reform: For What and for Whom?" In *The Land Question in South Africa: The Challenge of Transformation and Redistribution*, edited by L. Ntsebeza and R. Hall, 132–52. Cape Town: HSRC Press, 2006.
Walker, Cherryl, and Ben Cousins. Introduction to *Land Divided, Land Restored: Land Reform in South Africa for the Twenty-first Century*, edited by Cousins and Walker, 1–23. Auckland Park, South Africa: Jacana Media, 2015.
Weaver, John C. *The Great Land Rush and the Making of the Modern World, 1650–1900*. Montreal: McGill-Queen's University Press, 2006.
Weissenstein, K., and T. Sinkala. "Soil Pollution with Heavy Metals in Mine Environments, Impact Areas of Mine Dumps Particularly of Gold- and Copper Mining Industries in Southern Africa." *Arid Ecosystems* 1, no. 1 (2011): 53–58.
Wilson, Francis. *Labour in the South African Gold Mines, 1911–1969*. London: Cambridge University Press, 1972.
Wolpe, Harold. "Capitalism and Cheap Labour-Power in South Africa: From Segregation to Apartheid." *Economy and Society* 1, no. 4 (1972): 425–56.
Wood, Katherine, and Rachel Jewkes. "'Dangerous' Love: Reflections on Violence among Xhosa Township Youth." In *Readings in Gender in Africa*, edited by Andrea Cornwall, 95–102. Bloomington: Indiana University Press, 2005.
Worsfold, William Basil. *South Africa, a Study in Colonial Administration and Development*. London: Methuen, 1895.
Wylie, Dan. "//Kabbo's Challenge: Transculturation and the Question of a South African Ecocriticism." *Journal of Literary Studies* 23, no. 3 (2007): 252–70.
Yali-Manisi, D. L. P. *Imbongi Entsha: Iimbali Zamanyange: Historical Poems*. Translated by Jeff Opland and Pamela Maseko. Pietermaritzburg, SA: University of KwaZulu-Natal Press, 2015.
Yrjölä, Riina. "The Invisible Violence of Celebrity Humanitarianism: Soft Images and Hard Words in the Making and Unmaking of Africa." *World Political Science Review* 5, no. 1 (2009): Article 14.
Yudelman, David. *The Emergence of Modern South Africa: State, Capital, and the Incorporation of Organized Labor on the South African Gold Fields, 1902–1939*. Westport, CT: Greenwood Press, 1983.
Zwicky, J. "What Is Lyric Philosophy? An Introduction." *Common Knowledge* 20, no. 1 (2013): 14–27.

INDEX

Abantu Batho, 54–55, 209n55
Abrahams, Lionel, 76
accumulation, 15, 28, 30, 120
activism: cultural, 14, 20, 38, 66–68; environmental, 39; political, 74, 79, 88; scholarly, 5; suppression of, 91–93; union, 61, 65–67; women, 80–81, 83–84, 112. *See also* protest; resistance; strikes
African National Congress (ANC), 84, 91, 209n51; and chiefs, 149, 153; land policy, 143, 145, 170; leadership, 105, 107; party loyalty, 107, 153; party origins, 44, 56; social policy, 119; turn to the right, 32–33, 99, 149
Afrikaans, 24, 108, 138, 201
Afrikaner: colonialism, 40, 58; nationalism, 29
agriculture, 28, 30, 63, 64
Albany Museum, 148
Albany Thicket. *See* bushveld
alcohol, 40, 48; alcoholism, 46, 164; and colonialism, 29, 163, 164, 190; Eastern Cape Liquor Board event, 130–33
amaGcaleka, 21, 131, 157, 159, 162, 189. *See also* Gcaleka
amagqirha. *See* igqirha
amaMfengu, 21, 205n7
amaMpondo, 20. *See also* Mpondoland; Mpondo revolts
amaRharhabe, 21, 27, 37, 152, 157. *See also* Rharhabe

amaXhosa, 20–28, 73, 178, 199–200, 205n12, 208n44; and cattle, 166–67; cattle killing, 41, 218n26; customs, 51–52, 77, 122, 124–26, 130, 221n27; and environment, 23, 70–71, 155–60, 167–68; and fieldwork, 121–22, 124; imbongi, 7; and literature, 6, 10–11; and Mgqwetho, 46, 48, 50; politics, 91, 149–50; relationship with whites, 31, 40–42, 53, 57–59, 71, 163–64. *See also* isiXhosa; Xhosa
amaZulu, 21, 73, 91, 104–5, 158, 205n7; Zuma, 105, 110
ancestors, 1, 85, 136, 160, 209n71; ancestral lands, 47, 59, 99, 102, 148, 151–56, 160; ancestral presence, 7–8, 15, 71, 132, 160; ancestral responsibilities, 16, 125, 148, 176–77; assistance from, 57; and cattle, 166; and Christianity, 50; and iimbongi, 96, 98, 119, 125–30, 141, 169; names, 21–22, 26–27, 50–51; and poetry, 105, 142, 171, 174; and traditional leadership, 148, 150–56, 157, 161, 169; and women, 109. *See also* names; praise names
animals, 20, 152, 169, 205n4, 208n31; animal studies, 5; in dreams, 128; leopard skin, 104, 131, 164–65; in Mgqwetho's poetry, 37, 46; oppression, 3, 173; in poetry, 1, 6, 95, 198; in Poswayo's poetry, 167–68; proximity to, 58, 70, 177; skins, 9, 27, 100, 169; in worker poetry, 72, 82. *See also* birds; cattle; skins

242 / INDEX

anticolonialism, 46–47, 91. *See also* decolonization; resistance
apartheid, 6, 17, 28, 34, 62; and capitalism, 17, 30; development of, 29, 30, 38, 45, 62–65; environmental justice and, 30, 39, 61; and labor, 7, 61; literary response to, 7, 14, 31, 39, 60, 61–62; policies, 63; and unions, 61
Asvat, Farouk, 76
Attridge, Derek, 212n66

Bantu, 205–6n16; languages, 19, 22–23
Bantustan, 60, 63, 68, 121, 200. *See also* land reserves
battle. *See* war
Bechuanaland, 45
Bholotwa, 99–102
Biko, Steve, 91
birds, 2, 20, 48, 72, 220n78, 221n19; hadeda ibis *(ihahane)*, 167–68; hammerkop *(uthekwane)*, 158–59; hornbill *(intsikizi)*, 168
Black Consciousness, 66, 91
Black Mamba Rising, 61, 75–77, 81
body, 7, 42, 62, 73, 129
Botha, P. W., 92, 213n21
Botswana, 19, 45
Britain, 20, 28–29, 45, 100, 164
British Empire, 39, 44, 163–64
Brown, Duncan, 101
Bryson, J. Scott, 4
bull. *See* cattle
Bunbury, Charles, 70–71
bushman. *See* Khoisan; San
bushveld, 21, 140; bundu, 212n92; Fish River Bush, 70–71. *See also* mimosa
Buthelezi, Mangosuthu, 92, 213n21

Caminero-Santangelo, Byron 3, 4
Canada, 4, 5, 11–12
Cape Town, 36, 79, 82, 212n93, 214n55
capitalism, 120, 174; and Africa, 3; colonial and early twentieth-century South Africa, 35–39, 41–43; late apartheid South Africa, 65–66, 68, 73–74, 85; post-apartheid, 87, 92, 115; resistance to, 6–8, 61–62, 101, 179; in South Africa, 10, 14, 17, 28–34, 149, 177; and women, 80–82
Caribbean, 5
cattle, 221n17; amaXhosa relationships with, 21, 59, 138, 160, 166–67; bulls, 158–59, 167, 187, 193, 220n1; cattle killing, 41, 59, 208n31, 218n26; and colonialism, 20, 138, 164; colors, 219n69, 221n12, 221n16; and ecology, 160, 166–67, 174; in izibongo, 26, 152, 165–67, 170, 191–92, 197; kraal, 126, 155–56; *lobola,* 166, 219n72; Malange, 82; ritual, 155–56, 166; pastoralism, 19, 167; Qabula, 72–73, 85
censorship, 15, 31, 135, 141, 217n60; and gender violence, 109–12; Malange, 92–93; of poets/writers, 74, 76, 88–90, 93–95; and shifting traditions, 98, 114, 176
Chamber of Mines, 39, 40, 44, 54
chiefs and chiefdoms. *See* traditional leadership
Christianity and Christians, 8, 27, 44, 48, 50, 59; and colonialism, 52–54; missionaries, 53; and traditional beliefs, 37, 47–48, 129
Churchill, Lord Randolph S., 35
Ciskei, 36, 37, 121, 200
click (linguistic), 9, 22–24, 125, 216n35
climate change, 119
Cocks, Michelle, 70
colonialism, 2–8, 35, 110, 173–74, 200–201, 209n63; British, 14, 20, 29–30, 38–42, 70–71, 218n26; European, 20, 28–29; and iimbongi, 31, 71–72, 91, 121, 141–42, 163–64, 177; labor policy, 43–45, 54; and land or nature, 17, 143, 146; and language, 24, 101, 117, 138, 140; and literature, 17, 138, 204n20; Mgqwetho, 46–50, 53, 56–59; neocolonial, 32–34; positionality, 11–12; resistance to, 31, 61, 88, 148. *See also* postcolonialism
commodification (of izibongo), 15, 90, 93, 95, 99, 114
Congress of South African Trade Unions (COSATU), 61, 79, 84, 186
Congress of South African Writers (COSAW), 80–81
conservation, 3, 6, 174
conservative: ideologies, 3, 110, 136, 141, 178; politics, 55, 149
Cooke, Stuart, 5
Cooper, Brenda, 76
corruption, 34, 87, 94, 148, 176; resistance to, 121; and traditional leaders, 161, 170; and Zuma, 15, 107
crime, 75, 114, 142, 215n69; and inequality, 34, 87, 116
Cronin, Jeremy, 76
cultural workers. *See* Durban Workers' Cultural Local

INDEX / 243

d'Abdon, Raphael, 99
De Beers, 29
decolonization, 15, 32, 88, 101–2, 118, 173–74, 179
de Klerk, F. W., 86
de Kok, Ingrid, 80
democracy, 16, 138; labor movement, 61, 65–66, 74; and traditional leadership, 147–50, 171; transition to, 31–33, 87–89, 105, 115, 173
demonstrations. *See* protest; resistance
development, 8, 15–16, 102, 200; of capitalism in South Africa, 28–30, 38–42; and iimbongi, 117–21, 133–35, 139–42, 178–79; of language and culture, 101, 137; of literature, 8, 27–28, 36, 54, 89; literature in, 116–21, 137–39; underdevelopment, 14, 64–65; uneven development, 4, 10, 86, 143
dialect, 21–22, 27, 139–40, 199
dispossession, 3, 41, 148; and iimbongi, 2, 16, 121; legacies of, 110, 116, 143–45; in Mgqwetho's poetry, 36, 53, 56, 58; and worker poets, 15, 62, 88
Dlakavu, Simimakele, 112
Dold, Tony, 70
Dunlop, 60, 70, 73–74; "The Dunlop Play," 68
Durban, 15, 60, 73, 79, 91, 213n19; strike wave, 61, 65–68
Durban Workers' Cultural Local, 61, 66, 67, 75
Dutch, 19, 28
dwelling (human), 2, 7–8, 13, 151, 154–55; and ancestral, 151, 160, 164, 177
Dyakala, Mandlenkosi, 93–95, 108, 114, 132, 140

Eagleton, Terry, 79
Eastern Cape, 1, 13–14, 60, 62; and amaXhosa, 21, 160; colonialism in, 8, 27, 40, 53, 148; Eastern Cape Liquor Board, 130; fieldwork, 16, 117–18, 121–22; iimbongi, 37, 125, 99; and land reform, 145; landscape, 13, 115, 171, 219n50
East London, 102
ecocriticism, 2–3, 6, 11, 15, 174, 203n2–8. *See also* ecopoetics
ecology: ecosystem, 3, 20, 31, 70; political ecology, 62. *See also* nature
Economic Freedom Fighters (EFF), 146
ecopoetics, 4–6, 10–11, 13–17, 174; Mgqwetho, 45–58; Poswayo, 157–70; worker poets, 62, 68–75, 79–83; Yali-Manisi, 151–56
ecosystem. *See* ecology
education, 42, 107, 138; African language, 101–2; in development, 116, 119, 133; missionary, 50, 152; of workers, 66–68, 73
elections, 33, 112–13; of 1924, 45; of 1948, 45, 62; of 1994, 33, 173
emaXhoseni, 21, 41, 58–59
Engcobo, 26, 157, 161
English, 54, 201; colonialism, 29, 35; interviews, 13, 93, 122; and isiXhosa, 23–25, 102; linguistic hegemony, 102, 137–38; literature, 11, 108; translations, 2, 7, 10, 75–79
environmentalism, 2, 4–7, 61, 74, 174, 204n28
environmental justice, 3, 5, 6, 16, 37, 62
Ergin, Meliz, 5
extraction, 6, 15, 31, 38, 62, 65; of gold, 39, 44. *See also* accumulation; mining

Fanon, Frantz, 147, 209n63
FIFA World Cup, 99
Finnegan, Ruth, 95, 105
First National Bank, 99
Fish River Bush. *See* bushveld
forced relocation and forced removal. *See* relocation
forest: and Malange, 82; and Qabula, 60, 68–71, 74–75, 78, 181–82
Fritsch, Gustav, 167
Frontier Wars. *See* war

Gcaleka, 157, 217n52. *See also* amaGcaleka
gender violence, 49–50, 52, 79–81; and censorship, 109–14; and oppression, 135, 149, 173. *See also* rape
genealogy, 21, 22, 155, 156, 157
globalization, 6
global South, 4, 5, 200
Glotfelty, Cheryll, 3, 203n4
gold mines. *See* mining
gold standard, 44
Gordhan, Pravin, 105
Gordimer, Nadine, 76
Grahamstown. *See* Makhanda
grammar. *See* isiXhosa
Group Areas Act, 62–63
Guha, Ramachandra, 6
Gwadana, 164–65, 168

Hall, Ruth, 145, 147
Hart, Gillian, 33
Harvey, David, 33, 73
healer. See *igqirha*
health, 2, 115–20, 130–37, 142, 157, 183; of imbongi, 169, 196
Hertzog, J. B. M., 45
Hintsa, 40, 57, 157, 217n52
Hlatshwayo, Mi S'dumo, 61
homeland. See Bantustan
Huggan, Graham, 15, 120
Hume, Angela, 5
hybridity, 24, 139, 178

Idutywa, 157
igqirha, 199; and imbongi, 27, 119, 124–25, 127–28, 132, 176; initiation, 128. See also spirituality
Iheka, Cajetan, 2, 46
illiteracy, 67
imbongi: censorship and commercialization, 93–95, 98–100; ecopoetics, 7–8, 10–11, 16, 31, 140, 167–68, 171, 173–79; and emotion, 136–37, 144–45; fieldwork, 13, 121–25; freedom of speech, 96–98; labor movement, 60, 66–68, 71, 77; and language, 23–24, 137, 139–140; in politics, 102–8, 113, 174; and resistance, 10, 56, 74, 90–91, 120–21; spirituality, 27, 117–19, 125–33; tradition, 20, 24–27; and traditional leadership, 130–32, 150–51, 157, 159, 165, 169–71; in transition, 14–15, 88–90, 114, 134–35, 141–42; women, 27, 49–50, 52, 55, 108–9, 112, 175; Yali-Manisi, 1–2, 151–53, 155
imbongi yosiba, 125
imbongi zomthonyama, 11, 125–26, 128, 139
imperialism, 2–3, 28, 164; cultural, 31. See also British Empire
independence: African, 31, 102; amaXhosa, 41, 59; and decolonization, 173–74; South Africa, 32, 84, 87, 89; Transkei, 200
indigeneity, 5–6, 22, 125, 142, 199; languages, 137
inequality, 2, 10, 29, 116, 141, 173; economic, 64, 147; state sanctioned, 54, 86, 110
informal settlement, 65, 116, 174, 201
Inkatha Freedom Party, 91, 213n21
intellectualism, 16, 28, 36, 76, 92, 205n42; iimbongi, 8–9, 31, 74, 128–29, 142, 153
inthwaso. See *-thwasa*

intsomi (storytelling), 83
isiNdebele, 22, 138
isiXhosa, 200; deep Xhosa, 24, 137, 139–40, 178; and ethnography, 21–22, 50, 157, 199; fieldwork, 121–22, 124; iimbongi, 119, 136–37, 170; language politics, 137–40; linguistics, 22–24, 77; literature, 6–17; newspapers, 45, 54–56, 59; poetry, 1–2, 38, 105, 144, 153, 159, 167; relationship to print, 27–28, 36, 39, 54. See also linguistics
isiZulu: language and linguistics, 9, 22–24, 138; literature, 6, 61, 75, 77–78, 105–6; newspapers, 54. See also AmaZulu; Zulu
izibongo, 1, 7–9, 13–16, 20, 25–27; commercialization of, 90, 99; contemporary, 121–25; and development, 142; gender, 109; Malange, 79–84; Mgqwetho, 36–37, 58; Poswayo, 158–60, 162–63, 165–69; in print, 51, 58; Qabula, 71–79, 84–85; as resistance, 88; and spirituality, 117, 127, 144; in transition, 13, 90, 93, 175–78; in the union movement, 66–68; Yali-Manisi, 153–55; isiZulu *izimbongi*, 105

Japan, 64
Johannesburg, 14, 35–36, 44, 56, 69, 102. See also Soweto; Witwatersrand
Joza, 16, 121, 123, 126. See also Makhanda; township
justice, 3; African systems, 101; and emotion, 118; environmental, 5–7, 16, 30, 37–38, 61–62, 74; and iimbongi, 121, 171; land reform, 143–44, 146–47, 170; racial injustice, 10, 16–17, 37

Kaschula, Russell, 77, 107, 137, 183, 203n1
Kepe, Thembela, 145, 147
Khoi. See Khoisan
Khoisan, 22, 205n4; Khoi, 19, 22; San, 19, 22, 205n1
Kimberly, 29, 40. See also mining
King William's Town, 27, 95. See also Zwelitsha
kraal. See cattle
Krikler, Jeremy, 43
Kwa-Zulu Natal, 21

labor, 12, 78; and capitalism, 28, 30, 68, 73–74; control of, 29–30; exploitation of, 7, 110, 116; labor movement, 14, 54, 60–62, 65–68, 75–77; migrant, 14, 36–37, 39–40,

42, 45, 60, 68–73; segregation and apartheid, 30, 43–45, 63–65; unemployment, 64–65, 81–82, 133, 146; unrest, 88; women, 43, 59, 79–84. *See also* worker poets
labor movement. *See* unions
land act, 29, 42; of 1913, 41, 146
land expropriation without compensation, 16, 146, 170
land reserves, 63–64. *See also* Bantustan
languages, 4, 174, 199; African, 20, 22, 36, 54, 89, 101–3, 203n2, 206n16; colonial, 7, 24, 31, 88, 139, 101–2, 209n63; and ecology, 13, 167; *hlonipha*, 27, 50; imbongi, 8, 96, 108, 118–19, 121–22, 125–26; isiXhosa, 11–12, 14, 20–25, 27, 54, 200; isiZulu, 77–79; poetic, 5, 7–13, 15–16, 62, 76, 135, 144, 153, 156; politics, 32, 112, 114, 116–19, 137–42; transitions, 50–51, 54. *See also* Afrikaans; English; isiXhosa; isiZulu
liberation movement, 10, 31–33; psychological, 66
linguistics, 13; hybridity, 24, 139; isiXhosa, 22–24, 178
literacy, 116–17; illiteracy, 67
lobola. *See* cattle
London, 28, 36, 44
Lovedale, 27–28
Lovedale Missionary Institution, 152 (Lovedale Press)
lyric, 4–5, 8, 31

Magona, Sindiwe, 138
Makhanda, 90, 138, 148; interviews, 16, 117, 121, 136; and Dyakala, 93, 132, 140; and Mpupha, 104, 127. *See also* Joza
Malan, D. F., 45
Malange, Nise, 14, 61–62, 66–68, 73, 79–85, 91–93, 111–12
Malawi, 45
Malema, Julius, 146
Mamdani, Mahmood, 149
Mandela, Nelson, 22, 86; and iimbongi, 89–93, 99, 103, 123–24; in post-apartheid South Africa, 112, 149, 173
Manisi, David. *See* Yali-Manisi, David
Marikana, 87, 149
martial law, 44
Martinez-Alier, Joan, 6, 204n28
Marxism, 30, 147
Mathanzima, Kaiser Daliwonga, 153–54, 219n71, 221n15

Matsau, Nkutsweu, 76
Matthews, James, 104
Mbashe municipality, 121. *See also* Idutywa; Nqadu; Willowvale
Mbeki, Govan, 63–64
Mbeki, Thabo, 105, 107, 144, 149; administration of, 92
Mbuli, Mzwakhe, 74
metaphor: and affect, 15, 16, 62, 118, 144; and ecology, 8–9, 171; in izibongo, 25, 108, 121, 139–40, 150; rural aspects, 38, 69, 71, 73, 178
Mfanta, 154, 156
Mgqwetho, Nontsizi, 14, 36–39, 42–43, 62; ecopoetry, 45–47; tradition and change, 47–53, 79, 83; and resistance, 56–59; and *Umteteli waBantu*, 54–55. *See also* Christianity; *Umteteli waBantu*
Mhlakaza, 40–41. *See also* Nongqawuse; Sarhili
mimosa bush, 166, 220n78, 221n19. *See also* bushveld
mining: and apartheid, 64; labour, 68–69, 174; location of, 63; mining companies, 6, 29, 55, 87; mining industry, 39–40, 42–45, 86, 141; strike, 54, 87; Witwatersrand, 35
missionaries. *See* Christianity
Mkhonza, Sarah, 56
Mkiva, Zolani, 89–91, 98–103, 112–13, 148, 150–51, 218n26; in interviews, 124, 134
Mkiva Humanitarian Awards, 101
Mozambique, 45, 105
Mphupa, Dumisa, 104, 107, 127, 129; translations by, 184–98
Mpondoland, 64, 68, 77
Mpondo revolts, 65, 69–73
Mqhayi, S. E. K., 62, 127; and Mandela, 90–91; and Poswayo, 163–64, 190, 219n64, 220n10; transition to print, 51, 79
Mqolonzana, Thando, 137–38
Mthikrakra, Ntshiza Manzezulu, 153–55

names: beliefs concerning, 27, 49–51, 57, 109; of cattle, 167; clan names, 22, 27, 151; in izibongo, 2, 26–27, 49–50, 125, 131–32, 150–51, 155, 159–60; of kingdoms, 21; and police state, 70. *See also* praise names
Namibia, 19
Natal, 65, 68. *See also* Durban; KwaZulu-Natal
Natal Women's Forum, 81

National Assembly, 104
National Council of Provinces (NCOP), 104, 146
National League of Bantu Women, 54
National Party, 29, 86
Nation's Bounty, The. See Mgqwetho, Nontsizi
nature, 2, 4–5, 7, 13, 17, 38; exploitation of, 59, 173; and iimbongi, 74–75, 140, 157, 174
Ndaba, 153–55
Ndebele. *See* isiNdebele
neocolonialism. *See* colonialism
neoliberalism, 3, 6, 16, 31–34; in post-apartheid South Africa, 87, 93, 102, 115, 138, 140
Neser, Ashlee, 51
newspapers: and literary expression, 8, 38–39, 50–52, 54; and Mgqwetho, 36, 39, 45, 50–52, 54–56; 1980s, 67, 74, 75; nineteenth-century, 8, 36, 38–39, 54; in poetry, 186; and resistance, 54–55, 74, 91. See also *Abantu Batho*; *Umteteli waBantu*
Ngqika, 27, 49, 57, 154
Nguni: cattle, 156; languages, 22, 167, 205n16; people, 205n12
Nixon, Rob, 4, 64
Nkandla, 103, 106–7, 149, 184
Nongqawuse, 40–41, 148, 218n26
North America, 2, 34, 45, 174, 199
Nqadu, 130–32, 157–64, 165, 168
Ntshuntsha, Thokozani, 95–98, 127, 129–30, 132, 139–40, 151
Nxasana, Thulani, 49–50
Nyasaland, 45

Opland, Jeff, 10, 51, 124; on amaXhosa traditions, 26, 126–27, 151; on Mgqwetho, 37, 55; and Yali-Manisi, 2, 151–56, 203n1. *See also* transcription
orality, 8
oral literature, 6, 16, 66, 95, 117, 144, 178
oral poetry, 8–9, 11, 16, 24, 66, 77, 117. See also *izibongo*
oral poets, 7, 39, 67. See also *imbongi*
Orange Free State, 68
Osborne, Gillian, 5

Pan-African Congress, 64
panegyric, 24–25, 105

Pan South African Language Board, 170, 199
pass laws, 29–30, 42, 64. *See also* Group Areas Act
pastoralism. *See* cattle
Peires, Jeff, 149, 208n31
performance: affect, 117–18, 125–28, 132; iimbongi, 8–9, 12–13, 16, 31, 129, 175–78; Mkiva, 91, 99; Mgqwetho, 45; Mqhayi, 90–91; at Nqadu, 130; Ntshuntsha, 95–98; in post-apartheid South Africa, 88–89, 93, 139; Poswayo, 130–31, 165, 168–69; and print, 75–79; public perceptions, 123–24, 135–36; SONA, 104–5; traditional, 109, 139, 144; worker poets, 66–68, 72, 77, 83, 88; Yali-Manisi, 1–2, 153, 203n1
periodicals. *See* newspapers
Phalo, 157
Pistorius, Oscar, 111
place, 31, 38–39, 74–75, 151, 164, 171, 177; dwelling places, 155–56, 160; Great Place, 130, 157; marketplace, 89; place-names, 160; workplace, 37, 61, 65, 67, 69, 73, 80, 83
plants, 1, 6, 65, 72, 157, 171; grasslands, 21, 35, 46, 167; trees, 35, 96, 106, 115, 184
poetic devices, 9, 26, 58, 118; alliteration 9, 23, 24, 58, 118, 125 221n30. *See also* metaphor
poetic form, 11, 24–25
poetry: and affect, 66–67, 74, 118–19, 133; *Black Mamba*, 75–76; and cattle, 152, 167; contemporary, 108, 113; ecopoetry, 4–7, 10–11, 69–70, 156–57, 164, 174–75; education, 67, 73, *izibongo*, 13–16, 20, 24–27, 31, 199–200; Mgqwetho, 36–39, 45–51, 55–59; Mkiva, 99, 102; oral poetry, 8–9, 16, 66; panegyric, 105; poetic language, 8–9, 99; politics, 93–94, 117, 121, 142, 152–53; postcolonial, 201n20; print, 2, 54, 66, 77, 126; Qabula, 14, 60–2, 64–75, 84–85; and traditional leadership, 24, 150; women, 81–84
Pondoland. *See* Mpondoland
Port Elizabeth, 163
Portuguese, 19, 28
postapartheid, 14, 31, 33
postcolonialism, 3–8, 120–21; and imbongi, 10–11, 15, 89, 138–42
Postmentier, Sonya, 5

Poswayo, Thukela, 26, 130–2; at Gwadana, 164–71; at Nqadu, 157–64
power: abuse of, 101–2; apartheid state, 61; of arts and culture, 31, 62, 66–68, 71–72; of chiefs, 2, 22; colonial, 28, 45, 56; and context, 75–76; and imbongi, 8, 14–16, 24, 88; of language, 8–9, 26, 50–51, 74, 96–98; of popular movements, 10; in post-apartheid South Africa, 87, 90–93; power relations, 6, 84; religious, 50, 54; representation, 4, 7, 10
praise names, 26–27, 85, 125, 155, 167, 219n49. *See also* names
"Praise Poem to FOSATU" (also "FOSATU"), 60, 69, 77, 86–87, 181–83
praise poetry, 24–25, 199. *See also* panegyric; izibongo
praise singer, 25, 67, 92, 104, 107, 150. *See also* imbongi
print: introduction of, 27–28, 50, 54; growth of, 36, 39, 54, 213n18; and land concerns, 170; and literacy, 116–17; Mgqwetho, 43, 51–52, 54–56; relationship with oral, 8, 38, 50–51, 75–79; and workers, 67–68
private property, 2, 31, 146, 155
pronunciation, 23–24
protest, 33, 66, 87–88, 92, 112–14; pass, 54, 64; student, 61
proximity, 2, 6, 37, 46, 158
Puku Storytelling Festival, 138

Qabula, Alfred Themba, 14, 60–62, 64–75, 84–87; and *Black Mamba*, 61, 75–79, 81, 181–83
Qamata, 217n54, 220n9; and imbongi, 176; and traditional leaders, 131–32, 160, 168, 189, 193, 195; town of, 166, 191, 219n70, 221n14

race, 10; construction of, 29; and extraction, 62; and gender, 39, 146; geographical segregation, 62, 64; labor and, 39; oppression and unequal access, 12, 16, 29 146; race studies, 5; relations, 36; whiteness, 29
Ramaphosa, Cyril, 146
Ramazani, Jahan, 5, 204n20
Rand Revolt, 36, 43, 44–45
rape, 53, 107, 109–12, 116
Rawlings, J. J., 101–2
reconciliation, 92, 145, 150, 173

relocation, 42, 63, 64; from "black spots," 63; forced relocation/removal, 110, 116, 143; Group Areas Act, 62; homelands, 63, 73, 82
resistance: amaMpondo, 69–71; to colonialism, 40–41, 46, 61, 148, 205n4; cultural, 31, 66–68, 121; labor, 44–45, 54, 60–62, 65, 87; literary, 88, 116, 141; in the post-apartheid period, 141; to segregation and apartheid, 38–39, 64, 87; women, 43. *See also* activism; protest; strikes
Rharhabe, 157
Rhodes, Cecil John, 29
Rhodesia: Northern, 45; Southern, 45
rivers, 21, 140, 171, 219n50, 219n61, 220n3; Kei River, 41, 157, 194, 200; in poetry, 131, 158–61, 165–67, 187–88, 190–92, 197. *See also* Fish River Bush
Robben Island, 79, 91, 105, 154, 156
Rubusana, W. B., 138

San, 19, 22, 205n1
sangoma. *See igqirha*
Sarhili, 40, 131, 132, 162, 189, 217n53, 219n63
separate development. *See* development
serial publications. *See Abantu Batho*; newspapers; *Umteteli waBantu*; *Writers' Notebook*
Sesotho, 138
shack: dwellers, 88; settlement, 65, 116, 174, 201; uprisings, 88
shades. *See* ancestors; spirits
Sharpeville, 64, 87
Sigcawu, Nondwe, 157
siSwati, 138
Sitas, Ari, 72, 76, 79, 84
Sixham, Yakobi, 95, 114, 140
Slow Violence and the Environmentalism of the Poor, 4
Smuts, Jan, 44–45
Sotho, North, 63. *See also* Sesotho
Sotho, South, 63. *See also* Sesotho
South African Native National Congress (SANNC), 44, 54–55
Soweto, 82, 87, 213n96. *See also* Johannesburg
spirits, 6–7, 58, 70, 98, 126–28; ancestral, 27, 47, 50–51, 71, 155–56; and chiefs, 22; and iimbongi, 132, 160, 169, 171, 174–75, 177; *thwasa*, 119, 169. *See also* ancestors; spirituality; *umoya*

spirituality: colonial, 53–54, 57–59; effects of colonialism on, 46; forests and, 70–71; iimbongi and healing, 27, 122, 124–30, 132–33, 136; imbongi and *thwasa*, 128, 169–70; imbongi vocation, 8, 15–16, 20, 27, 31, 93–98, 117–19, 141–42, 175–77; initiations and, 128; performance and, 130–132; land and, 16, 145, 151–56, 171; oral poetry and, 7, 117, 144–45, 171; practices, 20; spiritual ecology, 46; traditional beliefs and, 27, 49–51; traditional leaders and, 149, 150, 161–62, 168–69, 177; rivers and, 159–60. *See also* cattle; Christianity; *igqirha*; names
State of the Nation Address (SONA), 146, 214n48; 2016 SONA poem, 15, 90, 104–7, 184–86; and iimbongi 104, 112–13, 123, 124, 175, 176
Steenkamp, Reena, 111
strikes: Durban, 61, 65–68; Johannesburg, 43, 44, 54; Marikana, 87; post-apartheid, 87–89
subaltern, 10, 205n42
suburb, 116
sustainable development goals (SDGs), 119
Swaziland, 105

Table Bay, 19
Thembu: abaThembu, 21, 159, 219n50; Thembukazi (Thembu woman), 188, 220n5; "Thembu Spatterings," 151–56
Thixo, 71, 162, 176, 189, 217n54, 220n9
-thwasa, 119; *amathwasa*, 128–29, 169; *ukuthwasa*, 128–29, 217n47
Tiffin, Helen, 15, 120
township, 11, 63, 80, 95, 115–17, 133, 136, 201; linguistic differences, 139–40, literature in, 11, 116–17, 133, 178; residents of, 13, 118, 123–24, 139; uprisings, 61, 82–83. *See also* Joza; Soweto; Zwelitsha
trade union. *See* unions
traditional leadership, 121, 132; controversy, 147–50; and iimbongi, 150–51, 159–62, 164–65
transcription: of interviews, 13, 122; by Jeff Opland, 2, 153–54; of oral poetry, 9–10, 75–79, 90, 104
transhumance, 20, 160, 167
Transkei, 15, 98, 200, 217n71, 221n15; fieldwork in, 121–25; and Malange, 82; performances in, 129–35, 157–70; and Alfred Qabula, 60, 63–64, 68–70, 74–75, 85; and Yali-Manisi, 152–53
translation, 25; isiXhosa literature, 2, 7, 12, 14; Poswayo, 158; SONA poem, 104; worker poets, 75–79
transport, 36, 39, 68, 115–16, 133
Tshivenda, 138
Tsonga, 63. *See also* xiTsonga
Tutuola, Amos, 46
Tswana, 63

ubuntu, 136, 176
umoya, 7, 98, 119, 201. *See also* spirits
Umteteli waBantu, 36, 45, 49, 50, 54–55
underdevelopment. *See* development
uneven development. *See* development
UN Human Development Index (UNHDI), 116
unions: 1980s movement, 60–62, 65–69, 71–75, 91–93, 181–83; post-apartheid, 87; restrictions, 45; union movement and women, 79–84. *See also* Congress of South African Trade Unions; labor
Union Defense Force, 44–45
Union of South Africa, 41
United Democratic Front (UDF), 61
United States, 5

Venda, 63. *See also* Tshivenda
Verwey, Herman, 113
Verwoerd, Hendrik, 62
Vetten, Lisa, 110
violence: apartheid, 72; colonial, 27–31, 39–42, 44–45, 57–58; domestic, 42–43, 60, 163, 175; environmental, 6–7, 58–59, 71–75; internal conflict, 46–47, 63, 65, 92; military, 27, 40, 44–45, 58, 148; police, 31, 44, 64, 71, 74, 82, 87–88; post-apartheid, 33, 87–88, 91–92; racial, 34, 72–73, 86; representations of, 34; slow, 4, 62; structural, 4, 10, 12–13, 64, 72–75, 143; township, 82–83, 91–92, 116, 213n96; Transkei, 69, 71–73, 82; against women, 49–50, 52, 79–81, 109–14. *See also* Mpondo revolts; Rand Revolt; war

Walter Sisulu University, 101–2
war, 66; First World War, 43; forest as shelter from, 75; Frontier Wars, 27, 40, 58, 71, 148, 154; and iimbongi, 97, 150; War of Mlanjeni, 40, 71

water, 21, 31; in poetry, 46, 55, 71, 75; quality, 116; shortages, 115, 144. *See also* rivers
wilderness, 2–4, 6, 174
Willowvale: interviews in, 15, 117, 121–23, 125, 133–35; and Mkiva, 99–102; and Ntshuntsha, 95, 132–33, 151; and performances, 130
Witwatersrand, 14, 29–30, 35–40, 55
women: and capitalism, 39, 42–43, 59, 73; cultural change, 48–50; and labor movement, 43, 79–84; oppression of, 36, 149; and poetry, 27; speech and erasure, 15, 27, 49–50, 90, 109–113, 175; rights, 54, 109; violence against, 49–50, 52, 79–81
worker poets, 15, 60–62, 67, 75–76
Working Life, A, 68
Worsfold, William Basil, 35
Writers' Notebook, 81, 212n89

xenophobia, 135, 140, 141
Xhosa, 21. *See also* amaXhosa; isiXhosa
Xhosa Oral Poetry, 124
xiTsonga, 138

Yali-Manisi, David, 1–2, 51, 62, 148, 152–56, 164, 176, 203n1

Zambia, 45, 105
Zanzolo, 131–32, 162, 189
Zemk'inkomo magwalandini, 138
Zimbabwe, 45
zomthonyama, 11, 125–26, 128–29, 139
Zulu, 63. *See also* amaZulu; isiZulu
Zuma, Jacob, 89, 103, 105–8, 110, 112–13, 144, 146, 184–86
Zwelitsha, 95, 140. *See also* King William's Town; township
Zwelonke, 23, 97, 130–32, 157–60, 165, 168; addresses to, 187–95

Recent Books in the Series
Under the Sign of Nature: Explorations in Ecocriticism

Scott Hess
William Wordsworth and the Ecology of Authorship: The Roots of Environmentalism in Nineteenth-Century Culture

Dan Brayton
Shakespeare's Ocean: An Ecocritical Exploration

Jennifer K. Ladino
Reclaiming Nostalgia: Longing for Nature in American Literature

Byron Caminero-Santangelo
Different Shades of Green: African Literature, Environmental Justice, and Political Ecology

Kate Rigby
Dancing with Disaster: Environmental Histories, Narratives, and Ethics for Perilous Times

Adam Trexler
Anthropocene Fictions: The Novel in a Time of Climate Change

Eric Gidal
Ossianic Unconformities: Bardic Poetry in the Industrial Age

Jesse Oak Taylor
The Sky of Our Manufacture: The London Fog in British Fiction from Dickens to Woolf

Michael P. Branch and Clinton Mohs, editors
"The Best Read Naturalist": Nature Writings of Ralph Waldo Emerson

Lynn Keller
Recomposing Ecopoetics: North American Poetry of the Self-Conscious Anthropocene

Serenella Iovino, Enrico Cesaretti, and Elena Past, editors
Italy and the Environmental Humanities: Landscapes, Natures, Ecologies

Christopher Abram
Evergreen Ash: Ecology and Catastrophe in Old Norse Myth and Literature

Elizabeth Hope Chang
Novel Cultivations: Plants in British Literature of the Global Nineteenth Century

Emily McGiffin
Of Land, Bones, and Money: Toward a South African Ecopoetics

CPSIA information can be obtained
at www.ICGtesting.com
Printed in the USA
LVHW031424230619
622081LV00002B/85